THREE-FIFTHS THEOLOGY

THREE-FIFTHS THEOLOGY:
Challenging Racism in American Christianity

Lewis T. Tait, Jr. and
A. Christian van Gorder

Africa World Press, Inc.

P.O. Box 1892

Trenton, NJ 08607

P.O. Box 48

Asmara, ERITREA

Africa World Press, Inc.

P.O. Box 1892 — P.O. Box 48
Trenton, NJ 08607 — Asmara, ERITREA

Book and Cover Design: Roger Dormann

Cover Artwork courtesy of
Life of Jesus MAFA,
24 Rue de Marchal
Joffre F-78000
Versailles, France

Library of Congress Cataloging-in-Publication Data

Tait, Lewis T.
  Three-fifths theology : challenging racism in American Christianity
  /Lewis T. Tait, Jr. and A. Christian van Gorder.
  p.cm.
Includes bibliographical references and index.
  ISBN 0-86543-989-3 — ISBN 0-86543-990-7 (pbk.)
  1. Racism—Religious aspects—Christianity. 2. Racism—United
States.
  3. African-Americans—Segregation. I. Van Gorder, A. Christian.
  II. Title.
  BT734.2.T35 2004
  261.8'348'00973—dc21

      2001006582

"From here, in the name of the Holy Trinity one could send as many slaves from Africa as one could sell...one could send 40 million, if there were enough ships to bring them here."
—CHRISTOPHER COLUMBUS,
On his third voyage to the Caribbean, 1498

O Lord, whenever I speak, I cry out proclaiming violence and destruction. So the Word of the Lord has brought me insult and reproach all day long. But if I say, "I will not mention the Lord or speak any more about his name," his word is in my heart like a fire, a fire that is shut up in my bones. I am weary of holding it in; indeed, I cannot.
—JEREMIAH 20:8-9,
After beating and imprisonment from Priest Passhur

Out of Africa, always something new.
—PLINY THE ELDER, 23-79 CE

Table of Contents

Preface

Preface by John W. Kinney, Ph. D., Dean
Samuel DeWitt Proctor School of Theology
Virginia Union University

Many times the best starting point for clarifying one's intent and purpose is to illuminate your desired conclusion. The conclusion of this probing work by Lewis T. Tait, Jr. and A. Christian van Gorder invites us to join them on the "freedom road." Preceding this concluding invitation to join the pilgrimage, they provide a sweeping engagement of the pain, problems, personalities, perspectives and possibilities encountered along the way. Confronting the unholy union of race and Christianity, the authors offer a critical, constructive survey and interpretation of history and Africa's Children and the conceptual frameworks that have informed and been formed by that history. We are invited to challenge a hierarchical system that demands that the different be deemed deficient, that value and dignity be biologically determined, that worth be assigned based upon position, power and possessions claimed within a perceived vertical order, and that universal and eternal cosmic validity be given to a singular cultural projection or pattern. With prophetic suggestion, this challenge is pointed particularly to the church and the people of Faith.

The road to freedom calls us to constant diligence, perpetual seeking, and faithful walking. Tait and van Gorger neither in their relationship nor their writing offer a finished product. What is offered is a suggestive and informative primer for all who would commit to the struggle for racial justice. The Psalmist says, "Let this be written for future generations that a people not yet created may praise the Lord" (Psalm 108:18, NIV). While wishing to neither diminish nor trivialize the significance of the Psalmist's pronouncement, may this work be written that an authentic community not yet formed may praise the Lord in word and deed.

Dedication

This book is dedicated to the memory of all of the martyrs, named unnamed. Remember:

Murdered, 30, January, 1885: Ebenezer Fowler, businessman
Murdered, 31, January, 1964: Louis Allen, farmer
Murdered, 3, February, 1989: John Jackson, student
Murdered, 21, February, 1965: Minister Malcolm X
Murdered, 26, February, 1965: Deacon Jimmy Lee Jackson
Murdered, 11, March, 1965: The Reverend James J. Reeb
Murdered, 25, March, 1965: Viola Gregg Liuzzo, homemaker
Murdered, 8, April, 1968: The Reverend Dr. Martin Luther King, Jr.
Murdered, 23, April, 1963: William L. Moore, CORE worker
Murdered, 25, April, 1939: Mack Parker, farmer
Murdered, 7, May, 1955: The Reverend George W. Lee
Murdered, 25, May, 1912: Dan Davis, fieldhand
Murdered, 7, June, 1998: James Byrd, part-time musician
Murdered, 12, June, 1963: Medgar Wiley Evers, NAACP worker
Murdered, 21, June, 1964: James Earl Chaney, CORE worker; Andrew Goodman, student; Michael Henry Schwerner, social worker
Murdered, 22, June, 1903: George White, worker
Murdered, 22, June, 1982: Willie Turks, age 34, Gravesend, New York
Murdered, 2, July, 1822: Denmark Vescey, revolutionary
Murdered, 7, August, 1901: John Pennington, worker
Murdered, 20, August, 1965: Jonathan Myrick Daniels, seminarian
Murdered, 23, August, 1989: Yusuf Hawkins, age 16, Bensonhurst, New York
Murdered, 28, August, 1955: Emmett Till, age 14
Murdered, 15, September, 1983: Michael Stewart, 25, artist and model
Murdered, 25, September, 1961: Herbert Lee, farmer
Murdered, 7, October, 1797: Gabriel Prosser, revolutionary
Murdered, 29, October, 1984: Eleanor Bumpers, ailing grandmother, 66
Murdered, 7, November, 1837: Elijah P. Lovejoy, printer/journalist
Murdered, 11, November, 1831: The Reverend Nat Turner
Murdered, 21, December, 1986: Michael Griffith, Howard Beach, New York
Murdered, 22, Dec., 1980: Luis Rodriguez; Antoine Davis; Richard Renner
Murdered, 25, December, 1951: Harry T. Moore, NAACP worker

And to the memory of four angels—Murdered at the Sixteenth Street Baptist Church, Birmingham, Alabama on 15, September, 1963: Addie Mae Collins, age 14; Denise McNair, age 11; Carole Robertson, age 14; Cynthia Wesley, age 14

And the Lord said, I have surely seen the affliction of my people which are in Egypt, and have heard their cry by reason of their taskmasters; for I know their sorrows; and I am come down to deliver them out of the hands of the Egyptians.
—Exodus 3:7-8

Acknowledgments

Highest praise to God who has united us in his Nija ("path")of faith.

However, as the Egyptian proverb says, "a person who does not thank other people does not thank God." We are thankful for our African and European ancestors who traveled long roads to bring us to this day. We are grateful for our parents, Bishop Lewis Thomas Tait, Sr., and his wife Ann Christine Tait and to Andrew and Erika Helena van Gorder. Asante Sana ("Thank you") to our respective wives, Lisa and Stephanie and to our children, Essence Ayana and Lewis Thomas Asante Tait III, and Patrick, Brendan, Keegan and Sean Michael. The way one says "thank you" in the Twi language of Africa is, "Me Da Ase," which literally means, "I will lie at your feet."

Asante Sana to the people of the Harambee Church in Harrisburg, Pa, and the New Life Church in Stone Mountain, Ga. Special thanks to Kler Jones, Steven Ross; Charles Ridgeway; Eric Jackson, and Barrymore Browne; friends at Messiah College: especially Tonya Baker, Jake Jacobsen, Terry Brensinger, Tyrone Wrice, Deborale Richardson-Bouie, Randy Blackford, Steve Cobb, Derek Lehman, and students Brian Scott, Zachary Jackson, Len Brown, Phil Bert, Malcolm Carr, and John Maher. Thanks also to Greg Webb, Charles Wang, Brendan McCauley, Yang Qi Kun, Xu Qin Sun, Gretchen Kohl, Jack and Sherryl Kribs, Pastor Dred Scott, Isaac Mwase, Paul Gifford, Lamin Sanneh, Joel Carpenter and to all who helped us as we traveled to Addis Ababa, Ethiopia, during the summer of 2000.

Asante Sana to the people who helped us in the preparation of this text, especially to our wonderful editor Ms. Patricia Allen, Roger Dormann, Damola Ifaturoti and to our kind publisher Kassahun Checole of the Africa World Press. We want to add a special word of thanks to La Vie Jesus Mafa, the consortium of West African artists based in France who graciously provided the cover artwork for this book. Thanks also to Dr. Cain Hope Felder, Dr. Wil Coleman, Dr. Mark Lomax, Dr. Jeremiah A. Wright, and Dr. John W. Kinney.

Asante Sana to you: our family, friends, and ancestors.

An enemy slaughters, a friend distributes.
—Fulfulde Proverb

Introduction

Three-Fifths America: Today's Dred Scotts and Judge Taneys

Almighty Savior, whose heavy cross was laid upon the stalwart shoulders of Simon the Cyrenian, a son of Africa in that sad hour of thine agony and mortal weakness....regard with thy favor this race still struggling beneath the cross of injustice, oppression and wrong laid upon us by our persecutors. Strengthen us in our determination to free ourselves from the hands of our enemy; put down the mighty from their seat, and exalt thou the humble and the meek; through thy mercies and merits who lives and reigns with the Father and the Holy Ghost, world without end. Amen.
—REVEREND GREGORY ALEXANDER McGUIRE, 1923

As long as the snake is in the house, one need not discuss the matter at length.
—Ewe Proverb

We are writing to educate, motivate, challenge, empower, question and inspire. From a Christian perspective, we will examine how the problem of contemporary racism relates to the three-fifths theology that holds much of American Christianity hostage. This book, while being very much an introduction to a multifaceted topic, is our contribution to the larger discussion. We look forward to others making helpful corrections and providing additional perspectives.

In the United States, there is a pressing need to challenge the injustice and inequality at the heart of our society. De-facto segregation is prevalent in residential communities, in many places of employment, and in most colleges. De-facto segregation is also the norm in most American churches. What does this reality say about our unity as Christians and our level of commitment to a God of justice? Without justice, there is no viable Christian witness that the church is being "salt and light" in our world. Jesus said that if someone held something against another they should leave their worship and work first to rectify what was causing enmity. American Christians have unfinished business demanding attention before they can discuss reconciliation and celebrate their worship of God.

History must teach us....

A chill wind blasts from America's heartland; a cold gale blows from a graveyard in St. Louis where Dred Scott, is buried. His story reaches its crescendo in 1856. At that time Scott was considered the property of John Emerson of Pennsylvania. Dred Scott knew, however, that he was not an object to be bought and sold. Scott demanded the respect due him as a human being. He laid claim to America's democratic promises. His hope was in vain. When Scott stood before Judge Roger Taney, he met a wall of vacillation and compromise. "Legalese" ground Scott's dreams into the powder of denial. All Americans were not equal. Dred Scott called for justice. He did not find it in America.

The United States did recognize that Dred Scott and millions like him had worth. But it was not the worth of equality. African-Americans existed to serve the whims of others. This injustice was law. Article 1, section 2c of the U.S. Constitution proclaims that Africans in America are not whole people but only "three-fifths" of a person. This constitutes recognition without respect; "three-fifths respect" is no respect at all. How can one be three-fifths of a person? Euro-Americans sought to determine what economic value the Africans were in relation to themselves. That slavery destroyed human dignity was not new. What was unique in America was the calculated audacity to establish, in the national Constitution, a way to quantify just how "human" these slaves were.

An African was not a "complete" person. Today, historians continue to use the disarmingly harmless phrase "Federal Ratio" to describe this crime against humanity. In 1783, the Continental Congress made the federal ratio of the Constitution the law of the land. Even at the time it was a mystery. James Wilson of Pennsylvania stated, "I do not well see on what principle the admission of blacks in the proportion of three-fifths can be explained. If the slaves are citizens then why are they not admitted on equality with white citizens. But if they are property then why is not other property considered into the computation." [Finkleman,15] As the Spanish painter Goya lamented, "the sleep of reason produces monsters."

Subsequent Constitutional amendments have addressed civil rights without formally rescinding the issue of an Africans human worth from the U.S. Constitution. Given America's devout "constitution-ology," this problem might never be resolved: the sacred words of the "document" may be amended but never changed. France, meanwhile, has redrafted its constitution five times during the same period of time.

It is clear that Madison, Jefferson, and Washington, et. al considered Africans to be sub-human. Imagine these leaders, familiar with the writings of Locke and Rosseau on the subject of human rights, approving such an abomination. Even those such as John Adams, who opposed slavery, chose political expediency over moral integrity. As the story of America proceeds toward greater civility it would seem appropriate to apologize for such detestable affronts and to castigate such actions as contortions of justice. Instead, America has chosen to honor these slave-owners on their currency and to name towns and cities after them. Some would say that these men should be excused because they were "people of their time." Similarly, then, are they to be forgiven for having only three-fifths of a conscience? They knew that slavery was immoral. There were many others "of their time", such as Samuel Hopkins and Thomas Paine, who openly challenged slavery. William Lloyd Garrison declared that the American government's attitude toward Africans in America meant that the Constitution of the United States was a "covenant with death and an agreement with hell." [Finkleman, 1]

When made law, the three-fifths formulation for Africans was already widely accepted as the "language of all America." [Fehrenbacher, 20] The three-fifths designation defines European attitudes toward Africans throughout American history. It blurred the line between property and persons; between economic worth and human dignity, into a single concept. Financial value replaced the Judeo-Christian concept that humanity was made in God's image. The Federal Ratio legitimized formally what was illegitimate morally. The United States Constitution used words to melt people into objects. It codified the "other-ness" of Africans. Even though the three-fifths designation represents a "ludicrous factional exactitude," [Fehrenbacher, 601] it remains a powerful metaphor for today's struggle.

In the 1856 Dred Scott Decision, presiding Judge Roger B. Taney disallowed Scott the opportunity to buy his own freedom based on the three-fifths logic of the Constitution. Taney said that the Declaration of Independence did not really mean what it said [Fehrenbacher, 351] when it stated that *all* people were created equal. Taney could come to such a conclusion in light of the fact that Jefferson, the author of these words, owned slaves and clearly ignored them when talking about his dreams for "all" Americans.

Judge Taney explained that the Founders must have been making a distinction between what he called "free inhabitants" and "citizens," adding that Africans were "separate and degraded people" [Walker, 19] who would never be suited for freedom. The "Judge Taneys" of our day continue to speak about equality while crafting distinctions based on economic or social status to maintain the status-quo against today's "Dred Scotts." Those who challenge this are said to be wallowing in victimology

What do Dred Scott and Judge Taney and the Constitution's partializing descriptions of Africans have to do with America today? Isn't America well beyond all that? What about the good news? African-Americans are featured on postage stamps and in advertisements. America has a holiday to honor Martin Luther King, Jr. and a month (the coldest and shortest) to honor Black History. The genesis of the latter idea began in the 1930s with an initiative launched by Carter G. Woodson, as a way to educate children. Woodson's efforts, however, were never meant to "ghettoize" African-Americans role in their nation's history.

Yes, there has been notable progress. Marches, protests, petitions and pleas have all had a positive effect. For everything that has changed, however, not enough has changed. We should commemorate the good that has been done. Unfinished business remains. So much business, in fact, that America will probably not be able to deal with it in only one or two generations. The problems are deeply rooted. Racism in America is as vast and varied as the country itself. This is why education is so important in it.

Children must be taught with a critical consciousness how to be advocates for justice and how, by our example, to live with moral courage.

Related Justice Issues: America's Women and First Nations People

If you love the children of others, you will love yourself.
—Wolof Proverb

Americans, like citizens of any other country, face a host of problems. Since the tragic events of 11 September, 2001 the United States has been in a time of transition as it evaluates its role in the world. America needs to recognize that it is not a "melting-pot" where cultures lose their distinctiveness to become subsumed into Euro-American society. Instead America is a multiethnic "salad-bowl" where each culture finds self-expression in the whole. The civil rights movement is primarily responsible for launching this shift in social perception by setting in motion a ripple effect that has encouraged all kinds of social groups to seek redress: women, First Nations People, Asian-Americans, Latino-Americans, homosexuals, and others. Ironically, some of these groups have benefitted more from the movement than have African-Americans. Additionally, the message of equality has become co-opted by an agenda of a contrived integration which has become the only vehicle for African-Americans to participate in America's segregated society.

We will look briefly at gender and First Nations/Native American rights issues. Christianity teaches that faith can speak with force to the challenges of the present day. The Church, self-confident in truth, is capable of being a dynamic agent for personal and social change. It announces that Jesus has inaugurated the "Kingdom of God" on the earth; bringing peace and justice to both individuals and societies. Jesus lived a revolutionary life. Many who claim to follow Him, however, are not interested in revolution and seek to maintain the status-quo. They are more interested in a religion about Jesus than the religion of Jesus.

The reality on which this nation was founded, i.e. the murder of at least twelve million Native Americans and the death by disease of countless others, must be confronted. Indeed, it is an ongoing problem. As recently as 1991, one fourth of the Yanomamos of Northern Brazil were wiped out by European introduced diseases [Loewen, 83]. Some historians suggest that there were as many as fifty million Native Americans when Columbus first arrived, while in the year 2002 fewer than three million First Nations people remain. The promises made and broken to these first people in America continue to affect us. Historical accounts must focus on these injustices so that our children can understand unresolved problems that linger.

Columbus did not discover America. Indigenous people claim they have been here since creation while others say they have "been in North America for only about 19,000 years." [Tucker, 116] The legacy of America's Manifest Destiny led to the genocide of many First Nations cultures while many of their nations are still caricatured without reference to their distinct cultural traditions. Sadly, casino gambling and New Age voyeuristic forays into Native American spirituality encompass how many other Americans think about the first people of this continent.

Native rights issues are important because all other Americans are guests in their homeland. African culture teaches that great honor is due to those who are first in the land. African tradition reminds us that those Native Americans who have died in this country continue to live on in the blood-soaked soil and in the on-going lives of their descendants. Further, it is important to remember that as many as thirty percent of all African-Americans have some Native American ancestry. Forbes writes that,

> The ancestry of modern-day Americans, whether of "Black" or "Indian" appearance, is often (and usually) quite complex indeed. It is said that many such persons have been forced by racism into arbitrary categories that tend to render their ethnic heritage simple rather than complex. It is now one of the principal tasks of scholarship to replace the shallow one-dimensional images of non-Whites with more accurate multi-dimensional portraits. [Forbes, 271]

Native and African-American cultures have interacted in countless ways within the last four hundred years of American history. It is a fascinating story. In 1526, five hundred Spaniards and one hundred African slaves founded the first non-Native settlement near the mouth of the Pee-Dee

River in present day South Carolina. Within a few months after the slaves revolted the Spaniards retreated and the Africans merged harmoniously into the nearby Native American settlements [Loewen, 138].

African-American Christians can be uniquely sensitive to the way that the Bible has been used against Native people because it was also used against them. Puritan preachers claimed they were a "European Joshua" people called into this new "American Holy Land" to "utterly destroy" the First Nations Canaanites. Only a few compromising native "Rahabs" who converted to European ways could avoid the wrath of God's chosen saints.

Gender issues are also important to all Americans. African-American women have suffered tremendously at the hands of men from all cultures. In contrast, women hold a high place in historic African traditions. Many African creation legends begin with God creating woman before he created man. African social values repeatedly affirm that an African man cannot have a position of honor in society if he does not honor the women in his life. African history is resplendent with the accounts of "Queen of Shebas" or "Queen Nzungas" who have led their people with wisdom and determination.

American women have also made progress while many gender issues remain unsolved. Equal pay for equal work remains a goal in the American workplace. Daughters are given Barbie-dolls and steered toward jobs traditionally designated for women. The women who constitute more than 50 percent of the population are represented by only a handful of female legislators. Pornography, portraying women as objects, thrives as a billion-dollar business. Women are victims of physical, sexual and emotional abuse in horrific numbers. Divorce is endemic and poverty-inducing single-parent homes abound. There are whole swatches of American Christianity that still teach that, "women should submit to their husbands as the weaker vessel," forgetting that those words were written almost 2,000 years ago and for a specific cultural context.

The Color-Line Has Become the Color-Wall

The problem of the 20th Century is the problem of the color line—
the relation of the darker to the lighter races of men in Asia
and Africa, in America and in the islands of the sea.
—W. E. B. DuBois, **The Souls of Black Folk,** 1903

DuBois wrote about the color-line between Europeans and Africans in America. Today's de-facto segregation suggests that DuBois "line" has become a wall. Modern comedians joke about how little Europeans and Africans in America relate to one another. At the root of the relationship is ongoing inequality and unresolved injustices. How do we begin to talk about relationships when African-Americans are expected to adjust themselves to the Euro-American majority in order to advance in society. This implicit demand goes forward even while many Euro-Americans build fortress walls of segregation in their churches and neighborhoods to avoid the "other." The situation is polarizing.

Ours is an arranged marriage from its inception. A contrived past affects a troubled present. What rapist would ask the one who has been raped about the status of their "relationship"? How can the Euro-American "rapist" take entire groups of people from their own lands, attack their societies, languages, music, assassinate their spirituality; isolate them in three centuries of forced labor camps and abuse them without regard to human dignity. Then, after only fifty years of relatively humane treatment, announce that everything is fine and expect that their relation with these people will be a healthy one?

The challenge is to get the one who is raped to trust and to have a "relationship" with the rapist. One of the oft-repeated arguments of contemporary Euro-Americans is that they do not understand the issues. Their objection is that they are not racist, and that they themselves never owned slaves. So, why are they culpable? How can they be compared with those who rape? These same individuals should not be offended or easily side-tracked when people take these laments at face value and try to address these very difficult dynamics.

What better place for Christians to begin to deal with racism than from inside the walls of our segregated churches? In 1900, there were more

African and European Christians worshiping together than in the year 2000. If the church cannot address these problems then it should not be surprising that Christians will not have a credible voice in the larger society. Today's "Judge Taneys" continue to change the subject and avoid taking the steps needed to effect change. They hide behind a smoke screen of words and spin spider webs with rationalizations to protect themselves. Three-fifths theology is filled with rhetoric but avoids the strenuous action needed to effect genuine equality and comprehensive social justice.

Living in Different Worlds

The revolution will not be televised!
—GIL SCOTT HERON

Lewis T. Tait and A. Christian van Gorder are two forty-two year-old American men (hoping to be) at the midway point in their lives. We were both born in cities and in hospitals and in the same year. Once our parents left those maternity wards, however, they took us back into different worlds. In elementary school, we had the same textbooks for American history and literature. One of us learned, however, that the country was "founded" by people who looked like he did, and one of us learned by inference that his ancestors played a minor role in its development.

We watched some of the same television sitcoms and, again, they helped reinforce who ran the M*A*S*H unit, the Bonanza Ranch, the General Hospital, the Adam 12 police station, the F-Troop, and everything else. We saw who had the deserted island named after him or who led the underground resistance at Stalag 13. We both cheered for football teams that seemed pretty inter-ethnic, at least until the camera panned over to most of the coaches and all of the owners. We both went to Sunday school, but our churches were almost completely segregated while both our Sunday school curriculums showed white angels and a blond-haired, blue-eyed Jesus. When we went to find jobs and attend college, America's segregating influences began to kick in with a vengeance. The difference at this point was that one of us became angry about injustice while the other continued, blissfully oblivious to the other's anger. That is until we met.

Van Gorder was returning from nine years of international mission service. Flying away from America for a number of years at a time could be described as the ultimate "white flight," because the problems of other countries do not have any personal effect on the expatriate. Tait was finishing six years of launching an urban church plant in a building abandoned by "white flight" and surrounded by government housing projects in desperate need for attention. His father had been a pastor for thirty-nine years and had poured everything he knew into his son.

When they met at Harambee United Church of Christ, where Tait was pastor and founder, van Gorder's obliviousness met Tait's experiences with well-meaning (do-gooding voyeuristic) white liberalism. Tait was in no mood to be "spectated" and to serve as someone's vehicle for education or intercultural entertainment. He had recently survived a terrible relationship with a Euro-American man who had promised to help the church but had only brought grief. That was behind him now. He had a job to do; change a community. Work for justice and awaken people who were struggling to keep their heads above water.

Tait was putting into reality a vision for an Afrocentric Christian church. Van Gorder thought all churches were supposed to be Christocentric. Maybe that was because van Gorder was part of a three-fifths theology that functions as if Christ lived in a culture-free vacuum. All Christianity is Christocentric. It is also incarnationally rooted in culture and not only some amorphous spiritual idealism. God relates to all people. God in Christ comes into time and becomes a Jewish carpenter in the Roman Empire. This was a specific, "once and for all time" miracle rooted in history. Through the Holy Spirit in the life of the church and through the sacraments, God is also "experienced" afresh in unique cultural contexts. God is in Christ, reconciling the world to himself. Culture is a vessel, and not a barrier, to God's redeeming work.

Tait called van Gorder a "Euro-American." Van Gorder didn't know what to call Tait. It had never occurred to van Gorder that he was a Euro-American. He thought he was a color: "white." The relationship could be seen as a microcosm of some of the larger realities of three-fifths theology. It is a difficult relationship, because we were raised in two different worlds. Both worlds call themselves Christian, but have a very different idea of exactly what it means to live as a Christian in a country which wraps its faith in the flag with blind patriotism. Another chronic problem in the relationship between European and African-Americans is the Euro-American assumption that there is no longer any major problem in this area because the civil rights movement resolved most inequalities. Many Euro-American Christians do not even recognize that their churches are segregated, and that their lives are being lived in isolation from the experience of African-Americans. These are the reasons that we began to write this book.

We Didn't Come On the Same Boat but We're In the Same Boat Now

Before shooting one must aim
—Nigerian Proverb

We do share a relationship; incoherent and insane as it is. Frederick Douglass warned:

> We shall neither die here in America or be driven out, but shall go with these people either as a testimony against them or as evidence in their favor throughout their generations...the white man's happiness cannot be purchased by the black man's misery....It is evident that the white and black must fall or flourish together. [Magubane, 70]

Douglass understood American cultural interrelatedness. We need each other, not only to survive, but to build a nation that is prismatic and vibrant. All Americans are inextricably bound together by a mutual citizenship and a shared history. Distinctiveness, as African and European-Americans, is to be respected. Our mutual American-ness must also be appreciated.

The relationship between African and European-Americans has often been more about rape than about mutuality. Interethnic mixing is a fact of American history. Pure bloodlines are only an illusion. The American census has no box entitled "mulatto." If it did, then every American should check it. A historical racist theory was that if a person had one drop of African blood then one was an African. According to this theory, many "Europeans" (through the male "Y" chromosome) are probably "Africans." Shipler writes:

A lot of white folks in their roots are black. Here's where the tables get turned. It is one thing for blacks to have some white in them but many whites shudder at the thought that their blood-line may have been infiltrated by even a touch of black ancestry. [Shipler, 113]

The idea of "racial purity" should be, by now, completely discredited. Even if this is not apparent to many, and, even if their ancestors were the raped as well as the rapists, there are still many other connections that link us together in this small lifeboat called America. To use another metaphor, the United States may be a dysfunctional family, but it is nonetheless a family. Recent national emergencies have brought that into focus. Once a little girl of a culturally mixed-marriage asked her mother if she could collect mermaids, because they are half one thing and half another as she felt that she was. Like the girl in the story, all Americans are part of each other and should see themselves as "mermaids."

Few Euro-Americans understand what it means to be of African ancestry in America. Most have never considered their own cultural identity at length, let alone how that identity relates to people of other cultures. Many Euro-Americans dismiss the notion of Afrocentricity while not being aware of their own constricting Eurocentricity. They might think of themselves as "universalists" in their faith and world view. The idea that European values are universal values allows many people to believe that their view is the only one that matters. Euro-Americans can learn from Afrocentric critiques of European culture from writers like Marimba Ani in her book, *Yurugu*. Ani's discussion of an ongoing syntax of cultural imperialism that Euro-Americans frequently impose while, at the same time, demanding from African-Americans a high degree of over-identification in order to share in the fruits of power, is seminal.

Does what we share as Christians and Americans enable us to talk about meaningful partnerships? The verdict is still out on this question. Social and institutional structures remain decidedly segregated. Many African-Americans are disillusioned about Euro-American rhetorical overtures that lack substance. Conversely, many feel that they have already done all that they can to "level the playing field."

Terminology for Understanding

*We die. That may be the meaning of life. But we do have
language. That may be the measure of our lives*
—TONI MORRISON, Nobel Prize Acceptance Speech

*My people should not be ashamed of their history, nor any name
that people chose in good faith to give them. Whether a person calls
a Negro a colored person or an African-American, makes no
difference if that person does not respect you.*
—W. E. B. DuBois

Finally, let's say a word about terminology. Care is needed here because so much carelessness marks intercultural discussion. People do not listen to one another; they infer, assume, deduce, imagine and mis-communicate with each other in seemingly every conceivable way. A West African proverb reminds us that God has given us "two ears and one mouth because he wants us to listen twice as much as we speak."

Substantive discussions about intercultural relations are often imprisoned by words. People supply different meanings for words like tolerance, integration, racism, and prejudice. Words also have symbolic as well as literal meanings. This is why Molefi Asante stresses that the one who controls the terms of the discourse will also determine the constructs of social reality. Perceptions will lead to how people act and not only how they speak. Terms have the potential to either empower or control others. It is telling that between cultures in America, social conversation is often stilted. There is often a frozen awkwardness in the way that many Euro-Americans speak with African-Americans about racial justice.

We will use the terms, "African-American" and "European-American." This does not mean that we are unaware of recent immigrants coming from Africa or Europe who feel very little connection to those who have lived here for generations. Americans who are recent immigrants from either of these two continents often also bear some of the weight of these two categories. The term "American" itself is multifaceted. We use it in reference to people from the United States.

We avoid the terms "black" and "white." It is interesting to see how long these terms have survived in light of the fact that the goal of many who use such categories is their desire to live in a world where color is not the primary way that people distinguish and define one another. The same proponents of a "color-blind" ideal use language against their fondest convictions. The terms are not even accurate. Children (sometimes using crayons marked "flesh colored") often remind their parents that skin colors are actually pinkish or brownish. It is unfortunate that children are taught labels of color, which divide instead of terms which celebrate the beauty of cultural heritage.

Jesse Jackson, one of the people responsible for emphasizing the term "African-American," stated that "Black tells you about skin color and what side of town you live on. African-American evokes discussion of the world" [Turner, 1]. Terms of color need to be intentionally pushed aside. In their place, we must examine cultural realities.

Malcolm X pointed out how American culture has vilified blackness. In cowboy movies and in films like *the Wizard of Oz,* the good witch wears white and the evil witch wears black. In *Star Wars,* that great cinematic Odysseus legend, the vile Darth Vader, is dressed in black and the valiant Jedi Knights are arrayed in white. An "acceptable" lie is a "white lie." People are "blacklisted" and "blackballed" as "black sheep" and "blackmailers." Politicians with little hope of winning are "dark horse" candidates and the 19, October 1987 stock market problem is called "Black Monday." Black is the absence of light, and white is the reflection of all light in the visible spectrum. Harvard sociologist Orlando Patterson in his landmark book, *Rituals of Blood* quotes Webster's Twentieth Century Dictionary definitions of the words "black" and "white":

Black: 1. Figuratively: dismal, gloomy, sullen, forbidding; destitute of moral light or goodness; mournful, calamitous, evil, wicked, atrocious (thus Shakespeare speaks of black deeds, thoughts, envies, tidings, despair, etc.) 2. Soiled or dirty. 3. Disgraceful 4. Without hope, as in "black" future 5. Inveterate, confirmed as in deep-dyed black villain 6. Humorous or satirical in a morbid, cynical or savage way such as in black humor.

White: 1. Having the color of pure snow and milk, the opposite of black. 2. Morally and spiritually pure; spotless; innocent 3. Free from evil intent; harmless as in white magic 4. Happy, fortunate and auspicious 5. Having a light colored skin-Caucasian; of or controlled by the white race as in white supremacy based on notions of racial superiority; Slang: honest, honorable, fair, dependable, favorite.

Patterson responds to these definitions by saying: "It is preposterous to assume that when Americans call each other "white" and "black" they are somehow able to mentally bracket these historically and culturally integrated and dictionary sanctioned, meaning of these terms...." [Patterson, 21]. We agree that it is time to do away with racist language.

Chapter One
Africa: Dark Continent or Cradle of Civilization?

*We are emerging from a time of ignorance and misunderstand-
ing....One of the consequences of this liberation has been, as a liberating force, the study of Africa's own history of social formation,
change and development over many centuries. That enlightenment has been the means of tearing down the veils and lies of
racism, of finally denying (if not yet destroying) the racist assertions of a natural and inherent black inferiority on the human
scale and of demonstrating the natural and inherent equality on
the human scale of black peoples with other peoples. It is a notable
conquest; it is the beginning of historical wisdom. Even the non-
African world has "re-discovered" the black continent. Explo-
ration of Africa has acquired a depth of human meaning that it
did not have before.*
> —BASIL DAVIDSON, **African Civilization Revisited.**

*What is Africa to me copper sun or scarlet sea, jungle star or jungle
trek, strong bronzed men or regal black/Women from whom my
loins I sprang when the birds of Eden sang? One three centuries
removed from the scenes his father loved/Spicy grove, cinnamon
tree, What is Africa to me?*
> —COUNTEE CULLEN, **Heritage**

Our Common African Origins

I've known rivers: I've known rivers ancient as the world and older than the flow of human blood in human veins. My soul has grown deep like the rivers. I bathed in the Euphrates when dawns were young. I built my hut near the Congo and it lulled me to sleep. I looked upon the Nile and raised the pyramids above it. I heard the singing of the Mississippi when Abe Lincoln went down to New Orleans, and I've seen its muddy bosom turn all golden in the sunset. I've known rivers: Ancient dusky rivers. My soul has grown deep like the rivers.
  —LANGSTON HUGHES, **The Negro Speaks of Rivers**

The Romans called it Libya, and early Greeks called it Aethiopia ("Aithiops" for "burnt faces") or Cush. Later Romans called it Africa, based on the Roman colony around Carthage (Tunis)that had the same name. It is believed that the word "Africa" comes from the Arabic, "Ifriqiya." Most Africans in antiquity referred to the general region as "Bilad al-Sudan", the "land of the Blacks." [Lamin Sanneh, lectures, 2000] All humanity should call her "Mother" (or some African language equivalent) because scientists and anthropologists around the world have confirmed, as far as it is possible, that the human story begins in Africa (4.4 million years ago!). "Denkneshi" (the Amharic word meaning "beautiful") is the Ethiopian name for "Lucy," the first known human ancestor found in Ethiopia's Rift Valley. These claims are widely accepted. Recently, even scientists in the People's Republic of China acknowledged that Africa was their probable ancestral home.

Racism has its roots in an assumption that "race is the primary determinant of human traits and capacities" [Webster's New College Dictionary, 1981]. The widely accepted notion of "race" emerged in Europe in the 1800s and concluded that there were three primary races (Caucasoid, Mongoloid, Negroid) in the human community. This is the view still presented in contemporary encyclopedias and textbooks,

These views developed from a racist scientism and are not an African notion. An African view would agree with Victor Frankl's claim in *Man's Search for Meaning* that there are only two races: those who seek to be virtuous and those who live lives of violence and selfishness. The Biblical narrative and contemporary science agree that there is only one race: the human race. Some humans simply have more melanin in their skin. Cain Hope Felder argues that the Genesis description of the Garden of Eden places it inside Africa. Felder shows that "the Gihon" is the term used by Ethiopians to describe the Blue Nile. He also claims that the Pishon River is probably the White Nile. The Bible seems to dramatize that God formed Adam from African clay and that all humans began as African.

African-Centered Values

Afrocentricity is simple. If you examine the phenomena concern-ing African people, you must give them agency. If you don't you are imposing Eurocentrism on them
—MOLEFI ASANTE

Does one have to be an African to share African-centered world view assumptions? The idea of Afrocentricity or African-centeredness is not only a meaningful concept for some 800 million Africans and for the over 100 million Africans of the diaspora. It is an idea with insights to be garnered for people from all cultures. This is because traditionally African rooted con-cepts of wisdom and spirituality exclude no one.

What does an African-centered perspective look like? Cain Hope Felder writes that it is "...simply the idea that Africa— and persons of African descent— must be seen as proactive subjects within history rather than pas-sive objects of Western triumphalism." [*Original African Heritage Bible*, 93] Molefi Asante suggests that, African ideas should be at the "center of any analysis of African culture or behavior." [Asante, 1988, 6] When focus-ing on things African we should begin with an African-centered perspec-tive. Similarly, when dealing with ideas and traditions that originate in Europe we should recognize that we often evaluate these from a Eurocen-tric frame of reference. To call a Christian an African-centered Christian is to acknowledge that the roots from which that person originates from, or in which that person now participates, begin in Africa.

Countee Cullen asked the question: "What is Africa to me?" What does Afrocentricity have to do with the day-to-day demands of life? Fords are made in Detroit, not in Dahomey; Silicon Valley is in California, not

Chad. An M.B.A. from a business school seems more pertinent to daily life than the ancient wisdom of Africa.

For some time, African-American consciousness of Africa was often superficial. Gradually, information and history are now being joined with hopeful idealism. Writers since Paul Gilroy have moved the debate from the limitations of race that were set out by thinkers like Martin Delaney. Afrocentricity is no longer only about the relation of Africa to European culture and issues of hegemony and value. It does not need the foil of Eurocentricity to define its parameters. Afrocentrists are no longer mono-culturalists but now embrace the "mixology" of both the African Diaspora and the great tapestry of African cultures. An African-centered world view is becoming an empowering tool for both individual and collective self-confidence. Increasingly, Africans are free from the need to respond to Euro-American agendas, levels of interest, and involvement in their lives. An African-rooted world view is self-defining and not dependent upon the approval of non-African peoples.

African-centered Christianity denies that Christianity inherently relates to European cultural values. As early as the third century, African theologian Tertullian was asking the question of Europeans: "What has Athens to do with Jerusalem?" Then as now, European Christians assumed that the Greek philosophical legacy they had inherited had made their faith somehow more substantive than that of people from other parts of the world. Robert Hood, in *Must God Remain Greek: Afro-cultures and God-talk*, explains:

> Christian reliance on Greek and Roman patterns of thought has been pervasive and overwhelming, even by those who joined in protest against that legacy. In councils and controversies and condemnations and crusades over 1500 years, the core notions of the Christian life and thought-fundamental notions of God, Christ, the Spirit, redemption-were forcefully if not always gracefully hammered into the Greek mold. And when Christian missionaries sailed from Europe and the United States to impart the gospel to native peoples in the colonies of Africa, they carried, along with their message and a host of other cultural assumptions, their almost visceral faith in the Greek way of thought. [Hood, preface, XI]

Eurocentric Christianity is only one expression of the world Christian movement. To speak of Afrocentric Christianity is to focus on world view assumptions rooted in African experience and does not claim that its experience is more valid than any other cultural expression. Cultures, not some misguided conception of "race," define world view assumptions. Cultures "provide arbitrary shared rules about emotional expression;" [Cohen, 99] define correct behavior; and provide other assumptions about the world. If the Bible is, as Theophus Smith says, "the model for post-modern ethnography," [Smith, 17] and if the divine theurgy ("God work") is the creation of different cultures, then we can come to appreciate the theopoetic nature of all cultural difference. It is as if the greatness of God demands the diverse mosaic of culture if humanity is to be made from earth's clay in divine image. Deculturation, the destruction of culture, inversely, a the work of greatest evil. In this context, the globalization war between what Benjamin Barber calls "MacWorld verses Jihad" is of moral as well as political concern.

Afrocentricity is important in that it holds great liberating potential for both African-Americans and Euro-Americans. The average person in the church or classroom needs to examine what Nai'm Akbar calls the chains that enslave the mind with false motivations, perceptions, aspirations, and a shallow understanding of identity. For Akbar this generates,

> ...a personal and collective self destruction that is more cruel
> than the shackles on the wrist and ankles. The slavery that feeds
> on the psychology, invading the soul of man destroying his loy-
> alties to himself and establishing allegiance to forces which
> destroy him, is an even worse form of capture. These are influ-
> ences that permit an illusion of freedom. Liberation and self-
> determination, while tenaciously holding ones' mind in
> subjugation, is only the folly of the sadistic. [Akbar, 1998, 2]

Historical oppression continues whenever any people remain divorced from the wealth of their own cultural heritage. This is a vital issue that an African-centered world view seeks to address. An example of how an African-centered perspective affects daily life is the idea that places are sacred because of the presence and lives of the ancestors in those places. This is not peculiar to Africans; Native Americans hold to this same value.

Europeans in America, however, have not always understood why others are so loyal to the land. Many did not understand, for example, why, after slavery was revoked, many African-Americans chose to live in the American South. The South was, as the song declared, the "Land where my Fathers died and the land of the Pilgrims (from Africa) Pride."

The Drum Major Instinct

One must touch a drum before it will speak.
—Hausa Proverb

The night is profligate with drums/that croak in the jungle/with their hoarse throats of skin/when some blaze awakens them....One hears of the white man lost in the jungle/It is as assiduous drum tone that runs imponderable through the immense night/At its conjuration bodes the obscure potentials/fetishes of the dance/ totems of war/and the thousand demons that swarm/through the sensual sky of the black soul...
—PALES MATOS (Puerto Rico)

In discussing the creation of culture in an African context we must turn our attention to the importance of the drum. When I (Lewis Tait), was a boy, my father used to take me to revivals all over the American South. He would preach, and I would play the drums. I remember the joy experienced in worship as people danced and worshiped the Lord. It brought such delight to my heart to watch people dance themselves into a frenzy; to dance themselves into joy; to dance themselves into healing. The worshipers may have come to church weighed down by oppressing challenges, but it was not long before they had danced themselves into a better future in God's glory.

There is an internal mechanism within us that beats out the rhythm of life. Our hearts beat with the power of all that we feel and experience. I have attended services where the congas were beating, and it seemed like the entire congregation fell into continuity with each other. The drums build the nation and bring us into focus. Drums call us together. They communicate something primeval to who we are as God made us. If God turned the drum of our hearts off for a moment, we would not survive.

When our ancestors came through the Middle Passage, they would find solace in beating their bloodied knuckles against the side of the slave ship wood. Their drumming sent out a wave of sound into the oceans that still echoes in the depths of the seas to this very day. When they broke their backs in American cotton fields, our ancestors lifted up their souls to God through the rhythm of their chant and the drumming that accompanied their words. Here they were powerful. Their song took possession of the land.

It is not surprising that the slave master often forbade the use of the drum. They could sense the power that the drum wielded. They sensed, perhaps, that the rhythm of the drums built bridges of communication. They feared people would send messages to one another that would foment rebellion. Drums empowered a sense of spiritual freedom, and the master did not want the slave to place any "god" in their lives above their own cruel authority (which puts Jefferson's call for secularism in a new light). There may be another reason: the universality of drums. Holy men beat the "bodhran" in Ireland, and drumming is deep in the psyche of the English and the German. Perhaps, listening to these African drums from their own ancestral links to Africa, and more recently Europe, evoked something too humane in their own hearts. They had to turn away from the of the beat to seek hellish solace in a silence free of music.

Drums remain a "glue" among African peoples worldwide. Drums echo the heartbeat of life. In Africa, spiritual traditions pulse with the sound of the drum. In the African diaspora this is also true. Segal discusses the "golpe" beat of the Venezuelans, the "tamborito" beat of the Panamanians, the fluid "guaguanco" beat of Brazil, the Afro-Cuban "mambo" (from the Kongolese word "mambe" which means "song") and Afro-Caribbean "bomba" beats that infuse the music of the African diaspora. [Segal, 389-392] The expression "give me some skin," according to Fox, is a reference to the skin on a drum. Too much of non-African evaluations of Africa have focused on skin color. Africans, as Zora Neale Hurston explained, brought the "drum in their skin." [Okpewho, 1999, 374]

All of us are called to take up the drum and communicate with one another and with God. It is a holy calling and a uniting vision. Our leaders have long known this to be true. When Dr. Martin Luther King, Jr. told his friends at Ebenezer Baptist Church what he wanted to have said at his funeral he asked to be called a "drum-major" for justice:

> I want you to say that day that I tried to be right and walk with them. I want you to be able to say that day that I did try to feed the hungry. I want you to be able to say that day that I did try in my life to clothe the naked and visit those who were in prison. And I want you to say that I tried to love and serve humanity. Yes, and if you want to say that I was a drum major. Say that I was a drum major for justice. Say that I was a drum major for peace. I was a drum major for righteousness. And all of the other shallow things won't matter. I won't have any money to leave behind. I won't have the fine and luxurious things of life to leave behind. But I just want to leave a committed life behind....If I can do my duty as a Christian ought. If I can bring salvation to a world once wrought. If I can spread the message as the Master taught. Then my living will not be in vain. [Lincoln, 87]

Critics of African-Centered Historiography

You made the earth as you wished to alone, All people's, herds, and flocks, All on one earth, that walk on legs or on high that fly on wings, the lands of Khor and Kush and the land of Egypt. You set every man in place and supply his needs. Everyone has his food, his lifetime, and his country. Their tongues differ in speech and their characters likewise. Their skins are distinct, for you distinguish the people.
—The Great Hymn of the Sun God Aten, circa 1330 B.C.E.

To be a critic is easier than to be an author
—Hebrew Proverb

Martin Bernal in *Black Athena: The Afro-Asiatic Roots of Classical Civilization,* and Mary Lefkowitz in her provocatively titled attack of this book *Not Out of Africa: How Afrocentrism Became An Excuse to Teach Myth As History,* have been at the center of an academic storm debating how African influences affected the development of European philosophy. The cover of Lefkowitz's book is graced with a statue of Sophocles in a "Malcolm X" baseball cap. The Introduction goes on to call Afrocentric ideas "strange" and "spurious," and before even beginning I (van Gorder), felt like I was dealing with the "Willie-Horton-ization" (Recalling George Bush's 1988 campaign "use" of Willie Horton) of Bernal's ideas. The question is not whether or not Bernal's thesis is correct but why serious ideas are cast as some sort of a sporting event where contestants "win or loose" or "strikeout at the plate" of academic acceptance. Is this "responsible scholarship"? Let the discussion go on with civility. No one is advocating historicity that is not based on thorough research and a balanced consideration of all points of view.

Bernal contends that there has been a longstanding assumption that Greek civilization developed from and, in relation to, the older civilizations of Africa. He calls this the "Ancient Model" and contrasts it with an "Aryan Model" which states that Greeks were primarily beneficiaries of Europe and without reference to Africa. He asks why scholars have difficulty accepting that Africans interacted with their contemporaries in the ancient world. Bernal attacks this as a contrivance with racist undertones rooted in European particularism. Bernal does allow for some possible influences from Aryan peoples (hence his "Revised Ancient Model").

Bernal asks why is it so difficult for Euro-American scholars to countenance the idea that Northern Mediterranean Greek culture did not borrow from Southern Mediterranean Egyptian culture? It should not be so difficult to accept that, "African influence on ancient Greece...was significant in art, architecture, astronomy, medicine, geometry, mathematics, law, politics, and religion." [Asante, 2001, 49] Lefkowitz accuses Bernal of revisionist history. Revisionism and myth-making is a reality that scholars of all cultures have to confront. The criticism of excess by Afrocentric historians could also be leveled against Eurocentric historians. Nell Painter, a historian at Princeton muses, "As someone who went to school in the fifties, don't talk to me about fabrication! What we had to put up with! I think you deserve a black everything for at least a decade!" [Shipler, 210] Lefkowitz, herself, admits to an agenda to support cherished cultural myths when she writes,

Any attempt to question the authenticity of Ancient Greek civilization is of direct concern even to people who ordinarily have little interest in the remote past. Since the founding of this country, ancient Greece has been intimately connected with the ideals of American democracy. [Lefkowitz, 71]

Is Bernal beyond reproach? Of course not. Frequent references to Heroditus should acknowledge that he openly admitted to being a storyteller as much as a purveyor of information. Plutarch even called Herodotus the "master of lies." [Mudimbe, 97] But this is a marginal issue which diverts attention from the larger scope. Herodotus, the father of history, is not the only historian who deals in inaccuracies.

Many scholars have taken issue with some of Bernal's conclusions. Bernal's ideas, however, do deserve a hearing if it is true that his ideas will "profoundly mark the next century's perceptions of the origin of Greek civilization." [Mudimbe, 104] Are some claims by Afrocentric historians overstated, i.e., relying on assumptions? Do some people describe positions that need further investigation as if they were fact? Invariably this occurs. These errors, however, should not lead to the dismissal of ideas that call for the rethinking Africa's role in the foundations of European philosophy and history. Noise should not be confused with music! Flawed reasoning that attack positions which affirm Afrocentric views of history must not be given more weight than they deserve. Assertion is not proof.

There is room for further inquiry. Continued research could focus on the Kushite, Ethiopian, and the Southern Nile Valley kingdoms. It is accepted that Mentuhotep was a Nubian pharaoh, but much less is known about other Nubian kingdoms. Little is known about the Kerma (Kermetic) civilization (circa 2686-1880 B.C.E.) in what is now the Sudan. Other African kingdoms distanced further from Egypt/Kemet have received even less scrutiny. The study of African history promises fascinating rewards and remains largely unexplored.

Conjuring the Dark Continent

There are no other savages in Africa than
some whites acting crazily
— FELIX VON LUSCHEN

Is Afrocentric history the story, as critics suggest, of "people deprived of a history seemingly keen to acquire a glorious past"? An African-centered understanding of history and theology can be an empowering resource. New possibilities rise from the clay of self-confidence. This is because an African-centered perspective draws from a vast history rooted in sustainable evidence. It is not "myth-making" any more than is any European-centered historiography. Literature and aesthetics offer important additional avenues for consideration. Wil Coleman, in *Tribal Talk,* has described how oral traditions and literature rooted in an African cosmology can be an invaluable source for shedding light on our relationship with God and with each other.

As the children of Israel crossed the Jordan River, Joshua told them to find stones in the middle of the river and save them as "teaching memorials." The stories and wisdom from Africa's past can be "stones" that can teach us. Africans must collect stones from their long sojourn in the American desert to serve as guides for the future. These stones will be the legends and poems of our ancestors. We must build with them and guard them as our legacy.

That should be obvious. African consciousness, however, seems to have often been dismissed in the church and in the academy. Textbooks widely used in North America and in Europe that claim to be comprehensive often omit African-centered theological perspectives along with African art, history, philosophy and religion saying, in essence, that things and views African are "not worth mentioning." These ideas are also expressed in the attitude of some Euro-American Christians who demonize African traditions and practices as primitive animism. Accounts focus on the bizarre and the garish while often altogether ignoring ideas that display deep moral values. Coleman writes:

Most Europeans and Euro-Americans believed that West Africans were extremely polytheistic and inclined toward demonism. Actually, they held a conviction in one supreme, over-arching being who could be contacted through many channels, both human and non-human and both animate and inanimate. [Coleman, 32]

The code word used to dismiss these kind of foundational religious ideas is "syncretism." But, where is Christian faith not, in many extensive ways, syncretistic? The problem is that no one ever says, "I am a syncretist." It is a term of approbation used to diminish other people with whom one does not agree or understand. In fact, Christians from many cultures, including Euro-American Christians, are quite syncretistic. They often comfortably accommodate a host of ideas about materialism, hedonism, individualism, and militarism that seem to other Christians to be clearly in opposition to biblical mandates for holiness. This fact puts a new light on their willingness to dismiss other people's faith as being syncretistic. When looking at early African-American Christians, Wil Coleman notes that it was the norm to attack African Christianity as being "something disturbingly un-Christian." Coleman argues these value judgements were,

Based on their own racist, ethnocentric and elitist interpretation of how the Christian faith should engender "appropriate" behavior within the context of worship (for all peoples, at all times). Most Euro-American catechists, especially among the upper class, stressed the rational acceptance of their doctrinal teaching along with a countervailing disdain toward any display of either emotionalism or irrationality, especially among African-American slaves. To them, such was the epitome of sensual bestiality." [Coleman, 50]

The idea of "discovering Africa" is well known in the annals of European geographical history. British museums staged exhibits showing their constituency the backwardness and savagery of the African continent. Some of these exhibits even included African participants dressed in animal skins as "performers." [Coomes, 85] Colonialists relished accounts by adventurers of Africa as a "dark continent." It was enlightening to visit Zimbabwe's *Mosokye-yi Onye* and note that even the local people only knew of the great cascade, "the water that thunders," as "Victoria Falls" instead of its actual African place name.

Arrogance combined with ignorance can be dangerous. Negative views of Africa can be documented ad infinitum in literary accounts. Writers created an Africa that never actually existed. According to Dorothy Hammond and Alta Jablow, "the British view of Africa appears to be, at best, quite absurd, and at worst, the result of malice and cynicism." [Hammond and Jablow, 15] This legacy remains to this day. Contemporary media portrayals of Africa advance colonial-era imagistic fantasies.

Early European theologians and anthropologists who "looked at Africa" promoted the image of impulse driven, instinctually sexual savage "Hamites" in spite what they actually found: Societies rich in cultural, ritual heritages and extensive litigious systems. Sadly, it was religious advocates of three-fifths theology who led the way in the promotion of this kind of denigration. An example of this is found in the footnotes of Bible commentators such as this widely distributed reading on Genesis 9:18-27 written by evangelical Finis J. Dake:

> All colors and types of men came into existence after the flood. All men were white up to this point, for there was only one family line-that of Noah who was White and in the line of Christ, being mentioned in Luke 3:36 with his son Shem...(there is a) prophecy that Shem would be a chosen race and have a peculiar relationship with God (v. 26). All divine revelation since Shem has come through this line.... [Felder, 1989, 40]

This long line of approbation also has contemporary expressions of unseemly conclusions about how the AIDS plague began. News accounts about the AIDS epidemic have at times been quick to accentuate how primitive African morality is, as if European and American moral values were more advanced.

In the United States, the legacy of this kind of recasting continues in the way that people evaluate the reasons for lower test scores among African-American students compared to Euro-American children or to explain the dearth of African-American scholars.

Behavioral scientists Charles Murray and Richard Herrnstein published a report in 1994 called the *Bell Curve: Intelligence and Class Structure in*

American Life. It purported that the least intelligent Americans were African-Americans. A lack of intelligence explained poverty. Writ large it was the bully telling the classmate that they were childlike. Such a study should have been treated with the same dismissiveness appropriate for theories about ancient tablets written by aliens. Instead, these ideas gained a wide audience. The gist of these portrayals, both contemporary and ancient, is singular: Africans and African-Americans are not whole persons from a whole culture. They are "three-fifths people" from a "three-fifths continent."

A Case Study for Afrocentric Christianity: "The Great Cloud of Witnesses"

Who would be free must themselves strike the blow.
—FREDERICK DOUGLASS

To be a Christian is to be part of a world-wide community of faith. The church, broad in its scope, is also rooted in specific incarnational contexts. These specificities are wonderful resources for learning for the entire Christian community. Often, one segment of the "beloved community" can provide valuable insights or needed correctives for another group of Christians. Examples of this abound. Here, we will introduce only one concept in African Christianity that can be helpful for Christians rooted in European traditions. This is the idea that there is some continuity between our lives and the lives of those who have come before us.

The greek in the Gospel of John talks about the Logos eternal way of God. The term "Logos" was borrowed from Greek philosophy. Chinese scholars have written about the Tao or path of life. In Swahili the term for the path of life and righteousness is *Nija*: the way. People the world over need to find the Nija/Logos way in life. Without such a foundation, people are aimless and float through life like ships without moorings. They have forgotten the path that the ancestors have made through the seas of life before they arrived.

Paul exhorts Timothy to honor his mother and grandmother who lived lives of faith before Christ's revelation. The book of Hebrews announces that we are "surrounded by a cloud of witnesses" and that our departed family watches from above, seeing how our lives build upon their work. They call us to live in the Nija of God's grace. This biblical idea is echoed in African understandings of the nearness of our ancestors. Wimberly writes, "Honoring elders is a deeply embedded value in African-American life" because they are repositories of the community's collective wisdom. [Wimberly, 5] Honoring makes "tangible the elder's experience of God's love." [Wimberly, 6] Remembering those who have gone before inspires us to follow in their example of lives lived in faithfulness to God's Nija.

The Apostles Creed avows that Christians are linked to the "communion of the saints" who, in heaven or on earth, are united in a common awareness. God is the God of Abraham, Isaac, and Jacob. The memory of these ancestors is kept alive through those who follow in their Nija of faith with God. This is a central idea throughout the Bible and Judaism celebrates this continuity. Catholics celebrate the constancy of the Pope's leadership to the present and Orthodox Christianity also finds strength in its heritage. The Bible confirms that people maintain a level of "relationship" with those who have left their legacies behind. This seemingly obvious idea is threatening to some American Protestants. How can Protestant Christianity take seriously, for example, the discussion in I Corinthians 15:29 without coming to grips with a seeming divide between Greek and Hebrew understandings of how the living relate to the dead?

Contemporary European world-views offer little help with these questions. The European Enlightenment seemingly offers only two options: the visible/known and the mysterious/spiritual. According to this dichotomous paradigm, there seems to be little interaction between the two worlds.

Job tells us to remember the wisdom of our ancestors and to build on the Nija of those who have gone before us. One cannot benefit from the wisdom of those in the past if they are not known or knowable. Contemporary physics even challenges the assumption that history is linear and as a result, in some way, nonexistent once it occurs.

Theologian Kosuke Koyama writes about a "cyclical-linear" view of time that allows for the "creation-to-Kingdom progress" of a linear perspective without excluding the cyclical patterns of the seasons of nature. Contemporary metaphysics asks if time even exists. The God of the Bible is above time and not bound to a linear world that pushes what has happened into irrelevance and secondary status. The God of "Abraham, Isaac and Jacob" is the "I AM" God of the present free from the linear constraints of both past and future. Christians should consider what in their world-view is actually biblical and what springs from European presuppositions about the nature of time and relation to ancestors.

The Afrocentric Vision: "Know Thyself"

The spell of Africa is upon me. The ancient witchery of
her medicine is burning in my drowsy, dreamy blood. This is not a
country, it is a world, a Universe of itself and for itself, a
thing Different, Immense, Menacing, Alluring. It is a great
black bosom where the Spirit longs to die...Africa is the
Spiritual Frontier of Humankind.
—W. E. B. DuBois

"Know Thyself" is a well-known axiom of classical Greek philosophy. It is also the oft-repeated wisdom of the ancient African empires. It was a statement that they carved into the front-pieces of their temples and at the top of their altars. It was the focal point of their epistemology. This message is important today, not only in our understanding of ourselves as individuals but also in our relationships and in our communities.

This proverb proclaims a vital truth. No people can attain social power without first being rooted in their own cultural identity. If a person believes they are inferior to someone else, they are defeated at the outset. Slavery brought Africans into America in a disruptive, traumatic, and violent way. Africans were cut off from normal ties of kinship and social identity. In Alex Haley's novel *Roots* there is a disturbing account of how the Mandinka Kunta Kinte refuses the slave name of "Toby." He is beaten until he renounces his name. The oppressor knows that Kinte's name was synonymous with his identity and a statement that he belongs to himself. When divorced from one's history, one's very identity is lost.

Kidnaped Africans were expected to forge new ties with their masters. This expectation remains. Slaves had their names changed and they were punished for using languages other than English. Perhaps worst of all, African cosmology was discredited. Africans were consistently told by Euro-Americans that all things African were inferior and boorish in comparison with European civilization. Africans were told that they were worthy of the curse of slavery. Today, variants of these themes keep some younger African-Americans from excelling in education and intellectual leadership. These kinds of indoctrinating arguments are what African-centeredness attacks: attempts to shackle the minds of African peoples.

In Ancient China, women had their feet bound because men deemed small feet to be attractive according to their sense of beauty and consistent with their low regard for women. Why did Chinese mothers allow this senseless brutality of their own children to continue even as they tottered in pain with each step to the end of their days? It was because they fatalistically embraced the lies of those who oppressed them.

A Xhosa proverb explains, "Once one has had a vision, he cannot return it." The book of Proverbs warns: "without a vision the people cast off restraint." When people lose their identity they loose that which brings direction and clarity. A blueprint for the future is contingent upon ones self-awareness. With self-knowledge one can proceed confidently. The Bible tells of Peter walking on the water toward Jesus. When Peter looked at the circumstances around him, he forgot what he was capable of doing (indeed, what he had been doing) and began to sink. African-Americans are in danger of allowing the waves of American racism to deter them from their proper path in life.

Healthy self-understanding fosters self-respect. Jesus told His followers to love others as they loved themselves. When you do not "love yourself," you dishonor the God who calls you to healthy self-understanding. When you do not love yourself, you destroy yourself and others in your life. As a dysfunctional person, you will fill the void that this lack of love creates by looking to others for love and by creating idols instead of embracing God's ways for your life. Dignity comes from living out the heart of the ancient command: know thyself! Not knowing yourself is living without the benefit of your birthright; separated from the confident power that flows through your long line of ancestry.

The idea of Americans of African descent reconnecting to their African ancestry is further compounded by the problem that "being an American" presents to African-Americans. Many African-Americans have developed a "Whoppi-syndrome" (named after entertainer Whoppi Goldberg) who proclaimed, "I am not an African-American. I am just an American." She is denying her heritage, her community and her identity. America, however, has never yet allowed Africans to hold such a view. Marcia Davis wrote that being "patriotic" as an African-American is "far more complex than flying old Glory and singing 'God Bless America.'" Indeed, it is often a "struggle waving a flag" [The New Crisis, 12/01, 30] in this country of contradictions. Not that long ago Richard Wright explained,

> The Negro is the only American in America who says, "I want to be an American." More or less, all other Americans who are born in America take their Americanism for granted...and since he lives amidst social conditions pregnant with racism, he becomes an American who is not accepted as an American, hence a kind of negative American. [in Magubane, 3]"

African-Americans have become alienated from their ancestral legacy. This dehumanizes in that it diminishes one's past so that it is no longer able to serve the present as a resource. The past must be recaptured so that people can once again envision what they can become.

Amnesia is a terrifying condition. People who forget themselves are quite vulnerable to being controlled. American educational, political, and religious systems, overseen by Euro-Americans, have been used to keep people separate from the sources of their own cultural power. Without history, current problems cannot be understood in their larger context. Repression can more easily take control. Saddest of all, victims of the theft of their own birthright may even strive to become like those who seek to rename and reshape them.

The unmitigated disaster of the African Slave Trade, as it proceeded for hundreds of years, worked to create a social amnesia among its victims. Amnesia creates, and then sustains, internal oppression. The tragedy of African-Americans who have been separated from the resources of their history is that it continues to keep them vulnerable to further abuse. It is the oppressor who tells the oppressed who they are. Amos Wilson, in *The Falsification of African Consciousness* writes,

> If oppression is to operate with maximum efficiency, it must become and remain a psychological condition achieving self-perpetrating motion by its own internal dynamics and by its own internal momentum. [Wilson, 3]

The promise of Christian faith is that God desires to "make all things new" and can restore to people that which has been stolen. Amnesia affronts the message that people are made in the image of God and enslaves them in a three-fifths self-identity. Amnesia breaks the connection with God by breaking with one's own history. It is a liar who seeks to deter people from the knowledge of their own God-given dignity.

Critics of Afrocentrism claim that its ideas foster prideful delusions, wishful fabrications, and spin a web of fantastical assumptions based on unsubstantiated boasts. Afrocentric values, however, are not the hopes of oppressed people who want to create myths to feel good about themselves. Africa is a vast, ancient continent; a land of kings and queens, scholars and poets, scientists, theologians, business-people and artisans. It is a world of builders, dreamers, workers, and soldiers. Africa stands with pride among the other continents as the cradle of human civilization.

The Afrocentric message is not merely about the generation of new symbols, although symbols have tremendous power. The primary value of having a story, is its legacy, whether that heritage be specific (i.e.,Dutch, Irish, Wolof, Mandinka, Fulfulde) or more general (i.e., European or African). Slavery has, until now, kept many of us from knowing who among us is Yoruba, Asante, Nuba, Shango, Ewe, Ogun, Xhona, Oshun or Obatala. In light of the prayers of many in Africa for a rise of pan-Africanism, perhaps it is God who is now returning people to an understanding of their heritage. To heed the African maxim to "know oneself" is to affirm the good as well as to be wary of the dangers of past errors. Jesus told us that knowing the truth about ourselves, whoever we are, would set us free. For those who have tyrannized, becoming free will mean becoming aware that condescension is inappropriate. For those who have been oppressed, knowing the truth will open up new vistas of optimism where, before, only fatalism had taken root.

"All That Is Hidden Shall Be Revealed"

And the Lord gave me "Sojourner" because I was to travel up and down the land showing people their sins, and being a sign unto them....You know children, I don't read small stuff as letters, I read men and nations.
—Sojourner Truth

What the slavers long thought would remain hidden is now coming to light. Technology is being developed that continues to open up new vistas of insight that would have been inconceivable until recently. An example of this comes from one of the founders of the American Republic. DNA testing done on the remains of Thomas Jefferson have determined that he had sexual relations with his slave Sally Hemings. What Jefferson long denied on the bond of his honor has now been shown to be truth. Justice now comes to the claims of one fourteen year old slave girl against the rebuttal of the President of the United States after 230 years of the truth being hidden. This kind of scientific advance makes it increasingly possible to learn specific details about our ancestry even from a sliver of skin, or from a drop of blood. This might provide information for those who have not been sure where in Africa their descendants are from. It may also be disturbing for those of any culture who may learn about ancestors of dubious reputation.

Jesus taught that "everything hidden will be revealed." The Revelation of St. John teaches that believers will be given new names in heaven. It offers the hope that justice will one day vaunt over the assertions of pride and prejudice. Would it not be wonderful if the names dispersed in the heavenly realms were the very family names that had once been cherished from generation to generation but have become destroyed or forgotten? It is a great reassurance of faith that a day will come when each of us will fully understand the truth about ourselves and our cultures.

Afrocentricity, Islam, and Christianity

We must take Afrocentrism from the sensational newspaper stories and emotional outbursts to a measured deliberation of why America continues to be confounded by race.
—GERALD EARLY

African-rooted values do not exclude or debase the values of other cultures. That is not necessary. Definitions of one's spirituality should not focus on what one does not believe. This stands in contrast with some evangelical traditions which stress their superiority over other faith communities. The world-view assumptions of African philosophy do not stand in opposition to any one religious tradition. One can be an African-centered Christian or an African-centered Muslim. Issues do arise, however, with ideas in other world-view assumptions that conflict with the idea of inclusiveness and mutual respect.

African-centered Christians should not be anti-Islamic. They should be quick to acknowledge that Islam has played an extensive role in the philosophical, historical and aesthetic life of the continent. African-American Christians who are trying to understand the varied legacies of Mother Africa need not be afraid to honor all that is commendable in the Islamic narrative, as it arrived in Africa beginning in the seventh century and expanded dramatically from the tenth century onwards. The fascinating story of Muslim slaves in the New World should also be studied.

African-American Christians should also not be afraid to examine the negatives of African Islam. The goal is a balanced appraisal that is neither interested in deifying or diminishing the role of Islam. The Muslim contribution must be affirmed. It also must not be overstated. Some viewers of the television series 'Roots' drew the mistaken conclusion that West African people were entirely Muslim. While millions of West Africans are followers of Islam, many are also African traditional religionists and even some were Christians as early as the beginning of the nineteenth century. This needs to be stressed so that those who would suggest that Islamic philosophy is interchangeable with a West African world view do not go unchallenged.

The claims of Islam should be considered by African-Americans in terms of Islam as a belief system and not in terms of Islam as being one with the prime cultural identity of Africa. Indeed, as we have stated, some foundational assumptions within an Islamic world view may even be opposed to African-centered perspectives. Molefi Kente Asante reminds us that, "Arabic is neither more or less significant as a language than Yoruba, Kswahili or Ebonics...if your God cannot speak to you in your language then He is not your God." [Asante, 1994, 4] Christianity, in contrast, assumes that the local cultures are capable of carrying within them the truth about God. The Bible can be translated into Yoruba or Swahili just as effectively as it can into any other language.

Those who called on the Creator with other names in the past were not calling out in vain to empty space. The Zulus call God the "Great Great

One" and the "King of Kings"; the Bacongo of Angola call God the "Marvel of Marvels" and the Yoruba of Nigeria call God the "the Mighty Immovable Rock that Never Dies"; the Ashanti of Ghana call God the "Eternal One." [Waters, 67] Christianity teaches that all of these names speak of the God revealed to Moses. The ancient historical names for the Supreme Being are still used by Christians in Africa and are seen as able vessels of truth. Lamin Sanneh observes that God among Yoruban Christians is called "Olorun" or "Oludmare," while Yoruban Christians use the Arabic word "Allah" to describe God. [Calvin lectures, 2000]

For Afrocentrists, there are other issues beyond the name that one should use to describe God. Asante also sees the Islamic ritual of the hajj, or pilgrimage, to Mecca and the practice of praying towards Mecca as ideas not appropriate to African-centered peoples. In the African tradition God is everywhere. Christianity rings with the agreement that God should be worshiped within the beauty of each and every culture in the world. Christians worldwide need not make pilgrimages to Bethlehem in the same way that Muslims are asked to pilgrimage to an Arabian city.

Some Muslims (and other detractors) are frequent in their criticism that Christianity cannot be described as an African-centered tradition, because it is so wedded to colonialism and Western influences. History and scholarship would suggest otherwise. Contemporary scholars like Dr. Cain Hope Felder (in *Troubling Biblical Waters*)have been instrumental in helping people see that Christianity is not "the white man's religion." Certainly, there is plenty of blame to be shared between both Muslims and Christians in Africa's troubled past. Positive statements about Islam in Africa should be balanced with the facts that it was one of the main contributors to oppression and the West African Slave Trade as were so-called Christians. It was the renowned Islamic writer Ibn Khaldun who (as early as 1377) stated in his *Prolegomena to World History:*

> God made Africa a natural source of slaves for the Negro nations are, as a rule, submissive to slavery, because Negroes have little (that is) essentially human and have attributes that are quite similar to those of dumb animals. [Sanneh, 1999, 1]

Islam conquered Africa by the sword, as did later European colonialists. As Asante writes, "the most crippling effect of Islam as well as Christianity for us may well be the adoption of non-African customs and behaviors, some of which are in direct conflict with our traditional values." [1988, 5] Indeed, the very reason that Islam expanded into Africa in the first place was the search for slaves rooted in the religious conviction that fellow Muslims could not be enslaved.

Afrocentric Christianity does not seek to exclude or attack others. It advocates that, instead of denigrating others, one should value and appreciate people of all cultures. God is not in competition with other gods and insecure enough that He needs to attack mortals who disagree with His ways. Christians are called to be humble in relationships. This Afrocentric Christian vision of others is possible because it is confident of the merits of its own rich and varied African tradition. This sure foundation for understanding other traditions comes into question when people lose sight of their own history and accept what others say about their identity.

Mark Twain said that when a country seeks to enslave people it must convince others and themselves that the people that they are enslaving are "subhuman." [Magubane, 16] Slavery dehumanizes. African-based Christianity is a vision to humanize and to accept one's God-given value. This process of affirmative "humanization" is one of appreciating and expressing all things African: philosophy, jurisprudence, sociology, ethics, music, poetry, stories, songs, dance and the fine arts. There is an ancient and multifaceted Kemetic term, "Ma'at," which Asa Hilliard says, "represents a singular whole for the concepts of truth, justice, order, righteousness, balance, reciprocity, and harmony." [Hilliard, 2] African wisdom calls people to live lives of balance and in harmony with others. Ma'at is a philosophy of affirmation; not of placing blame.

Christians rooted in an African-centered world view believe this call for mutual respect is a message whose time has come. It provides a fresh perspective to a world wearied with Eurocentric individualistic hedonism and materialism. Enlightenment-era scientism seeks to quantify the human experience, seemingly in an effort to root out mystery from understanding. It was the conceit of Aristotle that the "soul" of a person could be divided and named as if it were some object. It is the more holistic ideas from Africa and Asia that will return us to a more comprehensive understanding of personhood. An African world-view sees no distinction between the secular and the sacred. A persons soul is not divided or quantifiable. All life is part of God's creation. European-centered ideas have a history of being presented with an intolerance and a condescension that seeks to advance its own agenda through blame and critique. In contrast, African-rooted traditions hold that one should not advance one's own view at the expense of, or in competition with, others. This is well expressed in the Swahili proverb, "*muko vile mjiwakavyo wenyewe, si vile wengine wawawekavyo:* You are what you make of yourself, not what others make of you." [Asante, 1988, 9]

Afrocentric Christianity: "Stony The Road We Trod"

Then Peter began to speak: I now realize how true it is that God does not show favoritism but accepts people from every nation who fear God and do what is right.
—Acts 10:34-35

Let bronze be brought from Egypt and let Ethiopia hasten to stretch out her hands to God.
—Psalms 68:31

The biblical revelation is rooted in a specific multi-cultural context and tells a widely multi-cultural story of responses to God's promises. It shares with us different voices of both genders and of many different faith traditions. It certainly is much more than simply a Hebrew narrative. Africans are present throughout the biblical account. Cain Hope Felder after conclusively dismissing arguments regarding the so-called curse of Ham (Genesis 9:18-27) stated that the genealogies of nations (as provided in Genesis 10) provide us with a "theological catalogue of people" [Felder, 132] which frequently mentions African people groups, and places.

The Bible tells the story of many Africans. Some of these include Nimrod, Hagar, Asenath, Zipporah, Phineas, and the Queen of Sheba (Saba), Tirhakah, king of Ethiopia (II Kings 19:9; Isaiah 37:9) Zerah, and Zephaniah to name a few. In Genesis, Joseph went to Africa, where the Israelites lived for over 430 years and "became Africans" themselves through inter-marriage and acculturation. This process of inter-marriage continued after the Exodus (Judges 3:5-8; Ruth; I Kings 3:1; 11:1-4; I Chronicles 2:35; Ezra 9:1-2; etc.). Apollos was from Egypt (Acts 18:24) and other African leaders in Antioch were Lucius of Cyrene and Simeon of Niger. In an interesting passage even St. Paul was mistaken for an African (Acts 21:37-39).

Early Christianity was launched in the Afro-Asiatic world of Palestine. It is interesting to note how the formative world view assumptions of Christianity have developed in relation to the cultural legacies of Africa. Contemporary expressions of global Christianity, such as Pentecostalism (launched in the United States in 1906 through an African-American pastor in Azusa, California), have fascinating connections with African spirituality.

While it is true that prejudice is as old as humanity itself; racism as we understand it as prejudice under-girded by theology and philosophy plus power, did not exist in the first centuries of the Christian church. This explains why there is no mention of "race" in scripture. Frank M. Snowden, Jr. has written of the biblical era as being a time "before racism." The early church was free from assumptions that Africa was somehow backward. Tradition states that the apostle Mark went to the large Jewish community in Alexandria. This may have led to the eventual fact that a number of the early church patriarchs were African. Most notable of these are the martyrs Perpetua and Felicitis (d. 7, March, 203 CE), Tertullian (155-245 CE), Origen (186-255 CE), Cyprian (200-258 CE), Athanasius (293-373 CE), castigated as the "black dwarf" by his opponents [McKissic and Evans, 135]; and Augustine (354-430 CE), bishop of Hippo, author and theologian.

Some suggest that Jesus Christ's genealogy, through Rahab, Tamar, and Bathsheba show that he was "a Jew of black African decent." [Waters, 35] Felder has written that Mary was "Afro-Asiatic and probably looked like a typical Yemenite, Trinidadian, or African-American of today." [*The Original African Heritage Study Bible*, 14] This idea is often dismissed, because many are not aware that most contemporary citizens of Israel are much more light-skinned than those of the biblical era. Felder calls attention to the fact that Revelations 1:15 and Daniel 7:9 describe the Messiah as having hair "resembling wool" and feet "burned the color of brass." Jesus did not have blond hair and blue eyes as artists such as Werner Smallman have portrayed him. Moseley argues that,

To confront the issue and symbol of the white Christ is to confront the issue of how Christianity has been used to perpetrate
imperialism, colonialism and racism. It is a struggle to free
Christianity from its European American imposed definition of
whitey-anity." [Mosley, 5]

The genealogy of Christ shows that the blood of Africa flowed through
his veins and mixed with the blood of Israel. This was the blood poured
out for humanity's salvation. Shortly after the birth of Jesus, his family fled
to Africa to avoid persecution from King Herod. Jesus lived there for
many years and, in returning, Matthew said he fulfilled the prophecy
(Hosea 11:1) "out of Egypt I have called my son" (Matthew 2:15).

Early portraits, such as the second century catacomb of Dormitillia in
Rome, show Jesus as dark skinned. [Anyike, 77] Medieval European religious art has as many as "six hundred known depictions of a Black Madonna
with Child." [Johnson, 203] It was not until Leonardo Da Vinci and Rem-
brandt's day that Christ and the early disciples "became European." In the
area of Biblical scholarship, Euro-Americans would do well to heed the
warning of Walter Bruggerman; "We are discovering that what we thought
was objective scholarship really turns out to be white scholarship that is very
much limited by our cultural horizons." [McKissic and Evans, 50]

The Nija of scripture teaches that Jesus came for all peoples and is incarnated as all people through his church. God calls his people not to make
graven images of their own culture so that, in the end, we do not end up
worshiping ourselves. The religion of Jesus proclaims an inclusive message
of God's love that speaks of a divine miracle and a very human and daily
response to the concrete demands of history.

Chapter One — Questions for Consideration and Discussion:

1. Respond as appropriate: As An African-American/ Euro-American how should you understand your own Eurocentricity/Afrocentricity? In what ways are Eurocentricity different than Afrocentricity?

2. Describe how your own cultural legacy affects your understanding of patriotism and being patriotic. Respond to this quote by Roger Wilkins: "I have a little American flag on my car because it says to all the Yahoos who use it to sympathize with white supremacy 'it's not your flag, it's my flag too'"[The New Crisis, 12/01, 34].

3. How does cultural heritage relate to personal and social empowerment? What role does cultural heritage play in developing healthy self esteem in a child's education? Can you cite examples of this in your own life?

4. What evidence of honoring ancestors do you, see in your own church? Do you believe that you have fully heard the stories of the elders in the midst of your congregation?

5. Respond to your first impressions of the painting on the cover of this book? Are depictions of the historical Jesus in your church or home represent Him as a person who lived in the Afro-Asiatic world of Israel or do they present Him as a European? Why are so many depictions of Jesus as a European? How do you think these depictions affect our spirituality and the perceptions that our children have about Jesus?

Chapter Two
The Stow-away Rats of European Racism

Foundations for American Racism

I can bear no longer what I have borne.
— MARTIN PROSSER

What do we want? What is the thing that we are after? We want to be Americans, full-fledged Americans with all of the rights of other American citizens. But is that all? Do we simply want to be Americans? Once in a while through all of us there flashes some clairvoyance, some clear idea, of what America really is. We who are dark can see America in a way that white Americans do not. And seeing our country thus, are we satisfied with its present goals and ideals?
—W. E. B. DuBois

Whites are the victims of racism and blacks are the survivors. Places like this plantation and Black History month and things like it liberate whites. Lies have imprisoned them. If the whites could liberate themselves through our knowledge and information, then we could come together and develop a oneness as a human race and as a people
—H.L. BARNER

It will seem that, when we classify mankind by color,
the only primary race that has not made a creative contribution
to any civilization is the black race.
—ARNOLD TOYNBEE, **A Study of History**

The continent of Europe seems largely irrelevant to Euro-Americans in their understanding of themselves. People are ahistoric to a disturbing degree. Just as African ideas can provide strength for African-Americans, the legacies of Europe are invaluable resources for Euro-Americans. Yet, self-descriptions rarely include persons calling themselves a "European Americans" or describing themselves as "Eurocentric." Instead, people describe themselves as "white" or "just Americans." Most Euro-Americans do not grasp how they relate to accusations of "white privilege" and "white supremacy." Ask many Euro-Americans if they are "racist" in any way, and offence at the question is often expressed. In fact, most Euro-Americans, simply by being raised in a social context of privilege, have at least some vestiges of personal racism. All benefit from system-wide racism. These facts should be confronted.

Is it possible to be Euro-American and not be a racist? Yes and no. Racism is not only individualistic; it is systemic. Many Euro-Americans bristle at the idea that they are racist, while many African-Americans would agree that, "the anti-black idea is so contagious that it now affects, in varying degrees, almost every person in this society." [Griffin, 6] Racism presents itself as a response to the incomplete character of others. The corrosive cancer of racism concerns, "not the failures of the powerless, but the self-justification of the powerful." [Cohen, 187]

Many people in the "majority" expressed sympathy towards those in the "minority." Abolitionists such as politician William Wilberforce in England and William Lloyd Garrison, the controversial John Brown, and author Harriet Beecher Stowe in North America actively worked as evangelicals for justice on behalf of Africans in America. Their Christianity was based in the vision to bring the kingdom of God into daily life. That is why Wilberforce described his Christianity with these questions:

Is Christianity then reduced to a mere creed? Is its practical influence bounded within a few external plausabilities? Does it in essence consist only in a few speculative opinions and a few useless and unprofitable tenets? And can this be the ground for the portentous distinction which is so unequivocally made by the evangelist between those who accept and those who reject the Gospel? He that believeth on the Son hath life and he that believeth not on the Son shall not see life but the wrath of God abideth on him? The morality of the Christian Gospel is not of so slight a fabric. [Sanneh, 1999, 58]

Some Euro-Americans, especially during the Civil Rights era, even gave their lives for the cause of social justice. Yet, even these martyrs or the most sympathetic of Euro-Americans, were beneficiaries of a racist system at work in American life. Their very culture (at least until they chose to divest themselves of their privileges and to confront the racism within the system) allowed them to largely choose their own level of involvement in the issues. Whether their type of Christianity gave them this same choice, however, is a vital theological question that must be raised.

If it is true that racism is deeply rooted in the fabric of American "Christian" culture, then what ideas, or what group of people, laid the groundwork for this reality? There are many possible answers. Paul R. Griffin, in *Seeds of Racism in the Soul of America*, claims that the tenacity of racism after slavery and the unique characteristics of slavery in America are key factors that make inadequate the conclusion that slavery was simply an economic fact of the American South. The seeds of racism may have been sown "four centuries ago [but] they have proved to be perennial noxious weeds with deep roots." [Griffin, 22]

One of the most supportive forces in American slavery was American "Christianity." Not only were slavers accepted as "Christian" by the churches where they worshiped but they also used the Bible to justify their "business." They jammed ships with names like *The Jesus* full of slaves, and they did this believing they were doing God's will. Christianity in America functioned as a means to rationalize the trade but also as a way to deculturate the prisoners from Africa themselves. Europeans taught the slaves that they could hope for a savior in the world to come but had to submit to God's will in this life. Obedience was a moral duty for the good slave. God would bless them in the next life, where Jesus would reward them for being "good and faithful servants."

The next life, however, would include both a "Negro heaven and a white heaven" where Africans would be able to work in "heaven's kitchen" and remain serving as slaves. [Bay, 179] This was understandable coming from three-fifths theologians because, for them, slavery was already a sort of heaven with themselves functioning as gods. Slaves, in contrast, doubted if "white people could ever go to heaven or if whites would work as slaves for Africans" in the world to come. Most concluded that all slave masters and most other "whites would be condemned to the eternal fire" (Bay, 182). Eternity, if it was a place of perfect equality, could hardly contain "white people." Ultimately, believing slaves left these questions in the hands of God's perfect justice.

The conversion of the slave to Christianity incorporated these prisoners of economic warfare into the "Christian" world of the slave owner and the universe of the "white God." European and European-American missionaries sought to convert Africans supposedly for the benefit of the African soul. At the same time, however, other Africans continued to be enslaved and abused. Was this only an effort to assuage guilt? Organized religion in extreme insecurity with itself is often overtly confident and condescending with those of other cultures. These three-fifth theologians were not teaching liberation from a liberating Christ. Once religion began supporting slavery, the way was well established for the relatively unhindered cultural genocide of all things African.

Intolerance logically results from the idea that one group of people, in this case Christianized Europeans, is chosen by God to lead others of different and lesser "races." The fact that they are chosen means that they have a duty to lift those "beneath" them. It brings with it a mandate to rule over and enslave those in the "out-groups." Intolerance grows when people cannot see that there are alternative values or alternative perspectives of equal or even greater value than the perspective that they are holding. The divine imagination is not able to free the intolerant from their corrosive sense of "chosen-ness."

Is Racism a Uniquely Southern Problem?

Every time I saw a white man I was afraid of being carried away—Slavery is the next to hell.
— HARRIET TUBMAN

One of our hopes in writing this book is to raise questions about long-held assumptions. One of these which we will briefly address is the notion that racism in originated in the American South. In early America, slavery was very important in the North. In 1720, one out of every seven people in New York City was a slave and Wall Street was the place where owners went to hire out their slaves by the day or the week [Loewen, 142].

Griffin notes that it was northern New England Puritans, and not southern plantation owners, who first provided a theoretical and moral justification for slavery. Laws for perpetual slavery (as opposed to indentured servitude) were in place in Massachusetts in 1641. These ideas were not codified in the state of Virginia until twenty years later, in 1661; and, in the state of Maryland, not until 1663. [Griffin, 11] This raises a question for further consideration. Perhaps, perpetual slavery would have been replaced by the more common indentured servitude in the American South had it not been for the influence and theological underpinnings of Reformationist Puritans. Clearly, the Puritans held to a three-fifths theology that enabled them to turn the business of slavery into a religious mission for Europeans and a spiritual destiny for Africans.

The American southland vigorously accepted this New England-bred three-fifths theology that separated conscience and justice from worship and action. The American South clung for generations to what James Baldwin in 1961 described as,

> Two entirely antithetical doctrines, two legends and two histories....He is on the one hand, the proud citizen of a free society and on the other has not yet dared to free itself of the necessity of naked and brutal oppression. He is part of a country that boasts that it has never lost a war; but he is also the representative of a conquered nation. [Mazel, 48]

One sometimes hears from those in the American North that the plight of racism is primarily a "Southern problem." It is an American problem. It is more than, as James Baldwin called it, "the Southern way." It is also the American way. Interestingly, there is now something of a reverse-exodus in America with many African-Americans choosing to move their families back into the American South from other regions.

Martin Luther King, Jr. related that the racism he experienced in Chicago was much more entrenched and insidious than that which he dealt with in his native South. While the Carpetbaggers demanded that post-war Southern state governments include African-American representatives and leaders (even governors) there were no African-Americans in state office north of the Mason-Dixon line until Reverend Benjamin J. Arnett (an AME pastor) was elected to the Ohio legislature in 1885. The first Northern African-American was not elected to federal office until 1929. [Griffin, 41] There have been very few African-American governors since this era.

Three-Fifths Theology and "Race"

My view of Christianity is such that I think no man can consis-tently profess it without throwing the whole weight of his being against the monstrous system of injustice that lies at the foundation of all our society.
—HARRIET BEECHER STOWE

The "conversion" of Puritanism in the seventeenth century from a reli-gion in support of slavery to the eighteenth century version of New Eng-land Puritanism whose adherents became instrumental in Abolitionism is a fascinating study in transition. Pre-"Great Awakening" Puritanism is preoccupied with the status of the soul and the life of the world to come. This characteristic of the American communal faith allowed for social jus-tices to go largely unchallenged. In spite of this antinomian tendency, they were forced to explain the nature of the world. The fundamentalist Calvinism of the first Puritan Americans stressed that people were pre-des-tined either to rule or to be ruled. Curses from God had been set against certain people for their ancestral sins. This same logic should have relegat-ed all humans, marked with original depravity into a similar cauldron of miserableness. Instead, it was stated that the evil and suffering that Africans faced would cleanse their spirits from darkness. Slave-owning religious leaders like the Reverend Cotton Mather made much of how slavery actually helped advance the plight of the African, because it brought them the light of the gospel and the chance to learn from enlight-ened Europeans like himself.

Three-fifths theology taught that one deserved one's destiny and that everything that happened, including slavery, was the divine will of "Gott der Allmachtige" (to use Hitler's frequent invocation). If an African came to Christ, their black souls would be "purified to be white as snow" (not a very African idiom), and thus they were eligible to enter some form of heaven. Christian baptism, however, did not change their plight as slaves. This was their station in life; their "place." Today, this concept is applied by some that argue that the plight of the urban poor is inevitable. The belief that each person should maintain the status quo of social standing was supported by Paul's words in I Corinthians 7: 20-24. It was these verses, and others supporting slavery, that led Howard Thurman to warn Christians to read Paul's letters in the corrective light of the Gospels.

Griffin argues that racism is a religious confession of a distorted aberration of Christianity beholden to European political and social engineers of domination. Certainly, the Bible was a powerful tool in the hands of the slave owners. They told their slaves to "submit to their masters" and to co-operate with the ruling political authorities. The many references about slavery in the book of Leviticus were frequently quoted. Puritan three-fifths theology preached that Africans were the "miserable children of Adam and Eve who were created the vassals of Satan" [Griffin, 18]. They were the descendants of Ham mentioned in Genesis 9.20-27. Three-fifths theology determined that Africans were inferior to the new Americans, thus only worthy to function as servants.

Earliest Beginnings of Racism and the Irish "Test Ground"

The Irish are the Blacks of Europe.
—English curse against the Irish

It may be impossible to conclude when exactly racism began to infect European civilization. Certainly, while the question is complex in the extreme, there are many possible answers. Charles Copher cites passages in some versions of legends in the Babylonian Talmud, which assert that Africans received the "mark of Cain." The most often cited example come from the *Midrash Rabbah* (Genesis 22:6) and the *Tanhuma Noah* (13, 15), where Africans are seen to be cohabiting with animals [also Sanhedrin 108b; Felder, 147-148]. Others cite frequent anti-African statements in medieval Catholicism. Robert E. Hood's summarizes the development of the idea that there are different "races" of people. From this assumption comes the logic in Europe of genetic and eugenic categories of racism:

> Initially a category used to classify plants and animals, the innovative use of the term "race" was thought to have originated with a French physician, Francois Bernier (1620-1688). The Swedish botanist Carolus Linnaeus (1707-1778) taught that a factual scientific correlation exists between a person's outward appearance, and their intelligence and disposition. The German founder of modern comparative anatomy, Johann Friedrich Blumenback (1752-1840) maintained that through the study of skulls it is clear that Greek faces represent a superior standard of beauty and a higher culture compared to Ethiopians and Africans. Another Frenchman, Comte Joseph Arthur de Gobineau (1816-1882) wrote that Nordic races are by nature superior to Semitic and black races. [Hood, 10]

European, supposedly "Christian," travelers to Africa frequently chronicled how "beastly, mysterious, heathenish, libidinous, evil, lazy and smelly" [Griffin, 14] the Africans were. Clearly, they were inferior to Europeans. They were animalistic, and sexual. They were not entirely human ("homo erectus").

Snowden has established that the biblical era, was free of notions about racial superiority. It must be reiterated that, by our definition, racism per se, is very different from prejudice. We are saying that notions of destructive racial superiority cannot be described as a universal fact, even if ethnocentrism, e.g., the rulers of China's Middle Kingdom, is more widely held. The Chinese called those outside China barbarians, but they did not assert that these people were not human. Countless other examples abound. Our focus is on the enslaving racism that is rooted in a distinctly European-Christian construct. It is a form of racism that is undergirded with the theological underpinnings of a form of Christianity that is in conflict with itself. The fact that racism in Christianity has not always been present offers hope that it can be eventually overthrown or, at least, confronted.

Before the cancer of English racism came to North America and was leveled against Native Americans and legitimized the business of enslaving

Africans, an interesting "testing area" for methods and theological foundations was established in Ireland. As Walker states,

> In the eyes of the English, the Irish were a disgusting and unattractive people. Traveling to Ireland in 1860, Charles Kinglsey called the Irish "human chimpanzees"...By caricaturing the Irish as apes, the English defined themselves as superior. The Irish, in short, served the same function in the British Isles that Negroes did in America. [Walker, 16]

Historians such as Quinn, Jones, Canny, and Muldoon have drawn parallels between attitudes toward the Irish and Native Americans. British popular opinion relegated the Irish Catholic to the level of the brute savage and wondered if they were indeed human. Certainly, they were seen as a "different race." [Knobel, 88] The military leaders who had been used in England's Elizabethan war on the Irish were sent to launch a war of genocide on Virginia's indigenous peoples. Thanks to experiences with the Irish, the early settlers were preconditioned to maintain attitudes that reinforced their own sense of superiority.

The Irish in America, however, never formed an alliance with African-Americans. To the contrary, Irish-Americans exhibited some of the most racist behavior conceivable. If Marx's class analysis theory is accurate, this would not be the case. In America, however, race has always "trumped" class. The Jacksonian Democrats courted recent Irish immigrants while talking among themselves about the need to "promote outsiders and small men" as a way to maintain control in the South because of the frequent slave uprisings. Urban Irish, led by the Democratic Party's Tammany Hall, and later by the Hughes-backed American Catholic establishment, [Allen, 198] propagated supremacist attitudes in the North and pro-plantation bourgeoisie attitudes in the South. Was this because the Irish feared job competition? It was probably the Irish way of showing other Americans how "white" they really were. Acting "American" has often been synonymous with acting against African-Americans. The Irish in America embraced the same Ulster Presbyterian logic of chosen-ness with which they themselves had been attacked when they were in Ireland. A sad pattern repeats itself: The oppressed learning from the oppressors how to brutalize other.

The Racism of Three-Fifths Theology

Hypocrites and concubines/living Among the Swine
They run to God with lips and tongue/but leave their hearts behind.
—African-American Spiritual

Heaven! Heaven! Everyone talkin' 'bout heaven ain't goin' there!
—African-American Spiritual

Main-line American religion did not dramatically threaten racism until the rise of abolitionism. Instead, racism took root in the American psyche through the vehicle of three-fifths theology. There were few exceptions to this development in American church history. Anabaptists did not usually engage in the call for justice, because they believed that they were called to be "in the world but not of it." African-American Christians, obviously, stood against slavery but were ignored by other Christians. The Quakers were the "lone voice crying in the wilderness" that did respond to racism. Their numbers, unfortunately, were few. Their faithfulness in being a "voice and not an echo" meant that their moral influence far exceeded their numbers. It was among the Quakers, in Germantown, Pennsylvania in 1688 (already forty-seven years after slavery was legitimized in New England) that the first known Euro-American protest against slavery was presented in writing.

Perhaps, the best chance that Euro-American Christianity might have had to reject three-fifths theology may have occurred when John Wesley visited America and told his bishop Francis Asbury, not to allow any slave-owner to take communion. Wesley preached that slavery was an affront to God. His preaching in England greatly strengthened the burgeoning abolitionist movement. As time went on, however, slavery was rarely confronted by American Wesleyans. It was tolerated as a "necessary evil." By 1840, any mention of slavery as a sin had been deleted from American Methodist statements of faith and governance.

The abolitionist movement gained strong support among American clergy as the nineteenth century progressed. New Englanders, motivated by Transcendentalist and Unitarian voices, began to take the lead in this area. Among Methodist groups, holiness revivalists such as Charles Finney championed traces of abolitionist ideas. The stridency of these advocates,

however, was softened by the growth of their holiness, revivalist movements into the South. By 1859, the abolitionist movement was overtaken
by events such as John Brown's raids in Pottawatomie, Kansas and
Harpers Ferry, (West) Virginia. Brown's explosions of religious zeal were
seen in a positive light in the North. Thoreau compared him to Jesus and
Ralph Waldo Emerson said that Brown would make his execution gallows
as "glorious as a cross."

Even the abolitionist movement, for all of its bluster, was never at the
center of American Christian expression. Most pastors and people in the
pews were indifferent to the issues of the day. In a real sense, American
Christianity never threatened the social structures that supported racist
actions. It is not difficult to build the case that the "church" supported
racism and that, in America, a compromised church was the incubator for
racist ideas. In "Letter from Birmingham Jail" Martin King challenged
Euro-American pastors to "face their historic obligation" in the many
ways that they fostered racism. His rebuke came in response to Euro-
American Christianity's inability to remove the clear contradictions
between the teachings of Jesus and their own actions.

Three-fifths theology not only helped Europeans to rationalize their
actions; it was directed against African-American Christians and non-
Christian slaves with a vengeance. It helped the masters keep the slaves
docile. Catechisms were published to impart "plantation Christianity" to
the slaves. Presbyterian minister Charles Colcock Jones published one
such text in 1834 entitled *Catechism for Colored Persons* [Bay, 125].
Another example of this kind of control can be found in the *Southern Catechism of the Episcopal Church,* written in 1830 by pastors and owners for
their slaves:

> Q: Who gave you a master and a mistress?
> A: God gave them to me.
> Q: Who says that you must obey them?
> A: God says that I must.
> Q: What book tells you these things?
> A: The Bible.
> Q: How does God do all His work?
> A: He always does it right.
> Q: Does God love to work?

A: Yes, He is always at work.
Q: Do the angels work?
A: Yes, they do just what God tells them to do.
Q: What does God say about your work?
A: Those who do not work do not eat.
Q: What makes you lazy?
A: My wicked heart.
Q: How do you know your heart is wicked?
A: I feel it every day.
Q: Who teaches you many evil things?
A: The devil, and I must not let him teach me.
[Rutstein, 56; Newman and Sawyer, 26]

This sort of rationale continues to the present with the same logic of superiority. During the civil rights movement one saw "Christians" like Birmingham police Chief "Bull" Connor and Alabama Governor George Wallace (and many others) keep their compartmentalized faith far away from the reality of their lives. After all, common sense dictates that 'loving your neighbor" and "doing to others as you would have them do unto you" was not applicable to intercultural relations. People cannot be labeled other than hypocritical when they could fire-hose others on Saturday and, then, take communion in their Baptist churches on Sunday.

The greatest support for injustice has always been the silence and inactivism of America's "Christians." It was not unusual for churches in the American South to receive a small financial contribution from the Ku Klux Klan as a way of co-opting those churches into their racist agendas. Orlando Patterson reports that at one point before the Second World War there were almost forty thousand pastors enrolled in various Ku Klux Klan organizations. Sadly, Malcolm X was right when he said,

The Holy Bible in the White mans hands and his interpretation of it have been the greatest ideological weapon for enslaving millions of non-white human beings." [with Alex Haley, 241-242]

Chapter Two—Questions for consideration and discussion:

1. How would you define racism? How do you think racism is perpetuated in both church and society?

2. If it is true that much academic and religious training in America is rooted in Eurocentric assumptions, then how does that affect the theology and expression of the church?

3. How does considering the foundations of racism in the United States affect your opinion about its force and contemporary expression?

4. Can you cite examples of people who had once been oppressed becoming oppressors themselves? Why do you think this happens?

Chapter Three:
The Gray Between Black and White: Rethinking American History

*Some truths have to be really pounded into the national psyche.
And one of these is that history counts.*
—Roger Wilkins

*Comparing them by their faculties of memory, reason and imagi-
nation, it appears to me, that in memory, they are equal to the
Whites. In reason much inferior...and that in imagination they
are dull, tasteless and anomalous...never yet could I find that a
Black had uttered a thought above the level of plain narration;
never seen even an elementary trait of painting or sculpture.*
—Thomas Jefferson

Euro-American Historiography as "Whitewash"

*Traveled he back his proud ancestry to the rock on
Plymouth's shore. Traced I mine to a Dutch ship landing at
Jamestown, one year before.*
—James Edwin Campbell

You asked me if I was of your race. I am proud to say that I am of the same race that you are, I am colored, thank God for that. I have not the curse of God upon me for enslaving human beings.
—Sojourner Truth

What is it that we share? Both African-Americans and Euro-Americans are, in the words of Douglas Massey, "...trapped by race." [in Mazel, 100] Are we aware of this common legacy and what are the implications of this unity for dealing with the racism that mars the United States? If we do not seek solutions, a tragedy potentially worse than either Northern Ireland or Yugoslavia will be experienced in this country. We must move beyond rhetoric and work for justice.

Americans share a common history retold in two very different versions. Much of Euro-American historiography is brimming with whitewash. Because Euro-Americans still keep largely segregated from African-Americans in their social relationships, it should not be surprising that we also have our own separate histories. Difficult questions about the uses of American history in society must be asked. Why are slave-owners still honored on American currency? Why is Lincoln sometimes recalled in textbooks as a strident abolitionist? Why is it that historians do not consistently call to account supporters of the Ku Klux Klan such as Woodrow Wilson and others? Why is it even an issue that some American states still display a version of the Confederate flag enshrined on their state flags? All Americans should reexamine the particular version of the nation's history that we have been given. When this is done many of us will be forced to examine, not only many wonderful legacies, but also some of the most brutal atrocities committed in history. America is a wonderful, complex nation with a fascinating history, but it's relation to Native Americans and African-Americans is at the heart of its saddest contradiction: We are not what we aspire to become, "one nation under God, indivisible with liberty and justice for all."

Many citizens are uninformed about the extent of the nation's past atrocities. Conduct a survey among a group of Euro-Americans: Ask them how many Africans died in the Maafa and the subsequent years of enslavement. In the context of this ignorance it is inappropriate to glibly advocate "love and harmony among the races." At the Nurenberg trials of 1946, America demanded that Nazi war criminals first confront the nature of their deeds before judgment was proscribed. This same dynamic should mark the way that the government and Euro-Americans respond to Native Americans and African-Americans. The facts are that European-American "Christians" were often ruthless rapists and murders during more than three centuries of slavery.

It is important to remember that brutality leaves a terrible mark on both the victim and the brutalizer. The people who chose to come from Europe to the American colonies were eager for profit and a new life. These goals did not often coincide with being sensitive to the rights of the indigenous peoples and the damage that their arrival might bring to their cultures. Cohen writes that this fact,

> Made the colonizers often more racist than the people they left behind in the mother country...one should question whether the Pilgrims, Puritans and other Euro-American settlers were just seeking religious freedom, as our textbooks insist, or if this was just the most noble sounding part of the 'freedom' that some of them wanted. [Cohen, 187]

Lincoln's 1863 Emancipation Proclamation did not end the suffering of Africans at the hands of their European fellow-countrymen. To say this is to forget that, since the Civil War, more than five thousand African-American males were victims of lynching—ritual human sacrifices—often in the name of God. Over 90 percent of these murders, between 1880 and 1960, happened in the heart of the American "Christian" South, the so-called "Bible Belt." Most Euro-Americans have no knowledge of these lynching. They must never be forgotten. If they are, then similar events can occur again. It was not so long ago, on 7 June, 1998 that James Byrd was lynched in Jasper, Texas. This is not ancient history. The only "positive" out of that horrific tragedy was that people of all cultures in that little Texas town rose up to condemn the murderers. In a previous era, the killers might have gone free.

The goal of a comprehensive and accurate telling of American history from an African-American or a Native American perspective is not to be divisive. Feelings of guilt about past transgressions do nothing to constructively resolve present social challenges. Neither is the goal to foster a sense of victimhood or to nurse a sense of injury among African-Americans or Native Americans. That will not help our communities. History will become a proactive force for insight and a source for a healthy dose of humility. As Elie Wiesel stated, we must learn and benefit from having learned so that the tragedies of history will never return in our future together.

1585-1776: The Maafa

My brother tried to run away and received five hundred lashes when caught. They washed his raw back with salt and water and whipped it in, as well as rubbed it in with a rag; and then directly sent him to work in tobacco fields. I also have been whipped many a time on my naked skin, and sometimes till the blood has run down over my waistband; but the greatest grief I then had was to see them whip my mother, and to hear her, on her knees, begging for mercy....
—DAVID GEORGE (born 1742)

Alas! And am I born for this? To wear the slavish chain?
—GEORGE HORTON

Who were the first Africans to come to America? Were they the prisoners of war that we call slaves? Is it possible, as historian Lerone Bennett and Ivan van Certima of Rutgers University claim, that African traders came to the New World as early as the thirteenth century. [van Certima, 37-49] More research needs to be done on this important question. Waters notes that almost two hundred years before Columbus (1310-1311 CE) people from West Africa came, "from the motherland to the New World. They were led by the Mandinka King Abubakari II of Mali and his entourage. [Waters, 74]. The first Africans came, not as slaves, but as explorers and builders. These African mariners of medieval times may have been the first to encounter the native populations of the Americas; and the encounter was mutually beneficial, for it resulted not in conquest but in the exchange of culture. The impact of this encounter became diffused throughout Mesoamerica and Mexico. Even now, Waters claims, the pyramids of the Incas in Peru and the pyramids of the Aztecs and the Mayans in southern Mexico stand as a testimony to African influence. [Waters, 75]

How is it possible, sitting in a comfortable air-conditioned room in America, to examine the question of slavery? Without question, slavery has existed since the beginning of time. It is absurd to say that one form of slavery is "more brutal" or "less humane" than another form of slavery. These kinds of arguments are theoretical but invariably flawed for one reason: If one is a slave one lives in a terrible and dehumanizing situation. The slavery that existed in the United States, however, was unique in that it was rooted in a Christian theological paradigm. And the legacies of three-fifths theology remain with us into the present.

The word *Maafa*, comes from the Swahili word that means "disaster or catastrophe." It can also be translated, "The great suffering of our people at the hands of Europeans." [Ani, xxii] It swept an entire continent and threw many African cultures into disarray. Davidson projects that 13 million Africans crossed the waters with another 13 percent of that number dying even before the ships left the coasts of Africa. [1991, 96-97] Most of these were from West Africa, but perhaps fifteen percent also came from East Africa and South Africa. [1991, 121]

Witnesses of those years experienced something that was beyond words. Perhaps what is most amazing about the Maafa is that people survived at all and with a degree of faith in God and even hope in American democratic idealism. How can one talk about the Maafa without tears? Words fail to capture the reality of the rape, torture, branding, buying, selling, beatings, and murder of millions of men and women and children taken from Africa. Frederick Douglass wrote in 1852,

> I will, in the name of humanity which is outraged, in the name of liberty which is fettered, in the name of the Constitution and the Bible, which are disregarded and trampled upon, dare to denounce, with all of the emphasis that I can command, that everything that serves to perpetrate slavery in America promotes the greatest sin and shame of America! [Mazel, 27]

Slavery is America's original sin. It became the major moral issue that the signers of the Declaration of Independence faced. It is the defining event in the American story. It reveals American hypocrisy vis-à-vis justice and human freedom in its formative stages. The Bill of Rights and the Constitution were written for "all Americans" while at least 700,000

Americans lived in slavery. [Sanneh, 1999, 12] Benjamin Rush, one of America's true Revolutionary heroes, wrote:

> The American war is over. But this is far from being the case with the American Revolution. On the contrary, nothing but the first act of the great drama is closed.

> [Samuel Hopkins wrote:]Let it not be said that the pride of youth and the strength of our young Nation perished of a heart blackened by atrocity and ossified by countless cruelties to the Indian and the African." [Sanneh, 1999, 14]

Unfortunately, the rhetoric of genuine democracy for all people did not carry the day in the foundations of the American Republic. Much more common was the kind of rhetoric given below, which rationalized the "need" for the institution of slavery. The following two excerpts are taken from Drew Gilpin Faust's anthology, *The Ideology of Slavery: Pro-Slavery Thought in the Antebellum South, 1830-1860*:

> If pleasure is correctly defined to be the absence of pain then I believe our slaves are the happiest three millions of human beings on whom the sun shines. Into their Eden is coming Satan in the guise of an abolitionist....The slave is certainly liable to be sold. But, perhaps, it may be questioned, whether this is a greater liability for the laborer who is dismissed by his employer without the certainty of being able to obtain employment or the means of sustenance elsewhere. The line of a slave's duty is marked out with precision, and he has no choice but to follow it. He is thus saved the double difficulty of first having to determine the proper course for himself, and then of summoning up the energy which will sustain him in pursuing it....It is the duty of society to protect all its members....To protect the weak we must first enslave them.
> —GEORGE FITZHUGH, **Southern Thought**, 1857.

> Slave-holders are a people whose men are proverbially brave, intellectual and hospitable and whose women are unaffectedly

chaste, devoted to the domestic life and happy in it. My decided opinion is that our system of slavery contributes largely to the development and culture of these high and noble qualities.
—JOHN HENRY HAMMOND,
Letter to an English Abolitionist, 1845.

When slavery is discussed in textbooks and taught in classrooms it is often presented in general terms. Perhaps even more inexcusable, is that misconceptions about the nature of slavery are sometimes presented as fact. Contrary to some presentations, enslaved Africans were not always meek, docile "children" who "did not mind" their bondage. Freedom fighters such as Denmark Vescey, Martin Delaney, Harriet Tubman, and Nat Turner all had burning within them a bright passion to be free. This caused them to risk their lives. Their courage in the face of such odds should never go untold as children learn America's story. It is incumbent upon all Americans, perhaps for the first time, to confront the pain of this era and to trust that Jesus is right when he promises that truth will set us free.

1776-1865: African-Americans and the Founders of a New Nation

Blacks can see very clearly that America is a nation built on inhumanity. The signers of the Declaration of Independence put down their quills to go home and beat their slaves. Blacks have heard the noble words, while the whip shredded the skins of their backs. It is no longer possible to hide the resistance struggle that blacks have constantly waged inside America. The smoke from the fires of Detroit singed every white eyebrow and the message was clear: to die in the attempt to humanize America is preferable to being an American as America is now constituted.
—JULIUS LESTER

A fugitive slave while under examination was asked if his master was a Christian, to which he replied: "No sir, my master is a member of Congress.
—**Madison (NY) Journal,** August 7, 1850

It has been said that hypocrisy is the tax "that vice pays to virtue." American democracy is founded in the soil of hypocrisy. The Declaration of Independence was written as a proclamation of freedom while one third of the signers were slave owners. [Wright,59] Jefferson and Franklin, colleagues on the committee to draft the document both owned slaves (though Franklin later became president of the Pennsylvania Abolitionist Society). European racism is so deeply rooted in the American story that this should not be surprising. If you were alive at the founding of the American republic you might have read the entry in a noted encyclopedia that described the "Negro" as:

> One filled with treachery, lying, cruelty, and impudence, intemperance, and a penchant for stealing, debauchery and profanity...They are strangers to every sentiment of compassion and an example of man when left to himself. [Magubane, 23]

European and Euro-American thinkers of the time assumed these things to be true. German philosopher Georg Wilhelm Friedrich Hegel wrote:

> The Negro exhibits the natural man in his completely wild, untamed state. We must lay aside all thought of reverence and morality-all we call feeling-if we would rightly comprehend him, for there is nothing in this type of character....[Magubane, 24]

Just as Hitler did when he cited this quote two centuries later, Europeans in early America took Hegel's advice to heart and "laid aside all thoughts of reverence and morality for the Africans in their midst." With this kind of rationale, the early slavers believed what they were doing was somehow humanitarian, virtuous, and philanthropic.

When visiting Monticello and Mount Vernon, I (van Gorder) was surprised how little mention was made about the majority of the people who lived in those testaments to power. Sometimes there was only a token plaque that read, "location of the slave quarters." Tour guides made passing references to Mr. Washington's "servants" as if they were local Mt. Vernon-area teenage girls who needed some extra spending money that led them to work at the big house. George Washington is sometimes called the "father of our country." Why do we not call his slaves "fathers of our country" as well? One thing is certain; without the economic wealth accrued from his slaves there would have been no Washington. By 1789, "all five of his farms had black overseers. [Finkleman,164] In October 1775, after they had fought at Lexington, Concord, and Bunker Hill, Washington led the way in forbidding freed Africans in America to serve in the Continental Army.

Antiseptic is spread all over the myths of America's founding fathers. Evaluations of Jefferson should also take into account that he fathered five children with Sally Hemings, an underage slave (any context that includes slavery cannot be called consensual) even though he emphatically denied it and preached against "the races mixing." Not only did Jefferson own people; he maintained that Africans were inferior. Much is made of the fact that Jefferson's first draft of the Declaration of Independence included this clause against the slave trade:

> He (King George III) has waged cruel war against human nature itself, violating its most sacred rights of life and liberty in the persons of a distant people who never offended him, captivating and carrying them into slavery in another hemisphere, or to incur miserable death in their transportation thither." [Franklin, 13]

> A CHRISTIAN (sic.) king of Great Britain was so determined to keep an open market where MEN (sic.) should be bought and sold and used his negative to suppress every legislative attempt to prohibit or restrain this execrable commerce. [Finkleman, 115]

When these words were written Jefferson owned 150 people. By 1822, he owned 267 slaves. He freed only three slaves in his life and five more, all blood relations, at his death. As an eighteenth-century natural law theorist, Jefferson knew that slavery was wrong and he had numerous friends who were vocal abolitionists. He was "not ahead, but rather, far behind such advocates of emancipation as John Jay and Alexander Hamilton...." [Finkleman, 110]

Any notion that Jefferson might have had for emancipation was probably linked to a process of deportation, for he was certain that the two "races" could not peacefully coexist. In any event, emancipation was a prescription for social chaos. Jefferson agreed with St. George Tucker, professor of law at William and Mary College, that "black slaves, if allowed to remain, would become the caterpillars of the earth and the tigers of the human race." [Sanneh, 1999, 184] Even while he was writing the Declaration of Independence, Jefferson was noting with shock that Lord Dunmore's British plan to free Africans who joined the British Army had already cost Virginia some thirty thousand slaves [Sanneh, 1999, 32]. If Jefferson abhorred slavery, as some suggest, then why did he do nothing to abolish it in Virginia while he was governor or, in America as a whole, while he was President?

In his will, Jefferson freed only five of his slaves. Upon his demise, in contrast, Washington freed all of his slaves. [Kaminski, 277] One of Jefferson's freed slaves included a man named Joe Fossett, who spent the rest of his life trying to purchase his wife and four children; also Jefferson's "property" before they were sold away from Fossett on the occasion of Jefferson's death. The "Master of Monticello" talked about his slaves as "my family." This was empty rhetoric. Jefferson frequently sold slaves. From 1784 to 1794 he sold at least 85 slaves. [Finkleman,107] Others were given as gifts. When slaves escaped, he sought and then punished them once they were recaptured. Julian Bond says, "Some ask the question, was Jefferson a good slave master? That is an oxymoron. There are no good slave masters." [Mazel, 30]

Thomas Jefferson stated that the people who maintained his extravagant life style, who built his house, cooked his meals and tilled his fields were unusually ugly. He wrote that he could barely stand to look at the "eternal monotony of their offensive features." [Finkleman, 152]. Jefferson considered himself a man of science, and yet he suggested that "blackness might come from the color of blood" [Finkleman, 152] He wrote that Africans,

> ...Secrete less by the kidneys and more by the glands of their skin which gives them a very strong and disagreeable odor....They seem to require less sleep. A black after hard labor through the day will sit up till midnight or later though knowing he must be out with the first dawn of the morning....They are more ardent after their female, but love seems with them to be more an eager desire than a tender delicate mixture of sentiment and sensation. Their griefs are transient. [Franklin, 18]

Are Americans aware that their founders held such ugly sentiments? Would knowing these facts make people think twice before naming their elementary schools after Washington, Jefferson, and others. Of course, these men were not completely evil. Much of what they said has brought great hope to the world. The fact is that there are "two Jeffersons and two Washingtons" just as there are two Americas.

The Great Emancipator?

There is a physical difference between the two races which will probably forever forbid their living together on a footing of perfect equality. And the black man is not our equal in terms of intellectual or moral endowments.
—ABRAHAM LINCOLN,
vs. Stephen Douglas, Debates, 1858.

Abraham Lincoln is often presented as a strident abolitionist. He was a fascinating, complex person who seemed to hold varied positions on the issues surrounding slavery. His most famous speech, the Gettysburg Address of 1863, refers to the United States as a nation "conceived in liberty and dedicated to the proposition that all men are created equal." One wonders what an African-American, hearing those words in the crowd, would have thought. Obviously, he was affected by the prejudices of his time. Lincoln did author, and then enact, the Emancipation Proclamation. This was a military policy that promised to end slavery in the South, but not in the border states. An earlier draft of the document included the idea that Africans should be colonized in Africa or in the Caribbean.

Lincoln defies simplistic interpretation. Perhaps, Lincoln is to be seen at his best when, as a young man in 1846 he declared:

We feel that all legal distinctions between individuals of the same community, founded in any such circumstances on color, origin, and the like, are hostile to the genius of our institutions, and incompatible with the true history of American liberty. [Franklin, 58]

Abraham Lincoln, however, was not an advocate of the equality of African-Americans. He was primarily a pragmatist who was trying to save the Union. In response to the Dred Scott decision, and during his famous debates with Stephen Douglass Lincoln explained:

> I will say then, that I am not, nor ever have been, in favor of bringing about in any way the social and political equality of the white and black races. I am not nor ever have been in favor of making voters or jurors of Negroes, nor of qualifying them to hold office, nor to intermarry with white people; and I will say in addition to this that there is a physical difference between the white and the black races which will forever forbid the two races living together on terms of social and political equality. And, inasmuch as they cannot so live, while they do remain together, there must be the position of superior to inferior. And I, as much as any other man, am in favor of having the superior position assigned to the white race. [Magubane, 72]

His views on repatriating Africans in America or allowing them to live unhindered in America were mixed. In any event, he did not live to see any solution emerge and his successor, Andrew Johnson, was an avowed racist and former slave owner. At a recent educational program for African-American children that we attended, there was a presentation to the children about how Abraham Lincoln "freed us." The reality is that, at the time of Lincoln's assassination, there were proposals for the re-location of African-Americans to a separate state in part of Louisiana as well as repatriating them out of the country. In 1864, a plan began to take shape in Haiti. It came to nothing after the first thirty Africans died within the first months of the experiment.

At times, Lincoln seemed to transcend his own racism and the racism of the day. At his best, Lincoln was an anti-racist who recognized the humanity of "Negroes" and knew that slavery was morally wrong. At his worst, he was a man of his times.

1865-1898 — From Reconstruction to "Redestruction": "Jim Crow" Laws

Weel about, and turn about and do jis so.
Ebry time I weel about I jump Jim Crow.
—Song, THOMAS "DADDY" RICE, founder of Minstrelsy

Sanctified by religion and justified by philosophy and legalized by the Supreme Court, the "separate but equal" (ruling of Plessy v. Ferguson, 1897) was enforced in the day by the agencies of the law and by the KKK and company under the cover of night.
—JOHN HOPE FRANKLIN

Had Euro-Americans truly believed the rhetoric of the Emancipation Proclamation, they would have welcomed African-Americans into the mainstream of American life after the Civil War. This did not happen. A wonderful opportunity was forever lost. New laws were put in place to ensure that African-Americans would remain disenfranchised. Most of the freed slaves still found themselves in a dramatically subservient status. Many families have not moved that much since then from a social status of poverty. Reconstruction quickly turned into the "redestruction" of hope. Promises soon gave way to further betrayal.

At the outset, Senator Thaddeus Stevens of York, Pennsylvania, proposed a bold plan for land redistribution. He proclaimed, "How can republican institutions and free schools and free churches...exist in a mingled community of nabobs and serfs." [Steinberg, 206] The Freedman's Bureau of 1865 initially offered (and then rescinded the offer only four months later) every freed slave "forty acres and a mule."

An understanding of this era must be set in the larger context of the world at that time. Reconstruction was a short-lived (ten-year) period that allowed slaves in the American South to be given authority for the first time. There was even some support for Reconstruction in the South itself. Some former Confederates, including even General James Longstreet, became Republicans because they "had grown convinced that equality for blacks was morally right." [Loewen, 194]

By 1876, however, Reconstruction was stalled by the Hayes-Tilden compromise that gave Republican Rutherford B. Hayes the White House in exchange for honoring the demands of his Democratic rival Samuel Tilden. The basic ultimatum was that all Federal Troops be removed from the South and all restrictive reconstructionist legislation be revoked. This opened a floodgate for the formation of new terrorist groups and the enactment of new legislation intended to in effect reenslave African-Americans in the South. The Ku Klux Klan, a group of primarily poor Euro-Americans began a century of lynching and humiliations. This terrorism flourished through the subjugation of knowledge and the unrestrained support of most local governments. A de-facto "slavery" had begun for African-Americans called the "Jim Crow" (based on a popular minstrel song title) era.

Jim Crow laws legalized the inequality of African-Americans. Countless numbers of African-Americans were arrested for debt peonage and other disguised ways to reintroduce slavery. Africans went from slavery to chain gangs. The 1897 Plessy v. Ferguson Supreme Court case decided that de-facto segregation could be legalized as long as facilities were "separate but equal." This phrase became the new mantra to reinstate three-fifths democracy to African-Americans. "Separate but equal" continues to the present as de-facto segregation has come to replace de-jure segregation.

Is the Jim Crow era a thing of the past? Are U.S. policies now in place that encourage aspirations of subservience in exchange for some political or economic gain? America has a new context that inspires people to succeed through the denial of their cultural integrity: people such as Colin Powell, Congressman J.C. ("Jim Crow") Watts of Oklahoma and Clarence ("Supreme House") Thomas. Meanwhile, the majority of African-Americans remain isolated from American prosperity and are the first to suffer in times of economic depression. Many "black conservatives" talk about a new reconstruction at hand. What is actually taking place is another Hayes-Tilden Compromise, where promises for equality are bartered away in exchange for support from those in power. Examine the dynamics of racial profiling, unequal treatment in courts over drug sentencing, perpetual urban ghettoes, chronic underemployment and poverty. Communities are still "red-lined" and many African-American businesspeople continue to discover a "glass ceiling" in their careers.

1898-1954: The United States and Africa

The meek shall inherit the Earth; but not the property rights.
—BILL COSBY

Racial arrogance has been the pattern of Europeans long before journalist Henry Stanley sent reports back to London describing savage cannibals offering human sacrifices and living in polygamous lechery. Mission-sponsored journal articles called for further European colonial expansion. This literature usually promoted notions that Africa was a backward land littered with sensual, irrational pagans who were thoroughly incapable of governing themselves.

The United States has always seen Africa through the prism of Africa's vulnerability. The story of the American-supported settlement of repatriated slaves into Liberia and a similar British initiative in Sierra Leone is ably described in Lamin Sanneh's book, *Abolitionists Abroad*. Thousands of diasporic Africans went to Sierre Leone to begin life anew. Many of these served as Christian missionaries to other countries such as Nigeria. Sanneh notes that Liberia was, at worst, a repository for unwanted Africans and provided a way for segments of the American government to be less involved in solving America's own racial problems.

In 1898, Theodore Roosevelt charged San Juan Hill in Cuba, and Admiral Thomas Dewey steamed into Manila Bay. America had joined the fray as a world colonial power. Imperialism became the primary vehicle to reinforce notions of racial superiority. English colonial education policies advocated that English become the language of the world, and through education and policy, European assumptions were promoted as universally valid for humanity. Colonialism meant that three-fifths theology was now exportable worldwide. A poem from the era, written by Rudyard Kipling, told the citizens of the world to "take up the white mans burden" and happily submit to European rule.

At the turn of the twentieth century, white supremacy was dressed in the garb of American patriotism. An assertive nation led by Roosevelt followed England into an era of colonialism. Roosevelt preached, quoting an African proverb, that the U.S. should "walk softly and carry a big stick." How did Roosevelt view African-Americans? In 1895 he said that they were, "A perfectly stupid race can never rise to a very high plane; the

Negro has been kept down as much by lack of intellectual development as anything else." [Magubane, 33] This kind of rhetoric from one of "our four Mt. Rushmore greats" shows that none of them merit the honor of being carved into sacred Lakota Black Hills rock.

For the first four decades of the twentieth-century American foreign policy fully supported European colonial efforts in Africa without regard to the interests of Africans. The United States was the first country to recognize King Leopold's despotic reign in the then Belgian Congo and one of the last to withdraw that recognition long after ten million Congolese had been beheaded and massacred. Belgian policy, driven by profit, mandated that police should be paid for each severed hand of a Congolese villager that were seen as un-cooperative. This led to the widespread practice of cutting off anyone's hand available just to receive this reward. A few guilt-stricken Europeans told of the grisly mountains of severed hands but few historical accounts of this colonial era in Africa have been written. Some that have been done have been criticized for being revisionist and sensationalist. This is a perennial problem in understanding African history. As a Kenyan proverb declares, "the hunt will always glorify the deeds of the hunter until the Lion tells the story."

Imperialism, Marx asserted, was based on the model of slavery and was, in itself, a form of slavery imposed by Europeans on the three-fifths peoples of Africa. For the most part, the United States watched from the sidelines as European colonialism roared to its ferocious conclusion throughout the African continent. Massacres occurred, to greater or lesser degrees, almost everywhere that colonialism slowly gave way to emerging hopes for self-determination. Robert Love wrote, "Africa has been the carcass upon which the vultures of Europe have descended and which they have sought to petition among themselves without any regard whatsoever for the rights of the Africans." [Lewis, 25]

A vivid example of European disregard for Africa came when Ethiopia was thrown to Italian fascists in the early 1930s to appease Generalissimo Benito Mussolini's ravenous craving for power. As Ethiopian King Haile Selassie (formerly Prince Ras Tafari) pleaded for justice at the League of Nations, the American government chose not to respond. In contrast, the brutal pillage of Ethiopia captivated the attention of the African Diaspora and many African-Americans donated funds to aid the Ethiopian cause. It was, however, not a new story in the long line of colonial abuses toward

Africa. When Belgium ruled Rwanda, it elevated the 15 percent minority population Tutsi people over the Hutu majority in a way that brought crushing ramifications down on the Tutsi people long after the Belgians had left. Belgium had been "given" Rwanda after World War I. Britain showed this same disregard for territorial sovereignty when, before that war, "gave" Portugal's African colonies to Germany in hopes of sating their thirst for aggression. The enduring legacy of European colonialism in Africa has been chaos.

After the Second World War, American intervention in Africa began in earnest as efforts were made to cull the continent of its valuable natural resources. Despots of newly independent post-colonial African nations gladly made themselves pawns in America's anti-Soviet cold-war era foreign policy. Foreign aid was often steered by Central Intelligence Agency operatives who, among other misdeeds, were in the shadows of orchestrating the assassination of the Congo's first prime minister, Patrice Lumumba. The CIA loyally supported Congolese dictator Mobutu who managed to continue King Leopold's horrific destruction of that wealthy nation. In South Africa, racist "Apartheid" policies were supported by one American government after another. American companies grew rich in South Africa, while autocrats were given a free hand to subjugate their citizenry. Three-fifths theology supported these policies assuring that God had ordained the ways of history. Americans were the chosen people, and America was, as the Puritans had dreamed, "the city set on a hill" and the light to all nations.

1898-1954: African-American Leaders during the "Jim Crow" Era

Would America be America without her Negro people?
The nation has not yet found peace from its sin; the freedman has
not yet found his Promised Land
—W. E. B. DuBois

It would be instructive to examine briefly a few of the notable leaders in the Jim Crow era because of their role in helping to define the present intercultural problems of the United States. The lives of these leaders are already well known to most readers. They lived in a time of incredible turbulence, where people were lynched and abused in what William Pickens calls the "American Congo." [Franklin, 86] While each of them employed different methods, their goals—confronting the racism of America's three-fifth's society—were the same.

Booker T. Washington

No people have ever risen out of the shadows and into the sunlight without fierce opposition. We have been no exception to the rule...But we shall win in the end because we have God and justice and fair play on our side.
—BOOKER T. WASHINGTON

Booker Taliaferro Washington is a controversial figure in American history. He was a product of a distinct period and place, and he must be understood accordingly. Washington was the last of the "major black leaders to be born in slavery" [Franklin, 13] near Roanoke, Virginia in the spring of 1856. According to Molefi Asante, Washington made a clear commitment to an African-centered perspective when he founded the Tuskeege Institute to educate African-Americans in Alabama. [Asante, 1988, 8] His courageous commitment to seek education in the face of the systematic lynching of the era and the rise of groups like the Ku Klux Klan is a credit to his determination.

The Tuskeege Institute is the concrete embodiment of his vision to raise African-Americans through education into the mainstream of America's commercial life. Washington also traveled the country as a lecturer and even as "advisor" to Presidents Theodore Roosevelt and William Howard Taft. In his most controversial speech, at the Atlanta Exposition of 1895, he urged "whites to disregard black agitation for social equality while allowing and even encouraging black economic advancement." [Franklin, 17] African-American observers in the North did not understand the dynamics that Washington faced in Alabama. As a result, it was easy for them to label him an accomodationalist. In a sense this charge is accurate. His main focus was on economic independence, and this need was also Washington's blind spot. This is part of the troubled legacy of Washington's double heritage as both an African and as an American in an era of great social transition.

Washington is often contrasted with W. E. B. DuBois. Contrasting these two leaders, however, could also be seen as a divide-and-conquer strategy. These two men were focused on different areas and lived in different social contexts and had very distinct social networks upon which they could rely. Both were optimists who worked to strengthen African-Americans in society. Washington, undoubtedly, did encourage accommodation to Euro-American majority expectations. Supporters will say, nevertheless, that fact is only part of the picture.

W. E. B. DuBois

I sit with Shakespeare and he winces not. Across the color-line I move arm in arm with Balzac and Dumas....I summon Aristotle and Auerilus and what soul I will, and they come all graciously with no scorn or condescension. So wed with Truth, I dwell above the veil. Is this the life you grudge us, O knightly America? Is this the life you long to change into the dull red hideousness of Georgia? Are you so afraid lest peering from this high Pisgah, between Philistine and Amalekite, we sight the promised land?

Actively we have woven ourselves into the very warp and woof of this nation-we have fought their battles and have shared their sorrow. We have mingled our blood with theirs and generation after generation we have pleaded with a headstrong careless people not to despise justice mercy and truth lest the nation be smitten with a curse. Our song and our toil and our cheer and warning have been given to this nation in blood-brotherhood.
—W. E. B. DuBois

William Edward Burghart DuBois lived many "lives" in one lifetime. His critics added even more "personas" to him. Some considered him a Marxist; others, an African Nationalist. If he had lived in a different age, this stately academic, known as the "Professor," might have simply lived a peaceful life as a quiet scholar of literature and history.

History, however, had other plans for him. W.E.B. DuBois was born in Great Barrington, Massachusetts on 23 February 1868. He graduated from Fisk College, and then went to the University of Berlin before going on to become the first African-American to receive a Doctorate in Philosophy degree from Harvard University. Upon graduation, he taught Classics at Wilberforce College and later taught at the University of Pennsylvania.

To some degree, W. E. B. DuBois, like Booker T. Washington, recognized biculturality as a positive resource for personal development. DuBois believed people of different cultures could provide unique perspectives and illuminate each other's worlds. As a academician, he hoped to join a world community of scholars who would "dwell above the veil" preoccupied with race and not "wed with Truth." On his ninety-fifth birthday, however, he gave a radio address from his home in Ghana for Radio Beijing in China. In it he said that whatever else he had done in his life, in America, he was "nothing but a nigger." [Walker, 77]

DuBois became an articulate activist speaking with a strident voice for justice. He was a leader in the Niagra Movement and was instrumental in the formation of the National Association for the Advancement of Colored People launched out of their 1907 Harpers Ferry Conference. He wrote about both personal refinement and societal advancement. DuBois preached political activism and economic empowerment. As a rationalist, he respected the teachings of Jesus, but abhorred institutional three-fifths Christianity in its lack of commitment to social justice.

With the resources of an excellent education and financial support, DuBois was among the elite of his day and he interacted with many influential Euro-Americans. This may partly explain why Marcus Garvey accused him of being too tentative when it came to supporting a more confrontative approach to Euro-American attempts at continuing the racial subjugation of African-Americans. DuBois claimed that African-Americans should embrace their European and American identities as well as their African legacy. He was proud of being an African but was, as he noted in his book *Dusk to Dawn,* not interested in having his "individuality entombed in blackness." [Walker, 81] Garvey dismissed him as a "mulatto;" but DuBois would never apologize for who he was, including his Dutch and French Huguenot ancestry.

DuBois' Pan-African ideas evolved over time and in, some respect, paralleled Garvey's ideas. DuBois rejected Garvey's militant dismissal of democracy and, what DuBois saw as his lack of respect for other cultures. For DuBois, the heart of formative Pan-Africanism was the spiritual integration of Africans both in Africa and in the diaspora. It tried the difficult path of being a "race-conscious movement without being racialist" [Magubane, 147] and, as such, was open to people of all cultures. DuBois knew, however, that before people could be powerful they had to clear their minds of misconceptions about the need to be dependent on the good will of Euro-Americans. African-Americans, DuBois wrote, must be dependent on no one but themselves.

Carter G. Woodson

Carter G. Woodson, the son of slaves, was born in New Canton, Virginia in 1875 and is called the founder of the "black history movement." As a young man he went to Harvard University where he earned a doctorate in history. In 1915, he launched the Association for the Study of Afro-American Life and History which publishes the Journal of Black History.

Before he died in 1950, Woodson authored sixteen books and dedicated his life to educating America about the many contributions of countless African-Americans to American cultural and scientific advancement. Many scholars consider his full-length *The Negro in Our History* to be one of the most important books in early African American studies. Woodson's book, *The Mis-education of the Negro* challenged African-Americans to develop a more Afrocentric understanding of their world.

Woodson believed that education and history were tools to empower. He knew that people needed to feel confident about their past before they could stride with authority into the future. Woodson's educational focus was children. He wrote that, "to handicap a student by teaching him that his black face is a curse and that his struggle to change his condition is hopeless, is the worst sort of lynching." [Magubane, 27]

Marcus Garvey

Marcus Mosiah (nee Auerilus) Garvey was born in St. Ann's Bay in Northern Jamaica on 17, August 1887. Garvey, the enigmatic leader of more than two million followers, defies simplified statements. From 1919 until his death in 1940, he preached a message of self-respect, self-empowerment and support for Africa and for all Africans of the diaspora.

One of his followers praised him by saying that he gave his people a "backbone where before they only had a wishbone." [Walker, 34] Garvey was a powerful communicator who captured the imagination of the people by articulating their longings for self-determination and by speaking against the "second class citizenship" that had been given to them in American society. J. Edgar Hoover, former director of the Federal Bureau of Investigation, stated that the leader was "one of the most powerful personalities I have ever seen on a platform." [Lewis, 77] The heart of Garvey's message was that African-Americans should remove themselves from the manipulation of a system set against them.

Perhaps Garvey's biggest problem was his lack of consistency. On one hand he taught that all "races" should be treated with respect regardless of color; on the other hand he said that,

> There is a need for a pure black race just as all self-respecting whites believe in a pure white race….Slavery brought on us the curse of many colors within the Negro race. Mulattos are evil and in the future the Negro race should not be stigmatized by bastardy. [Walker, 45]

For this reason he felt that the NAACP was an "enemy of the race," but that the Ku Klux Klan and the Anglo-Saxon Clubs were "friends" because they did not hide their true intent, dispelled any illusions about the true intent of Euro-Americans and galvanized alertness among his followers:

> Between the Ku Klux Klan and the Morefield Storey National Association for the Advancement of "Colored" People give me the Klan for their honesty of purpose toward the Negro. They are better friends to my race, for telling us what we are, and what they mean, thereby giving us a chance to stir for ourselves, than all the hypocrites put together with their false gods and religions, not withstanding. You may call me a Klansman if you will but potentially, every white man is a Klansman, as far as the Negro in competition with whites socially, economically, and politically is concerned, and there is no use lying about it. [Walker, 54]

Marcus Garvey had been accused of many things in his tempestuous life. Finally, in 1926, the FBI accused him of mail fraud in connection with his Black Star Steamship Company. The government deported Garvey to Jamaica where he lived out the rest of his life. Detractors accused Garvey of being an egotistical "virtuoso." Certainly, Garvey's view of history was static, but his message of the need for African redemption was dynamic. Contemporary Afrocentrism owes a debt to Garvey's, "Back to Africa" Movement, even if it was overly idealistic. He taught that Africans had no future in America. His awareness of the crippling effects of racism are still instructive. In that he preached a message that combined spiritual and psychological emancipation, he was a forerunner of Malcolm X and other Afrocentric activists. His emphasis on self-reliance and trans-national African identity laid the foundation for future African diasporic nationalism.

1954-1968: The American Civil Rights Movement

The only thing we did wrong; stayed in the wilderness a day to long. But the one thing we did right was the day we began to fight. Keep your eyes on the prize! Hold on!

I love everybody! I love everybody! I love Hoss Manucy
(KKK leader in St. Augustine, Florida) *when he'd just beat us up! I love everybody*

You know I would not be Governor Wallace and I'll tell you the reason why, I am afraid my Lord might call me and I would not be ready to die.
—Civil Rights Freedom Songs

The end of the Second World War did not significantly improve the legal standing of Africans in America. It did, however, enhance their economic position and empowered a greater degree of assertiveness. African-American soldiers, who had risked their lives for their country, were shocked to see Nazi prisoners of war housed in the United States being treated better as prisoners than they had been treated as soldiers and citizens. [Franklin, 90] Veterans called for, and received under President Harry S. Truman, the genesis of an integrated American military.

It is interesting to note a correlation between the timing of the rise of the American civil rights movement and the dawn of the newly independent African nations. Many of the issues that civil rights leaders struggled with in the United States were the same ones that leaders in Africa were facing. Just as colonizers warned that Africa "was not ready yet," Dr. King heard this same warning from his critics. They were content with incremental progress and expected African-Americans to gratefully appreciate what they were given. While some African-Americans were lulled to sleep, others sought justice over comfort and resisted calls not to "rock the boat" or press issues to an untimely conclusion.

One day, 5 December 1955, a woman named Rosa McCauley Parks in Montgomery, Alabama, changed the country by getting on a bus. She was tired of going to the back of the bus and always being asked to be the one to accommodate Euro-Americans. Parks, a forty-two year old seamstress, had decided that she did not care any more about those who threatened her. Her action began the process that shook the foundations of racism in American society. Impatient anger plus wise courage is a daunting combination for any enemy to overcome.

Once Rosa Parks began to fight, many others followed her example. Thurgood Marshall, and the legal arm of the NAACP, began looking for other test cases to challenge unjust laws. Civil rights leader Medgar Evers worked until he was murdered on 12 June, 1963. James Cheney, along with two Euro-American civil rights workers, Michael Schwerner, and Andrew Goodman, were murdered in Philadelphia, Mississippi. James Meredith took great risks by enrolling at the University of Mississippi. African-Americans decided not to settle for second-class citizenship, realizing that power could be effected through unity, organized protest, determination, and wisdom. The civil rights movement also developed a coalition between an emerging "beloved community" increasingly aware of its own power and the aid of supportive allies.

The movement generated hundreds of martyrs and thousands of committed activists. Sixteen-year old Brenda Travis was arrested in Macomb, Mississippi for sitting at the Greyhound lunch counter. Diane Nash was arrested for marching in Tennessee. Linda Brown, a third-grader accompanied by her welder father, Oliver, was stopped while trying to enroll in the local elementary school in Topeka, Kansas. The Reverend George Lee, gunned down on 7 May,1955, was working to organize Mississippians to register and vote. Perhaps the heart of the civil rights movement is best personified, however, by four little girls: Addie Mae Collins, Denise McNair, Carole Robertson, and Cynthia Wesley. They were studying and worshiping in their 16th Avenue Baptist Sunday School class when it was bombed by terrorists at 10:22 in the morning of 15 September, 1963. In ashes of their unrealized future is our on-going mandate for action.

Martin Luther King, Jr. and Malcolm X: United Against Three-Fifths Theology

Talk! Talk! Talk! That will not free the slaves. What is needed is action! Action!
—JOHN BROWN

Those who profess to favor freedom and yet deprecate agitation, are people who want crops without plowing up the ground." / "If there is no struggle there is no progress.
—FREDERICK DOUGLASS

Martin Luther King, Jr.

The Black family for three hundred years has been on the tracks of a racing locomotive called American history; dragged along and mangled and crippled. A nation that continues year after year to spend more money on military defense than on programs of social uplift is approaching spiritual death. The bombs in Vietnam (van Gorder: Afghanistan) explode at home. They destroy the hopes and possibilities of a decent America. I am disappointed with our failure to deal positively with the triple evils of racism, extreme materialism, and militarism. We are presently moving down a dead-end road that can only lead to national disaster.
—MARTIN LUTHER KING, JR.

The Rev. Dr. Martin Luther King, Jr., was a man whose life focused on social justice. He was born Michael Luther King on 15, January 1929 and was nurtured in a church in which his father and grandfather, A.D. Williams, had served. As a youth, "ML" did so well in school that he skipped both the ninth and the twelfth grades. His formative years, at Morehouse College in Atlanta, Georgia, exposed him to many voices for justice such as President Benjamin Elijah Mayes. Mayes showed him that " a minister could be a rational moral agent who was socially involved, widely read and well spoken"[Walker, 106]. God had called him, and his calling was not merely to inspire; his calling was to bring a message of liberation and social change. This calling had its genesis in an African-American church history dedicated to Biblical justice. King's development was further enhanced by time at Crozier Theological Seminary in Chester, Pennsylvania and at Boston University, where he studied the philosophy of personalism. Later, he recalled that he had also been moved by transcendental writer and abolitionist Henry David Thoreau, who confronted injustices with moral authority. At this time, King also studied Mahatma Gandhi's nonviolent satyagraha strategy that brought political change to India.

King began to see, with Rauschenbusch, that the church should be a prophetic, vibrant force in the redemption of society. These times of intellectual ferment, however, were only reinforcing what had already been deeply imbued with the rich soil of his spiritual heritage. He was a man made by the love of his family and his community. Whenever he did not know where to go and when troubles mounted against him he would return home to his Atlanta home church, Ebenezer Baptist. There, the parishioners said they, "knew Martin before he knew himself and knew him better than he knew himself." [*A Knock at Midnight,* Time-Life Audio Series. Tape 6,1995]

People often quote his 28, August 1963 "I Have A Dream" speech's call for a "racist-free nirvana" in some distant future. They should also remember that in the same speech the preacher said, "The whirlwinds of revolt will continue to shake the foundations of our nation until the bright day of justice emerges" [King, 1963] King was not about a dream. He is terribly misunderstood by those who would try to encapsulate him, referring to one speech. Critics who say he was too tentative also do not understand King. He did not preach an integrationalism that was assimilationist.

He worked for equality and full citizenship. He never once called for the negation of his African tradition. His life was a testament of his love of that heritage. This love was not exclusive, i.e. against others. It was inclusive because he believed that all people were made in God's image. For King, racism, along with poverty and militarism, were America's three systematic evils. His life's work was dedicated to dismantling America's foundational racist construct that had disenfranchised people of African descent.

King's life unfolded in a synergy of integrating passions. He was a scholar who was pastoral and an idealist who was pragmatic. He was an introspective author of five books and a social activist who, in 1964, won the Nobel Peace Prize. He was murdered on April 4, 1968 in Memphis while leading a campaign for justice on behalf of the local garbage-men.

King had profound faith in God and a deep suspicion of three-fifths theology. He preached that Christianity must be prophetic in its call for God's glory in the midst of our challenging lives. There could be no separation of the spiritual and the secular. Christ called us to work faithfully to bring change toward justice. He patriotically loved America, but it's injustices grieved him greatly. He wrote: "We feel that we are the conscience of America. We are its troubled soul. We will continue to insist that right be done because both God's will and the heritage of our nation speak through our echoing demands." [Walker, 138]

Malcolm X

Second-class citizenship is only a modified form of slavery, which means the Civil War did not end slavery and the Amendments did not end slavery. They didn't do it because we still have to wrestle the Supreme Court and the Congress and the Senate to correct the hypocrisy that has been practiced against us by whites for the past umpteen years. We who are Muslims....do not think that an integrated cup of coffee is sufficient payment for 310 years of slave labor.
—MALCOLM X

Malcolm X, born Malcolm Little on 19, May 1925 in Omaha, Nebraska was a revolutionary intellect and leader who defiantly gave voice to African-American anguish. He articulated the pain that people felt from a system intent on destroying them. Walker writes that "like a pulsating cultural archetype, he lives in the unconscious of every Black American." [Walker, 75] He called people to unity around that anger. As preacher, Malcolm X carried out a jihad with words. [Turner, 184]

His messages to America rang with clarity. Malcolm called for financial reparations for African-Americans that would be overseen by international authorities, perhaps the United Nations or the World Court. He initially believed that Euro-Americans were "devils," at least corporately even if they were kind and supportive in certain individual instances. How could the perpetrators of the slave trade and Jim Crow Apartheid be called anything else? As he embraced Orthodox Islam, in the last year before his assassination, he came to believe that racism was not inevitable in all Euro-Americans, and that people of noble character could rise above the morass of "white privilege."

Perhaps there are three "Malcolms." Malcolm Little became Malcolm X for most of his adult life. Shortly before his death he assumed the name, El-Hajj Malik el-Shabazz. His mother was from Grenada and his father was a Baptist minister who preached both the Gospel and a Garveyite message of self-empowerment. His preaching led the Ku Klux Klan to burn down his house and threaten his life. Malcolm was separated from his mother after his father died (under suspicious circumstances)and, as a teenager, he became a hustler before being arrested and sent to a juvenile detention home in Mason, Michigan. In prison he became a member of the Nation of Islam led by Elijah Muhammad. There were fewer than a thousand members when he joined the group; when he left it had, with no little thanks to his efforts, over forty-thousand members.

Malcolm X's life is a fluid metaphor, of what it means to be an African man in America. He experienced, learned, suffered, hoped for, fought for, worked for, and believed in, so much in his short life of thirty-nine years. Malcolm was able to transform the broken shards of his life into a beautiful mosaic through intellectual determination, personal discipline, and cultural education.

Throughout his spiritual pilgrimage he sought to cultivate his African identity. Malcolm fought against blind conformity to smothering systems and narrow assumptions. His social vision stressed community economic self-determination as well as spiritual independence. Faith must be, first and foremost, liberating. Euro-American Christianity, mired in three-fifths theology, did not offer a message of freedom to Malcolm X. His deft sense of pragmatism led him to conclude that the solutions for the African diaspora were not to be found by physically leaving en-masse to Africa. Instead, he taught that the inherent pride and eternal dignity of the African spirit could be nurtured in America. Malcolm came to believe, after his trip to Ghana, that Africans could not be free anywhere in the world until all Africans had achieved freedom. He described himself as a "black Nationalist freedom fighter" [Cone, 1991, 195]. Cornel West states,

> Malcolm articulated black rage in a manner that is unprecedented in American history....The substance of what he said highlighted the chronic refusal of most Americans to acknowledge the sheer absurdity that confronts human beings of African descent in this country—the incessant assaults on Black intelligence, beauty, character and possibility. [West, 1993, 83]

The Photograph: Martin and Malcolm

The white man's Christian religion further deceived and brainwashed this "Negro" to always turn the other cheek, and grin, and scrape, and bow, and be humble, and to sing, and to pray, and to take whatever was dished out by the devil white man. He was told to look for his pie in the sky and for his heaven in the hereafter while, right here on the earth, the slave-master white man enjoyed his heaven.
—MALCOLM X

They met only once and then very briefly by accident in a hallway. It was only for a few minutes. As they were going their separate ways someone with a camera suggested that they take a quick photograph. Not long after, Malcolm X was shot dead at the Apollo Theater in New York City. Both men were murdered at age thirty-nine. Both men were shaped by profound spiritual convictions and sought to embody in their lives the values of "justice, love and hope." [Boesak, 170] The love of their community and the forces of time have linked Malcolm and Martin inexorably into the fabric of America's visions. Martin focused on justice, while Malcolm keyed on Euro-American hypocrisy and the need for African-Americans to build their own community within America.

If the Christianity that Malcolm had known had not been based on three-fifths theology, he might have found in it enough to energize his passion. The same story mirrors Mahatma Gandhi's claim that he had not rejected Christ, but Christianity when he faced terrible racism in South Africa. Islam, in its call for universal brotherhood, won Malcolm's heart. Today, it is Malcolm's nation-building insights that African-Americans need combined with Martin's justice-based Christianity. American Christians must welcome Malcolm into their pulpits. He has been demonized and held at arm's length for far too long. Some have contrasted Martin's call for "redemptive suffering" with Malcolm's call for "reciprocal bleeding." Others have noted that Malcolm represents the anger of the poor while Martin emerges from a more cautious middle-class community. These dichotomies are divisive. The passive, fearful, tentative, and compromising in our churches need to be "Malcolmized" while the theoretical and intellectual advocates of the new African conscious nationalism need to be "Kingized." This will mean that American Christians will recognize, as Asante says, that it is through the agency, advocacy, and instrumentality of the church that ideas of nation building and efforts for social justice will best flourish.

What American Christianity needs is a Martin-Malcolm balance; a Martin-Malcolm agenda for this generation. The "yin" of Christian idealism needs to join with the "yang" of angry passion and sober realism to keep us in a balance and prevent us from toppling off the narrow tightrope wire that we are balancing across. The alternative to this kind of "prophetic-accomodationalism," to borrow a term from theologian Kosuke Koyama, is for the church to have no relevance in an increasingly polarized context. Ours is a time of urgency requiring strategic action.

It is telling that when three-fifths theology is determined to maintain control it most fears the "Malcolmization" of African-American Christianity. This is because Malcolm advances an agenda that is independent from Eurocentric America and thus beyond the scope of Euro-American influence. Defenders of what South African theologian Zolile Mbali calls "status-quo Christianity," who are both Euro-American and African-American, prefer to advance a safer, more sanitized version of St. Martin of the Poor that allows that King is a hero of the past, but not a prophet with a relevant message for today. Status-quo Christians honor Martin Luther

King because he is dead. They iconicize him on postage stamps and with a national holiday's because King can be seen as a model of restraint.

This is a legendary King; not the post-Washington D.C.-speech-King who attacked the war against Vietnam and the brutality of capitalism. Literally, King has been placed in a box. At his funeral, the Biblical passage was read which asked: "let us kill the dreamer and see what becomes of his dream?" Perhaps the speaker meant this phrase to be a challenge to those who laid him to rest. In actual fact, it is a taunt against the way that his dream has been turned into a harmless ideal without applicability to today's inequality. His tomb at Ebenezer Baptist reads "Free at last, free at last, thank God Almighty, I'm free at last" but in a real sense, he is not yet free.

By taking Martin back to that hallway with Malcolm we see both of them, together as partners in a way that circumstances prevented them in their own lifetimes. Listen to the rhythm of their heartbeats beating along with the prisoners of war in the Maafa who are still pounding out the rhythms of Africa with their bloodied knuckles on slave ship walls. Listen to the call and response of their voices. Listen to Martin's "Amen" to Malcolm and watch Malcolm place his arm around the broad shoulders of his brother Martin. By themselves they are only part of the picture. Together they have, in their lives, a message of action and inner strength. They offer a powerful, balanced perspective for revolution.

1968-2002: Recovery from Betrayal and Assertion of Identity

By age thirteen, I had intuitively developed the cardinal
guidepost for emotional health: the "Never-wanna-be" rule.
Never want to be with the people who do not
want to be with you.
—RANDALL ROBINSON

The genius of our black foremothers and forefathers was to
create powerful buffers to ward off the nihilistic threat, to equip
black folk with cultural armor to beat back the demons of
hopelessness, meaninglessness, and loveless-ness.
—CORNEL WEST

The murder of Martin Luther King paralleled the rise of the anti-Apartheid movement in South Africa. The fact that Euro-Americans see the end of the civil rights movement coming with King's death says much more about the shallow nature of their perspectives than it does about the realities of today's racism. Some lament that African-Americans have been without leaders since Malcolm and Martin were murdered. This is not only presumptuous but preposterous. African-Americans have never been without leaders. The prime leader is now, and has always been, Mother Africa. She is much greater than any one person. God, her Creator, spoke through Jesus, who said that "unless a grain of wheat fall into the ground it abides alone." The grains of wheat that are Medgar Evers, Emmett Till, Malcolm X, Martin Luther King, Jr. and thousands of others have become a field of one hundred million diasporic Africans. They are growing not only to rescue themselves, but to also revitalize Africa, America and the world.

Immediately before his death, Dr. King made an obvious illusion to himself as a Moses to his people. He declared, "Even though I might not get there with you, I have been to the mountaintop." What Moses did not see was how God would bring the miracle to pass. These past forty years in the wilderness have been a time for the grumblers to pass from the scene. The African nation is rising to its feet as it learns from theologian-warriors like James Cone, John Kinney, Jeremiah Wright. Gauyard Wilmore, Cain Hope Felder, Carlyle Fielding Stewart, C. Eric Lincoln, Wil Coleman, Robert Hood, Bell Hooks, Karimu Welsh Asante and Katie Cannon. Lessons are being learned from politician-warriors Jesse Jackson, Ron Brown, LeRoi Jones, Mwufe Kumei, Maxine Waters and John Conyers. The emerging nation is benefitting from scholar-warriors like Randall Robinson, Orlando Patterson, Marimba Ani, Molefi Asante, Asa Hilliard, Basil Davidson, Nai'm Akbar, Cheikh Anta Diop, Maulana Karenga, Yosef A.A. ben Jochannan, Charles Finch, John Hendrik Clarke and countless others. Each of these leaders continues to learn with their hearts and minds and shape their teachings for further levels of empowerment.

Living History: Contemporizing the Maafa of Africa's Millions

Is White America really sorry for her crimes against the Black people? Does White America have the capacity to repent and to atone?

Does the capacity to repent, to atone, exist in a majority, in one-half, in even one-third of American White society?...Indeed, how **can** *white society atone for enslaving, for raping, for unmanning, for otherwise brutalizing* **millions** *of human beings for centuries? What atonement would the God of Justice demand for the robbery of the Black people's labor, their lives, their true identities, their culture, their history—and even their human dignity?*
—MALCOLM X

The Maafa, the African Holocaust, is not only a historical event. It is a resource for vital healing and the restoration of collective memory. One can never forget that the people who bought and sold slaves were "Christians." They were church-members who quoted Paul's writings about slavery. The slaves were objects destined to serve. America's three-fifths theologians said that slavery was not evil but was in fact God's will and God's design.

Three-fifths theology was born to bridge evil acts with holy belief. In order to be true to Jesus, who taught us to love one another as we love ourselves, the "righteous" purveyors of slavery needed to rationalize slavery and de-humanize the slaves. The main obstacle that three-fifths theology needs to overcome is that slavery was an affront to God's created natural order. In Genesis, God commands Adam to have dominion over the animals. The Creator never intended Adam to dominate or subjugate other human beings. Three-fifths theology was based on the notion that Africans were not human but animals that needed to be controlled.

Contemporary three-fifths theologians seek resolution without repentance. Shelby Steele worries about a "politics of memory" that entrenches African-Americans as victims and keep them preoccupied with the past and unprepared for the future. Steele claims slavery should be placed in the "cold storage of history." [Steinberg, 163] This is the voice of the offender asking the offended to forget without making restitution.

George Santayana warned that those who forget the past are condemned to repeat it. Past lessons should be used to fight present injustices. Forgetting a past not yet fully confronted, is injustice in itself. The past forgotten will reap the wrath of lessons unlearned. One obvious lesson that needs guarding is the reality that social solidarity must never be surrendered to another ethnicity. Mutual respect, not arrogance, must define future intercultural partnerships. This is an ancient message from Africa.

Asa Hilliard writes that Kemetic tradition teaches that "before any substantial healing can take place we Africans must begin at the beginning and pursue the wisdom of our ancestors." [Hilliard, 2]

Without the collective contemporizing and memorializing of the African Holocaust there will be a collective unconsciousness and an invariable dismissing of the terror of past events. To be unconscious is to be in a vulnerable state where one can be hypnotized away from ones own sense of dignity and destiny. People living in ignorance about their own stories are kept from being restored to mature self-understanding. Unattended wounds will never be healed. The anger of African-Americans must be dredged up from deep within our social consciousness, in order to experience resolution and forgiveness.

At the heart of African-American social consciousness is a biblical world view which teaches that individuals share a deep connection with their collective past. African tradition teaches the idea of *Sankofa;* that one must go back and "retrieve" what has been lost or stolen. The Bible reminds the Hebrews ("Habiru") that they are not isolated in time but are related to their Abrahams, Isaacs, and Jacobs. We are part of our ancestor's ancient prayers, cries, and hopes.

Every autumn, Brooklyn's St. Paul's Baptist Church led by Johnny Ray Youngblood, stages a re-enactment of the tragedy of the Maafa. Services such as these are springing up all over the country. The Harambee United Church of Christ in Harrisburg, Pennsylvania first staged such a program to lead the congregation and the community into a greater recovery of collective memory. The Maafa re-enactment becomes a mechanism for African-Americans to deal with their collective denial of the horrors of the past in order to find healing in the present.

To do full justice to the Maafa would make any drama so overwhelming that it could not be staged. Efforts must be made, however, just as Jewish Americans have done at the Holocaust Museum in Washington. D.C., to connect people with history. Germany, in order to progress as a healthy civilization, continues to seek to come to terms with Hitler's pogrom against Europe's Jews. American Christians must also confront the myriad abuses and war of genocide against America's First Nations and against her African slaves.

Keeping the memory of the Maafa alive in churches is one way to guard against the encroachments of three-fifths theology and teach invaluable lessons about today's challenges. One lesson is the call to ensure that such a tragedy never happen again. Today, slavery remains in many nations, particularly in the southern Sudan. Other forms of slavery flourish worldwide through the international sex-trade and through sweat-shops where many, often children, slave as indentured servants. Global businesses advance a new form of colonizing imperialism. Meanwhile, developed nations continue to dump weapons into Africa; "the three-fifths continent," where there are more wars than any other region of the world. Hilliard warns that without collective consciousness, "the Maafa continues to take its toll." [Hilliard, 3]

Pressing issues for African-American leaders should continue to be viewed through the prismatic lens of the Maafa. African-Americans must not allow themselves to be enslaved again for some slight benefit offered by potential oppressors. Africans are heirs to a legacy that promises a rich future but an ongoing Maafa of hearts and minds threatens that destiny.

The Nightmare of History

The fact is, that unless it is recognized that there is a dilemma with the historical record of the Euro-Christians, in regard to the way they have treated black people and with respect to certain self-serving theological presuppositions proliferated in the white church, then all of my solutions will be found to be problematic, flawed, unnecessary and exclusionary. This book will be found to be a work of "Black Nationalism" rather than a work of "black liberation." [Spencer, 27]

Martin Luther King predicted that "one day the South will recognize its real heroes." As we sit together writing these words "beneath" Robert E. Lee and Stonewall Jackson and J. E. B. Stuart here in Nathaniel Bedford Forest's Stone Mountain, Georgia, we wonder just when that day will be? Where are the monuments for Emmett Till, murdered in 1955? Where are the statues for Andrew Goodman and James Cheney and others killed in Mississippi in the cause of justice? Why do Confederate flags still fly and why do people who resent these symbols spend their vacation dollars to patronize states that commit such effronteries? It is good that

America has museums in Birmingham, Memphis and Atlanta honoring the civil rights movement. It is good that there is a Negro Leagues Baseball Museum in Kansas City. But why is there no museum in Washington, D.C. commemorating the Maafa?

Progress against racism in America has been slow. Many advances have been symbolic. College African-American Literature and History classes, for example, have been introduced, but they remain "segregated" from the larger curriculum. Diasporic Africans such as Alexander Dumas (author of *the Three Musketeers*) or Alexander Pushkin (Russia's greatest writer) are rarely presented as being of African ancestry.

African-Americans appear in textbooks pocketed in the context of slavery and the civil rights movement and are portrayed as victims. Ennobled in their suffering they are models of patient tolerance. These portrayals are negative. The history of slavery, as described in textbooks, does not often make any connection to the great African heritage and culture of these prisoners of war. Worse yet, historians present the picture of Euro-Americans as the sole builders of the nation. African-American scientists and inventors are frequently ignored. Many people have never heard of noted African-Americans Garret A. Morgan or Norbert Rillieux or Granville T. Woods or Lewis H. Latimer or of cowboy Bill Pickett. When African-Americans are mentioned it is often on the margins of what was "really meaningful" in America's history.

It is true that every culture has terrible legacies to confront. Few of those who celebrate the Thanksgiving holiday and present a morality legend about the "Pilgrim Fathers" (a term first used in the 1870s)mention that within four days of arriving in America they were robbing Native American graves and villages and went on to enslave Natives; massacre them and rejoice in their demise [Loewen, 91]. Bill Maher of the television show "Politically Incorrect" says that the ethnocentric Thanksgiving holiday, a day of mourning and fasting for many Native Americans, is an example of rewriting American history: "Yes, the Germans had Auschwitz and the Turks have Armenia but at least they do not have a holiday to celebrate them!" [*Politically Incorrect*, 20, November 1999] This holiday is an exercise in Euro-American civil religion with God clearly on the side of the Pilgrim Christians among the marginalized Wampanoag Native People.

Do Americans stop on the highways of the American South and think that the roads on which they travel were probably first built by slaves? Do they think that the food they eat probably grew in fields first cleared by prisoners of war? Facing history can overwhelm us or it can cause us to change. It has great potential to divide when confronted. It also has potential to foster mutual respect. The people in the parable of "Plato's Cave" saw shadows but thought that they were real. When the light shone on the walls, they had trouble turning their misconceptions into an accurate grasp of reality. To deny that one is in a "cave of shadows" leads to deluded, arrogant ignorance.

What does it say about the power of history that it is often the case that those Euro-Americans who are often trusted among African-Americans are also people who have faced the facts of history, the fact of their own racism, and their own relation to the Maafa? What does it say about the nature of Euro-Americans that those "handkerchief-head Negroes" who are ahistorical and tend to minimalize their own relation to their community are often the same ones who are welcome into America's halls of political, cultural, or economic power?

Our portrayals of history are, to some degree, portrayals of ourselves. History can offer the deceptive impression that it is a science set in stone; when in actual fact it is a quite malleable art form open to interpretation. The exaggerations of some revisionists, both African-American and European-American, are just as harmful as the pernicious silences that we have illustrated.

History tells us who we are and where we come from. If you take away a people's history, it is then possible that they will believe lies about themselves. The Bible promises that God will give "beauty for ashes." Out of the ashes of the past, a new sense of expectation can arise. Recapturing the powerful resource of the past is what lies behind the observance of Kwanzaa. The principles of "umoja" (unity); "kujicahagulia" (self-determination); "ujima" (collective work and responsibility); "ujamaa" (cooperative economics); "nia" (purpose); "kuumba" (creativity), and "imani" (faith) are guideposts for families of all cultures. The values of the past empower the present and inspire the future.

As the Irish writer James Joyce lamented, "History is a nightmare from which I am trying to awake." [Magubane, 229] The nightmare of history casts a long shadow. Yet, it is to history we must return to answer the questions of who we are as a nation. As the Bible reminds, we must "look again to the rock from which we are hewn" and see where we should next be going in our future.

Chapter Three—Questions for consideration and discussion:

1. What is your response to the idea that memorializing the Maafa is divisive and retrogressive? Why are these criticisms also not valid for memorializations of the Jewish Holocaust? How would you best deal with the past as a vehicle to deal with the present and the future? Can joint memorializations between African-Americans and Jewish Americans be a bridge between our two communities?

2. Do you and your church celebrate Kwanzaa? What does it say about you that you do or have not yet decided to celebrate this holiday of tradition and culture? Is this a holiday that only African-Americans should celebrate?

3. Respond to the Malcolm X quote at the beginning of this section. Is there any reason why his pessimism should be amended decades later?

Chapter Four
America's New Subtle Racism
The Cancer Spreads

*"When I use a word," Humpty Dumpty said in a rather
scornful tone, "it means just what I choose it to mean. Neither
more nor less! The question is" said Alice, "whether you can make
words mean so many different things." "The question is," said
Humpty Dumpty, "who is to be master. That is all."*
—LEWIS CARROLL, **Alice in Wonderland**

*In order for Africans to understand the nature of the world in
which they live, they must first understand the nature of the people
who interpreted the world for them.*
—ANTHONY BROWDER,
Survival Strategies for Africans in America

The Bible testifies that there is nothing new under the sun. While prejudice has existed since Cain and Abel, racism is a relatively new plague on the
world scene. "Racism" is a slippery term. There are many definitions about
what it actually is. The definition that we are using, prejudice plus power
equaling racism, is widely contested."The risk is that the word racism
begins by designating everything and ends up denoting nothing." [Wein-

ter, 92] In the nineteenth-century, the term "racism" was widely used for a host of ideas about cultural differences. Some sought scientific and biological proofs to explain how people were dissimilar. Hitler, and in the United States Margaret Sanger and others, made this use of eugenics infamous.

Racism has political, cultural, ideological, sociological, and theological interpretations. Racism exists today for one important reason: It works. It is always institutional before it is personal and leads to dominance and insecurity. Its apogee was in centuries of slavery that dehumanized millions and left deep wounds. Racism spawned three-fifths theology; the distortion of the message of Genesis (i.e. that God created all humanity in His image) is recast in the notion that God Himself is made in the image of European males and European ideals.

Racism is so misunderstood that it often eludes many peoples'"radar screens." Many tune out the idea whenever "racism" is mentioned. It is seen as a way for others to complain about their problems and rationalize their own failings. To others, who consider themselves well beyond the designation "racist," the idea is seen as a caricaturized and, thus, trivialized phenomenon. In this view, racism is primarily a problem held by white southern males who have drunk too much or who have probably spent too much time out in the sun at the NASCAR race-tracks waiving their confederate flags. If some 'Red-necks' are white-supremicist racists they are, no doubt, much less harmless than those C.E.O.'s in America's cities who forge business strategies, live in segregated communities and attend segregated churches in the suburbs. The latter's racism may be more subtle, but it is also usually more deadly.

Racism is growing in many places in the United States. One of these locales is the American College campus. In a 1996 article in the Journal, *Thought and Action* Noel Jacob Kent writes about what he calls the "new campus racism." In 1997, Amy Elizabeth Ansell tracked the rise of this same problem of new racism in Britain as well as in the United States. Both authors may have been borrowing the term from Sivanandan's 1988 book, or from Barker's book entitled *New Racism* from as early as 1982. It would seem that the "new racism" is simply the old racism repackaged in new disguises. The main difference is the deft subtlety in which it is communicated. Cultural differences replace crass biological notions of inferiority. Advocates disseminate paranoid fears about social trends at work that undermine "American values."

On the opposite side of the spectrum, racism is expressed with inappropriate "compliments" such as the statement that a certain African-American is "really exceptionally intelligent person" when the same kind of patronizing compliment would not usually be paid to a Euro-American colleague. Another comment some people make is that they "do not even notice that someone is black." This idea would sound ridiculous to the speaker if someone out of the blue said to them that they "just wanted them to know" that they did not notice that they were short or fat or Jewish or female or ugly or rich or educated. The very fact that people are singled out and told by others of their "blessed assurance" is indicative of racist views.

People who make such statements often say that their goal is "color-blindness." What they are really blind to is the culture, and thus the dignity, of people who are not like themselves. Instead of being color-blind we need to be aware of the effects that color plays in contemporary American society. Orlando Patterson states,

> To argue that we should begin to solve the problem of racial exclusion by assuming a color blind world is to assume away the very problem we are trying to solve: only voodoo priests and rational choice theorists can get away with this kind of mumbo jumbo....It is disingenuous in the extreme to argue that because the ideal of the Civil Rights Movement and of all persons of ethnic good will is a color blind world. Any policy that takes account of African ancestry betrays this ideal. [Mazel, 127]

Racism as pathology is constantly reinventing itself. A "color-blind world" is only another phrase in a long series that have been used by those with prejudice to keep others from power. It certainly demands a good degree of social blindness to maintain this position of a color blind world. The "disneyfication" of social issues allows Euro-Americans to confront the extent to which they, and their children, benefit from the present social configuration.

Defining Characteristics of the New, Subtle Racism

*On occasion, people move from trying to ignore race
to explicitly announcing it as irrelevant. A typical claim is:
"I don't think of you as Black." When I am on the receiving end of
such a "compliment" I am tempted to respond,
"Really? What do you think of me as?"*
—HARLAN DALTON, **Racial Healing: Confronting Fears
Between Blacks and Whites**

An important first step in identifying the "new racism" is to know that it actively disavows being racist. No one is parroting blatantly derogatory statements such as those made by the nineteenth-century scientist Louis Agassiz, who said Africans had brains that paralleled those of orangutans. [Wright, 31] Today's racists do not see themselves as racists but "realists" who do not look, as "liberals" do, through "rose colored glasses" or from "ivory towers." New racists eschew violence and distance themselves from racist organizations. They rely on sociological themes in place of the discredited ideas of biological racism.

The new racism is reactionary. The Reverend Jerry Falwell writes: "It is important to remember that what is being observed is a reaction to the action begun by the liberals as they sought to dismantle our moral heritage." [Conservative Digest, 1/81, 28]. When reading this quote the question arises to whom exactly does the "our" refer to! Whose cultural norms are being put forward as exemplary. Falwell's iconographic historiography portrays the founders of the nation as righteous idealists free from the taint of wrongdoing.

Listen to American radio commentators, and you will hear an oft-repeated refrain. Rush Limbaugh discusses personal responsibility and the lack of this virtue as the reason why most urban Americans remain mired in marginal lives. This kind of rhetoric is rooted in what Kofi calls the "politics of class envy," where others are expected to seek what the advocates already enjoy. [Kofi, 64] Advocates of these views claim that they are merely responding to a backlash of abuses that they, are not the millions in America who live below the poverty line and are last in the job line but first in the front lines when America goes to war. The new racists are suffering persecution for righteousness sake as did their Puritan fore-bearers.

Contemporary racism is a perpetrated with a new vocabulary. In this language the notion of power is completely absent. New symbols are used to restate well-known positions such as scapegoating. At the same time, they condemn racism as being irrational and cannot fathom how they can be accused of being racist. They maintain that anyone, from any group, can be a racist. In fact, the greatest racists in society, these "soft racists" contend, are the "affirmative racists" who, in effect, are attacking "white people." New racists reject the fabrication of "white privilege."

New racist believe that the government has no responsibility to interfere in correcting peoples racist perspectives. New racists argue that race should not be a factor in making public policy. Enough has been done already. Laws have been passed. People should be judged by "the content of their character." Individuals rise or fall on their own merits. One only has to look at Michael Jordan, Oprah Winfrey and Bill Cosby to see how effectively the meritocracy works. In this way, Euro-American dominance over the mechanisms of society are preserved. The social status-quo is maintained while being gradually fine-tuned. In their view, anything but a "color-blind meritocracy" insults African-Americans.

Education is the solution that focuses on changing attitudes. Student should be taught to "love" African-Americans even though they will never probably meet any African-Americans in their neighborhoods or churches.

When African-Americans object to this re-casting of old racist ideas in this new user-friendly variety, those who raise objections are viewed by the new racists as frustrating to deal with, irritating and demanding. The responses of the new racists reveal how far America needs to progress.

The Mantra of Individualism and its Racist Implications

*What every Black American knows, and what every White should
try to imagine, is how it feels to have an unfavorable and unfair
identity imposed on you every waking day.*
—ANDREW HACKER

No White person, even when he wants to, can
understand what it means to be Black living in America today,
any more than a combatant can understand what
it means to be a non-combatant.
—MARGARET HALSEY, 1946.

American literary accounts and images of media celebrities like John Wayne or Humphrey Bogart have long celebrated the idea of the rugged individual who fights on the frontiers of life and succeeds of his own accord. Individualism is the rallying cry for those who want to maintain the present social status-quo. It was the main argument that Ronald Reagan and Senator Barry Goldwater raised against the Civil Rights Act of 1964. It was the reason that George Bush attacked the 1964 proposal in Texas during a failed bid for Congress. It is the same argument used in calls to end affirmative action legislation. The Constitution, according to this logic, provides for individual rights against the threat of social controls. It is ironic, in light of this interpretation, that any African-American and Native American advances have been made vis-à-vis constitutional amendments have all been group initiatives.

From the pride of place given to individual rights in American political culture, it is easy to see how group entitlement initiatives, e.g. school busing to promote integration, are seen as illegitimate. An increasingly libertarian America calls for limited federal government and maximum individual self-determination. Government should only underwrite services rendered to the taxpayer and not help those who are unable to keep jobs or are heading toward prison. Government should stay out of social justice issues rooted in individual dysfunction; not social conditions.

It is increasingly rare to hear about the collective good of American society while the mantra of "individualism is everything" spreads like poison ivy across the political landscape. The advocacy of this view reached an absurd nadir with William Bradford Reynolds, (the paleoconservative chosen by Reagan to lead the Justice Department's Civil Rights Division) who declared: "We are all—each of us—a minority in this country: a minority of one." [Ansell, 115] "I" replaces "us" in the political conversation, but it is a distinctly European "I." In this logic, if you happen to be sinking on America's Titanic, you have no one to blame but yourself for buying the ticket. If you are an African-American, you have no one to blame but yourself that you were not born as a Euro-American.

This paradigm explains why, in the minds of the new racists, rhetoric against racism coincides with the assertion that nothing should be done institutionally to implement any changes that might be needed. In fact, the brunt of hostility in the preaching of the American Right is against the "State" as a liberal establishment. Anti-racist bureaucrats are cast as social engineers with unpatriotic and non-Christian intent. The rights of the citizen must be protected against the tentacles of the "State." American government should not dictate to schools what to teach or tell employers whom to hire. Their vision for an ideal America echoes what the Bible says about a society that had reached its lowest point imaginable: "And each man did what was right in his own eyes."

Subtle Racism Used to Promote Power

I was, for all practical purposes, a "made-in-America" person. Yet, the making itself had not convinced me that I was truly part of the process that governed the society. Black and White, two colors, two origins, two destinies; that is what intervened in the midst of reflections on place for a young African in the south of Georgia.
—MOLEFI KETE ASANTE

Is racism on the decline? Between January 1995 and October 1996 more than one hundred African-American churches were the target of arson attacks. [Goldberg, 36] Environmental racism is growing as toxic landfill dumps and waste sights are repeatedly placed near African-American communities. Hate groups that used to terrorize with white sheets and burning crosses now pour out venom over internet sights that are broadcast all over the planet. The African-American prison population is growing while the economic gap between African-Americans and Euro-Americans continues to expand.

The great triumph of the Civil Rights Movement removed legal barriers. The substantive transformation of social and even religious structures, however, remains unfinished. Racism is kept alive through the dynamics of de-facto segregation. Social segregation is so distinct that it has been estimated by some that 95 percent of Euro-Americans do not even have any African-American friends. A similar percentage of Euro-Christians worship in congregations that are entirely homogeneous. Money is segregated. Few economic dollars are spent by Euro-American individuals, in distinctly African-American owned businesses.

Americans have been gripped with fear as terrorists struck New York and Washington, D.C. The storm troopers on the American Right, however, continue to blame even the latest threats to the "American way" on internal enemies who are rotting away the heart of all things American. The idea of creating enemies so that one's own power is necessary to stop them is an old story for both right and left-wing extremists. The basic idea is that there are "insiders and outsiders" in America. The "outsiders" are the ones who are trying to destroy the values of "true Americans."

The "insider-outsider" model explains why some politicians in America are calling for an end to Affirmative Action programs after they have had only forty years to take effect. That seems hardly rational in light of the fact that the previous slavery-Jim Crow economic program toward African-Americans had a full three hundred years to take root. The new racists see Affirmative Action as, "leaking poison in the American soul....America must once again try living with inequality as life is lived." (Ansell, 109)

Another expression of the insider-outsider model is the way that welfare is discussed. Just as the *Bell Curve* worked to "root" African-Americans again in the stereotype of un-intelligence; rhetoric about welfare affirms ideas about indolence. Welfare policies are paraded as examples of the government creating dependants. This accusation, ironically, affirms the economic justice half of the civil rights movement agenda stymied by critics of the 1965 Civil Rights Act. Meanwhile, de-facto segregation in the United States continues to flourish.

Exactly what do these conservatives offer African-Americans? "They" can become just like "us." "They"are welcome to come to our party, after all, it is "our" country! "We" built it, didn't we? At the price of becoming "pseudo-whites" African-Americans will be entitled to a few token benefits. These rewards, however, are always given on a probationary basis. African-Americans can be thrown out of this precarious social lifeboat whenever they are rocking the boat with a little too much vigor.

Subtle Racism and Republicanism

Being Black is like skating on ice but not knowing the location of the thin places. It is like going to war without weapons or holding a hand-grenade and searching for a target beyond the ten-second interval allotted after pulling the pin. To be Black is a confusing proposition. Not the color itself, but the complexities brought to it by the cold, harsh realities of a nation filled with all-encompassing whiteness. We are caught in the briar patches of white power and institutional controls, and there is no escape.
—CHARLES H. KING

The new American racism is a "thoroughly mischievous soft racism" [Dolton, 95] that argues that there is actually no racism problem. Instead, there are different tribes (multiculturalism) that are waging a battle for power. This is why Affirmative Action programs should be removed. The claim is that the reality of equal access to the American Dream already exists for all of her citizens. These affirmations of the great meritocracy bring to mind Frederick Douglass' comment about the nature of European optimism as an expression of self-delusion:

This self-deception is a chronic disease of the American mind and character. The crooked way is ever preferred to the straight. All Americans are masters of the art of substituting a pleasant falsehood for an ugly and disagreeable truth and of clinging to a fascinating delusion while rejecting a palpable reality. [Wright, 9]

The palpable realities of American racism are recast by new racists not because of failures within society, but because of the personal inadequacies and splintered families of those who "choose" to remain marginalized. This "survival of the fittest" social Darwinism came into prominence in the Republican Party with the failed presidential bid of Barry Goldwater and from his supporter, California Governor Ronald Reagan. It resurfaced in the Republican Party when Richard Nixon crafted a policy of "benign neglect," which sought to "milk white backlash" against the civil rights movement. [Steinberg, 100] Republican Presidents Reagan, George Bush and George W. Bush have since continued this policy of solving the problem of racism by declaring it solved. They have, at the same time, "milked the white backlash" by infusing their political agendas with code words such as crime, busing, welfare, and quotas that under-girded social Darwinism. Nixon probably saw the political potential of this strategy by watching the meteoric 1968 Dixiecrat presidential campaign of George Wallace. A blatant racist with an inexcusable track record of offences, Wallace won the ear of the American voter by calling himself a "law and order" candidate and assiduously avoiding race baiting. Nixon parroted this approach in his 1972 presidential campaign. This so-called "Southern strategy" brought Wallace's rhetoric to the center of American politics.

1980-1992, 2000-2004: A Kinder Gentler Racism— The Reagan-Bush-Bush Era

There are some today who, in the name of equality, would have us practice discrimination. They have turned our civil rights laws on their head claiming they mean exactly the opposite of what they say. These people tell us that government should enforce discrimination in favor of some groups through hiring quotas, under which people get or lose jobs or promotions solely because of their race or sex. They couldn't be more wrong....
—RONALD REAGAN, June 15, 1985

Old Satan am a liar and a conjurer too and If you don't watch out he'll conjure you too!
—Spiritual

Special honorable mention for advancing the cause of the new, subtle racism is reserved for the grand-fatherly warm-hearted Ronald Wilson Reagan. Dyson said: "It was a new era where the thinly veiled contempt for racial minorities during the Reagan-Bush administrations unleashed a racist backlash" [Dyson, 154] in American society. It was not until Reagan's election that the all-out assault on the key gains of the civil rights movement began. Reagan gave the country a happy, upbeat, and patriotic version of racism that won wide support across Euro-America.

This was done was by invoking, as Reagan always did, the pure, fundamental, and "true America." He was a gregarious spokesman for non African-America in its struggle to reverse any progress that African-Americans had made in society. If it is true, as the old axiom states, that "politics and patriotism are the last bastions for scoundrels" then this actor-turned-President raised patriotic politics to a new level. George Lipsitz writes that:

> Reagan succeeded in fusing the possessive investment in whiteness with other psychic and material investments-especially in masculinity, patriarchy, and heterosexuality. The intersecting identity he offered gave new meanings to white male patriarchal and heterosexual identities by establishing patriotism as the site where class antagonisms between men could be reconciled by in national and patriotic antagonisms against foreign foes and internal enemies. By encoding the possessive investment in whiteness within national narratives of male heroism and patriarchal protection, Reagan and his allies mobilized a cross-class coalition around the premise that the declines in life chances and opportunities in the United States, the stagnation of real wages, the decline of basic services, and infrastructure resources, and the increasing social disintegration stemmed not from policies of big corporations and their neo-liberal and neo-conservative allies in government but from the harm done to the nation by the civil rights movement, and anti-war, feminist and gay liberation movements of the 1960s and 1970s. By representing the national crisis as a crisis of the declining value of the white male and heterosexual identity, Reagan and his allies and successors (the Bushes) built a counter-subversive coalition mobilized around protecting the privileges and prerogatives of the possessive investment in whiteness....[Lipsutz, 72]

Lipsutz's argument was that, without sounding blatantly racist, Reagan spoke directly to Euro-American males and offered them a vision of a society crafted in their image and for their benefit. He dealt with Afrocentric issues in the same way that Jefferson and Washington did; by ignoring them. An example of this is the way that Affirmative Action policy was recast. During the Reagan-Bush years the momentum of Affirmative Action was turned around and the huge gap that is now seen between power and powerlessness began in earnest. George W. Bush is reviving that trend. Reagan slashed federal enforcement efforts, denounced Affirmative Action quotas, and addressed reverse discrimination. Reagan lulled the country to sleep, proclaiming how life had never been better. He was a wolf in sheep's clothing, unleashing other ravenous wolves into society against the policies launched by civil rights era reformers.

Reagan eliminated countless social welfare programs that emerging urban African-Americans had relied upon. Welfare flourished while big business and the upper classes enjoyed new tax breaks and greater prosperity. The work was so complete that by 1991 the top one percent of all Americans have more wealth than the bottom ninety percent of Americans combined. [Ansell, 222]. Long-term unemployment increased 2 percent among Euro-Americans during that time while it rose 72 percent among African-Americans. [Ansell, 222] And, Reagan accomplished all of this while not giving the appearance of being a mean-spirited racist.

It should not be surprising that Reagan, Bush, and Bush, Jr. admirers claim that these statistics are misleading. A mountain of evidence remains to counter their arguments. Steven A. Shull summarized the Reagan-Bush era of race relations by saying: "By playing on the fear and frustration of lower-class Whites, both Reagan and Bush left a substantial civil rights legacy, but it was not a kinder and gentler one." [Schull, 229] The selection by George W. Bush's of John Ashcroft to serve as Attorney General promised America more of the same. These leaders were leaders for only part of America; that part which was concerned with maintaining their majority social and economic status quo in America.

A word about the Republican Party's great enemy: Affirmative Action. People who have been marginalized before they begin, need to have something done on their behalf. Fairness demands that Affirmative Action is not abandoned. That Euro-Americans regard Affirmative Action programs as unfair is a reflection on their unwillingness to see how inequitable this country has been toward African-Americans. These three Presidents have tried to make the issues theoretical by complaining about "reverse racism." Reverse racism is an ahistorical fabrication. John Hope Franklin has observed that "as long as Affirmative Action was functioning the other way then there was no opposition at all." [Mazel, 120]

Some say that Affirmative Action insults the genuine merits of African-Americans. There can be nothing more demeaning than pre-determining that a person will fail in life even before they can begin to make an effort. Affirmative Action is not a perfect tool for justice but it is one of the few plans at work against racism, and as such needs to be given further opportunity to succeed. Affirmative Action does not "give something;" it recognizes that something must be corrected. The average Euro-American household has a net worth more than ten times that of the average African-American family. Businesses, government offices, and banks are predominantly in the hands of Euro-Americans. Affirmative Action should remain a tool for social change until the justification for its existence is no longer a reality.

"Reaganism" was built on the assumption that government spending was the cause for economic stagnation and even for moral decline. Both Bush Presidencies have followed this view. It is a backward-looking argument presented with an optimistic forward-looking rhetoric.

Distrust of government was the foundational reason given for attacking Affirmative Action; yet, these three Republican Presidents have spent unprecedented amounts of Federal money fighting terrorism, drugs and sending people to prison. Perhaps Reagan's greatest legacy was the way he defined the terms of the debate on racism in America. Justice was replaced by fairness, and the color-blind vision of the American meritocracy replaced civil rights era rhetoric about justice and equality. What W.D. Wright said of Ronald Reagan could also be said of both George Bush and George W. Bush; these men served as, "the white people's president" [Wright, 111] using the authority of the White House's to serve their constituency; America's powerful majority.

The presidential election of 2000, however, did not even secure a majority of the popular vote for George W. Bush. Further, the electoral vote was inconclusive with a host of improprieties in the Florida state election that forced America to learn that our government is not always a government "by the people." The final vote that mattered, in mid-December, 2000 was the vote of nine Supreme Court justices. Not surprisingly the vote was cast five to four along party lines forever eliminating any presumption that the American judicial system was impartial. George W. Bush is the first resident of the White House in American history to be appointed, not by popular mandate, but by the Supreme Court: Resident Bush.

The United States Supreme Court should not even have been considering the case as there was arguably no substantial federal question. The process of voting is fundamentally a state issue. Taking a larger view, it is clear that discouragement is a luxury. Many African-Americans suffered and even died for the right to vote. Perhaps the same must be done to bring just election reform measures to ensure uniformity and access for all citizens. The power of the ballot must be utilized. This is as true today as it was in 1866 when Frederick Douglass went to President Andrew Johnson and told him, "as you gave us the musket to free the nation, now give us the ballot so that we can free ourselves."

1992-2000: "Big Clouds, No Rain"— Clinton-Gore Social Justice Rhetoric

The State of the Union has never been better!
—PRESIDENT BILL CLINTON, 2000

Sadly, the Clinton-Gore Democrats gave only tepid support for Affirmative Action and maintained Reagan and Bush's focus denying empowerment and substituting "fairness:" a new racist code word for inertia.

It would seem that many of Bill Clinton's ideas about racial inequality parallel the arguments of Harvard professor Cornel West. West largely shifts the blame from societal structures to what he calls "nihilism" among African-Americans. For West, African-Americans are the primary problem. What is needed is new leadership and a rejection of hedonism in the African-American community. Steinberg reports:

> In a speech delivered to a Memphis church in 1993, Clinton practically echoed West in asserting that there is a crisis of the spirit...legitimate spiritual concerns (are)used as a subterfuge for political and moral abdication. The irony is made still more bitter by the fact that Clinton gave his speech in the same Memphis church where the Reverend Dr. Martin Luther King, Jr., delivered his last sermon on the night before his 1968 assassination. [Steinberg, 132]

The 1992 Democratic Party platform was the first in almost fifty years to make no mention of redressing racial injustice [Kofi, 96]. The question must be asked if Clinton-Gore Democrats were actually working for the best interests of the African-American community or if, in fact, they were supporting another "Hayes-Tilden" compromise. These politicians were part of a larger trend that shifts the central point from the deeply rooted facts of discrimination to a focus on total individual responsibility for one's destiny. They have also used the high sounding term "color blindness" to assure voters that they need not fear change.

The Democratic Party's lack of advocacy is a fact because, to use Kofi's phrase, the sentiment is that, "we got you under our control" [Kofi, 51]. African-Americans tend to describe themselves as Democrats. This blind loyalty has become counter-productive and confining. On party affiliation Malcolm X declared, "I am not a Democrat. I am not a Republican. I do not even consider myself just an American." [Dyson, 91] The Democratic Party has been able to "assume" that African-Americans will vote Democratic without much question because most of the Republican Party was disinterested in African-American voters. Democrats have mostly chosen to rely upon symbolic gestures and cautious social programs without taking stands that confront the issues of structural inequality. Clinton was willing to open a "dialogue on race," but was not politically motivated enough to work for the healing of America's deep racialist wounds.

Although it is frequently maintained that these leaders were the lesser of two evils, it can also be charged that Clinton and Gore were actually Democratic-Reaganites. Their rhetoric proposes recovering the center of the social debate. Early in Clinton's national career that meant the candidate playing the race card by attacking the lyrics of rap-singer Sister Souljah in June of 1992. Clinton played one ethnic group against another throughout his tenure and in so doing lost the opportunity that he might have had to forge a progressive alliance that could have worked for meaningful change. Dyson wrote,

> Clinton is just the sort of political figure that Malcolm often warned us against. Clinton's public positions on race encourage clever, often unprincipledly manipulative, even distortive, words and phrases that are an attempt to distract us from the issues of race relations in our national life. [Dyson, 152]

New Racism: The Code-words Differ; The Message is the Same

I was eight years old when I saw a photo of Emmett Till's body. The murder shocked me; I began thinking of myself as a Black person for the first time, not just a person. And I grew more distrustful and wary..., I could be hurt or even killed just for being Black.
—KAREEM ABDUL-JABBAR

Code words are nothing new. During the American Civil War, the government talked about "Free States" and "Slave States" when in fact African-Americans in the northern states at that time had clear restrictions that made them less than free, if not more than slave. One cluster of code-words converge around high-sounding phrases such as "family values" which should really be rephrased as "my family values." Do we really want our families to have values such as silence about inequality and injustice and condescending non-involvement with people of other cultures? New racist political rhetoric seeks to remind Americans "who we are" and who and what threaten our cherished "Amerikaaner" homesteads. New racist rhetoric would suggest that what is at stake is the erasure of all that is characteristic of the United States. Their essentialist undercurrents, however, are exclusivistic. It is their America, made in their image, in which all of us are invited to sustain.

How does this "we" preaching relate to claims that racism is individualistic? This simple question lies at the heart of what is contradictory about the way many Euro-Americans view racism in its social forms. The solution to this problem is explained by the new racists who conclude that racism is not even part of the picture of modern America. Racism is described as only a "coat of paint" and peripheral to the real issues of the day. Optimists project that racism will eventually die of its own impotence. This is because life is improving for all Americans as the country grows wealthier. Facts indicate otherwise.

The new racists announce that their agenda is the best hope for Africans in America. They insist that they are not exclusionary. Their truth, like the three-fifths theology of the early Puritans, is a universal truth available with equal access to all. What is hindering African-Americans from enjoying wealth is not their "blackness" but their inability to be "white." The problem is that African-Americans will not give up their notions of community and accept the American notion that each person is a king. Instead of investing in this great American creed, African-Americans have cursed themselves by claiming to be victimized and by resorting to fantastical arguments about contemporary links to past injustices to explain the nature of their wide-spread poverty and social powerlessness. The new racists challenge African-Americans, instead, to concentrate on their own social behavior. They maintain that African-American poverty and incidences of criminality are resultant primarily from inferior personal values. With this logic, long held prejudicial stereotypes are affirmed without being seen as racist.

A New American Racist "Sermon"—The Dangers of the Slippery Slope!

Wake up America! Can't you read the hand-writing on the wall indicating where our country is going if we keep pandering to special interest groups like African-Americans, gays and liberals who are trying to rip this country apart at the seams? Will we experience the same fate as Sodom and Gomorrah? Heed the warnings: America will become like Rome and destroy itself in a whirlwind of crime, violence, and chaos. Recent terrorist attacks are the judgement of God! Foreign religions are growing. The enemy is within. Satan in dark skin is at work in our midst to undermine our godly heritage. Wake up! The enemy of our cherished American way of life is near. He thrives in godless colleges spouting hated "political correctness" (Bush) and in the secular humanist public schools and even in churches where sneaky liberals spew forth sermons of hatred against us and promote divisive cultural identity.

Wake up America or we will be living in Bosnia U.S.A. filled with foreign gods (presumably worse than Mammon and Moloch). The enemy will get to your children through his godless, immoral music; then he will sell your children his ghetto drugs and seduce them with his wanton women on cable television. America will no longer be America; it will become Babylon. Even now, political correctness is sneaking into your children's PBS morning television programs.

Real Americans must be vigilant. The enemy of all that this coun-
try is founded upon is trying to take over America. Things must be
kept the way they were when Columbus and our Fathers, Jefferson,
Washington and Stonewall Jackson led us with their virtue. Thank
our lucky stars that a few Americans are still out there to speak as
Patrick Buchanan says, "for the real Americans who founded this
country." [Ansell, 128] Leave the rotting cities! Move into the
country where it is safe and quiet and white. Leave the public
schools and home-school to give your children a strong Christian
education! Buy a gun and keep praying! We need every one of you
to circle the wagons and every one of your precious children to
ensure that our great nation under God has as bright a future as
its glorious past. Let's not watch America go down the tubes. Let's
take America back! God Bless America!

Such arrogant attitudes of cultural dominance are alive in America today.

"Culture Wars" and "White Privilege"

Turn now and look at Black America. We are not only
separated from the rest of the country by geographical and
discriminatory containment, but we are also isolated in spirit. We
have become a separate people, both in philosophy and experience.
That Black experience is unknown to White America.
—CHARLES H. KING, JR.

Real community is based on reciprocity of emotion
and relation between individuals sharing a common vision of the
possibilities and potentialities of man. The basic fact of race rela-
tions in America is that White people and Black people
do not belong in the same community.
—LERONE BENNETT, JR.

How united is America? How true has "E Pluribus Unum" (From out
of the Many, One) ever been in the United States? Are we decaying in our
monocultural unity or are we coming to learn that we have never really

ever been unified in a monolithic culture? African-Americans have always known the answers to these questions. The wisdom of the street has long been that the "White man's ice is colder."

Social commentators have noted that Muslim terrorists are tribalist while the rest of the world is globalist. In America, the new racists preach Enlightenment era individualism but actually live by the rules of tribal communitarianism. Their tribal God and their tribal religion, complete with its ancestor worship-shrines in Washington, D.C. and historiographic iconography, is assumed to be the one way to define American society. In addition, their god and their way of life should be universal exported as truth to all of the people of the world. Their rhetoric about American family values is tribal language. New racists talk about the "culture wars" when they are actually advocating the maintenance of "white privilege."

What is "white privilege?" It is a term used to describe the privilege to be ignorant about other people's history and to be ignorant to other people's children. White privilege is getting served quickly at a restaurant while people from other cultures have to wait. White privilege is not being followed in a shopping mall for no apparent reason. White privilege is not needing that credit check that is required of some African-American customer. White privilege is never having to worry that a policeman will pull you over for the crime of "DWB" (driving while black) White privilege is well expressed in the epigram, "Don't worry! Be happy!" It consists of making little effort to learn about others while expecting them to make tremendous efforts to learn about your culture and beliefs.

Privilege is least apparent to those who posses it. To those who do not have it, it is easy to recognize. Americans have long used terms such as "the disadvantaged" to describe the poor and others in American society. This implies that there must also be some people in America who are "advantaged." Paul Kivel states,

> There is nothing that we do as whites that is qualified, limited, discredited or acclaimed simply because of our racial background. We do not have to represent our race, or be a confirmation of its shortcomings or inferiority. [Mazel, 98]

People have automatic "credit" in the culture of America if they happen to be Euro-American. People with this kind of advantage should not then have the audacity to assume that this advantage is because of their own intelligence or skill.

The main function of racism in American society is to maintain the domination that Euro-Americans enjoy. Maintaining this status as "gate-keepers" and guardians of the American ideal, requires the development of special terminology. This is where the idea of the "culture wars" emerges. It is a phrase that builds the ghetto wall of segregation by keeping people "in their place" and out of "our place." New racists talk about how welfare mothers (interesting the gender choice!) are "piranhas that feed off the sweat and toil of the honest workingman" and homemaking mother. Conservative prophets warn of America's decline, fighting tooth and nail against every state and federal dollar for entitlement programs. How do conservatives reconcile these complaints with all of the corporate welfare that the government doles out? In 1988, the American taxpayer subsidized the bailout of the Chrysler automobile manufacturer. NASA, the American military complex, and many other institutions are direct beneficiaries of massive government funding. There is no greater welfare program in American foreign policy than the incredible amounts of foreign aid paid to Israel and Egypt.

Every symbol that many Euro-Americans cherish as "American," from the Statue of Liberty chiseled with European features to Mount Rushmore and the heroes on American currency, all look like themselves. American conservatives reject the assertion that the "culture wars" posture is, in effect, advancing a racist position. African-Americans are welcome to act like Euro-Americans, eat the same American pie and dream the same Euro-American dreams if they so wish. This is, after all, America: the great meritocracy set on a hill, where anyone can become a President or a billionaire. What stands in the way for African-Americans to achieve the American dream? First of all they would have to abandon Ebonics and their African-ness and think of themselves solely as Americans. It would also be helpful if African-Americans dispensed with those un-American Kente garments and ceased taking "un-American" names like Asante and Kareem instead of keeping their good American names like Jefferson, Davis, Jackson, Lee, or Wallace. Africans, to melt into the American pot, must avoid contrived holidays such as Kwanzaa when Martin Luther King Day should be holiday enough. Constantly complaining about injustices and discrimination is also very "un-American."

In America's culture wars between the right and the wrong, tokenism replaces the pursuit of equality. The new racists are quick to point out the heart-warming anecdotes of success stories-people like Condelezza Rice or Secretary of State Colin Powell, who have "overcome the odds"and gained America's praise. Stories about people like Clarence Thomas affirm for believers the correctness of their own rhetoric. America is a meritocracy set on a hill. The culture wars will be won once rebels surrender with a white flag. This declaration of "our independence," at the expense of everyone else's dependence, is well articulated by many Uncle Tom liaisons who serve as diplomats between the two cultures. Their primary allegiance is to those who pay their way. American political conservatives are often heard speaking out against "free-rides." It would seem, however, that Clarence Thomas is getting just that. These African-American voices against African identity not only support their sponsors but are also part of a long-held divide-and-conquer strategy. It was Malcolm X who said that, during the time of slavery, when the Big House was burning, the "house Negro" would say, Massa, our house is burning"; while the "field Negro" would say "let it burn!" If the slave master was sick, the "house Negro" would say, Massa, we sick!; while the "field Negro," seeking liberation from the oppressor standing on his neck would say, I hope he dies! Malcolm X reminded us that there are black as well as white snakes that can deliver a poisonous bite.

American conservatives say that the fact that a small number of people of color do succeed is proof that those who have failed have not tried hard enough. African-Americans, the logic goes, are the main reason for their own failure. Individual failure is also evidence that African-American culture is inferior to Euro-American culture. Because these problems are not the fault of the government, it cannot be the source for the solution. Conservatives say that African-Americans should pull themselves up "by their own bootstraps." As Dr. King said, however, that is cruel advice to give to a person who has no boots.

Liberal Paternalism

America is false to the past, false to the present, and solemnly
binds herself to be false to the future.
—FREDERICK DOUGLASS

Just as there are many forms and expressions of "conservatism" there is also a wide range of what is called "liberalism." This chapter will consider what Stephen Steinberg calls the "new liberal orthodoxy" that begins with Franklin Delano Roosevelt and proceeds into the present with politicians like Bill Clinton. During the Civil Rights movement Dr. King wrote from the Birmingham jail that the greatest enemies African-Americans faced were not members of the Ku Klux Klan or the John Birch Society, but "the white liberal, who is more devoted to order than to justice and who prefers tranquility to equality. " [DeLoria, 184]

As early as 1963, Murray Friedman wrote an article in the *Atlantic Monthly* entitled, "The White Liberal's Retreat," which recognized that liberalism was bailing out of King's vision for economic, as well as civil, rights. This liberalism is as toxic as conservatism to the cause of racial healing in America. Part of the emerging black conservatism (Walter Williams for example) has developed as a response to the racism of the paternalistic liberal left. Advocates of the idea of color blindness must to recognize that it leads to cultural suicide and identity meltdown. African-Americans may have been thrown into a melting pot; but do not need to seek annihilation. The ideal of color blindness promotes an abstract liberal universalism and has been pirated by those opposed to Affirmative Action. Liberal and conservative poles come together when they discuss color blindness. Senator Bill Russell called these liberals the "I didn't notice" liberals [Boxill, 10], because they act "sweet and innocent" about the tensions between Africans and Europeans in American society.

Talk of color blindness is meaningless as long as structures of power and privilege remain intact. Euro-Americans have access to social and economic networks that many other Americans do not. As Greg Loury has stated: "To be blind to color, given our history and our social structure, may well mean that one must be blind to justice as well." [Ansell, 108] In Miguel Cervantes' book *The Man of LaMancha,* Don Quixote finds himself attacking windmills while fantasizing that they are giants. Quixote joins bold courage with misguided fantasy. Liberalism offers help to the weaker, childlike African-Americans. It is rooted in assumptions about inferiority. Who are Euro-Americans to help African-Americans (at least, not without being asked for help)? Liberals assume that they have the answers that others need. Other cultures are "sick," "we" are "healthy." Many well-meaning social initiatives are top-down in character with little regard for local sentiment. Little time is wasted in garnering local input. Is it any wonder that these liberal initiatives, thrown like bones to a dog, are often rejected as inherently paternalistic?

One of the most irritating traits of many Euro-American liberals is their smug assumption that they know what it is to "be black." They know "both worlds." They lead organizations trying to help African-Americans and relate with other Euro-Americans as "experts on us." [Tucker, 138] They benefit in the process by having their consciousness eased, a good feeling about helping humanity, and maybe even some prestige or economic benefit from being an expert in an area where other Euro-Americans have little or no information whatsoever. These liberals may fool some ostriches whose heads are stuck in the sand, but they do not fool most African-Americans. As people with the traveling circus have learned, if you spend enough time backstage watching the magician rehearse it becomes rather difficult to remain impressed with the magic act. In the history of relations between African and European-Americans there has been too much "sleight of hand" to be deluded by magical words and theatric gestures.

African-Americans realize that most liberals are usually only "visitors" to their world. Until the biblical motive for justice replaces calls for self-displacement of vested interests, nothing much will happen to change that. Courage will disappear at the first sign of inconvenience if courage is not rooted in something beyond self-interest. Those who call themselves Christians, however, have more than enough incentive to buy a one-way ticket into the realities of American Apartheid, not the least of which is honoring God. The Bible is clear: One's motives determine the effectiveness and value of ones actions. The Bible calls people to relate with each other in humility. For Euro-Americans that may mean gaining trust over time as a learner, a listener, and a pride-free participant divested of personal gain.

Children raised in Euro-American suburban ghettos still have only their stereotypes to rely on in understanding the "alien" African-American. The extent of their segregation is so extreme that they cannot even understand why African-Americans respond to the idea of color blindness as if it were a cruel joke. That even well-intentioned Euro-Americans begin with entirely different reference points on vital issues should be evident. Liberals have long "used" issues of racism and poverty to carve out a secure place for themselves in the political landscape. It's role as champion of the "little guy" is calculated to contrast them with their heartless Republican rivals. With this posture has come a "father knows best" paternalism in relation to the "little guy." Flourishes of compassionate rhetoric are usually cancelled out by inactive timidity once elections have been secured. For many, dealing with racism is a sideshow without much coincident determination to effect change.

The Pervasiveness of America's New Racism

If we tell ourselves that the only problem is hate, we avoid facing
the reality that it is mostly nice, non-hating White people
who perpetrate racial inequality.
—ELLIS COSE

Racism is so universal in this country, so widespread and so deep-
seated that it is invisible because it is so normal.... The difference
between de-jure and de-facto segregation is the difference between
open and forthright bigotry and the shame-faced kind that works
through unwritten agreements between real estate dealers, school
officials, and local politicians.
—SHIRLEY CHISOLM

There are two languages about racism. For Euro-Americans, racism is almost a peripheral artifact of the distant past. For African-Americans, dealing with racism is an everyday occurrence. At colleges, Euro-American students view the efforts of African-American students to form student unions as a form of racial exclusion and not attempts to recover a sense of dignity. Campus enclaves are often the only supportive environments that students can run to in an increasingly new-racist campus environment. The same dynamic is at work when African-Americans worship and socialize apart from Euro-Americans.

One of the most pervasive expressions of racism in America today is fear. Fear is often the parent of cruelty. Some Euro-Americans are afraid of African-Americans, particularly young African-American men. This fear springs from stereotypes deeply rooted in the Euro-American psyche. The

Bible says that "perfect love casts out fear." People fear others because they do not love them. Another reason for fear is ignorance. There is a West African proverb that states: "Perhaps you do not understand me because you do not love me!"

Euro-Americans also fear African-Americans because they are unrepentant, which leads to a coldness of heart. The Bible declares that God's heart is sympathetic to the oppressed. The Bible, the book that Zola Neal Hurston called the "greatest conjure book in the world" [Smith, 42] because it has the power to challenge world view assumptions, claims that injustices will not go unpunished. God will judge the evil in the world. For three hundred and fifty years their ancestors initiated constant violence against Africans in America. In light of that fact, it is ironic that Euro-Americans fear "black power."

The prevalence of the tentacles of racism seems all-pervasive. A 1967 survey found that Euro-American children as early as six years old most often told psychologists that "they did not want to be Black and were least like people from Africa" when asked who they do not want to be. [Lambert and Klineberg, 208] More recent surveys are also instructive in this regard. Many respondents guessed that most welfare recipients were African-American while, in actual fact, two-thirds of those who live below the poverty line are European American. One study of 1,200 respondents, including 150 African-Americans, discovered that 53.2 percent of the people believed, "blacks were less intelligent than whites while 40.5 percent said they were equally intelligent and only 6.2 percent said that they were more intelligent than whites. 62.2 percent of the entire sample rated blacks as lazier than whites...." [Shipler, 278]

Another researcher underwent the intriguing assignment of analyzing Victoria Secret catalogues. Only twenty-five people of color appeared among the 2,198 Euro-American models. Most of the twenty-five had lighter skin tones, which is "intentionally ambiguous." [Shipler, 243] This is true in most advertising. African-Americans are sometimes "placed" in advertisements in contrived ways and with careful attention to ratios and with roles meticulously defined.

What does this new racism have to do with Euro-American three-fifths theology? Church and society are increasingly interdependent. The ranks of the new right fill America's evangelical churches every Sunday. There is preaching from pulpits about how American culture is being eroded as if that culture was in some meaningful way Christian. Do these Christians realize that their homogenous Euro-American cultural assumptions may not have universal merit? Does not God call these Christians to a spiritual warfare (Ephesians 6) instead of to a cultural war?

In the presidential election of 1992, Pat Robertson and Patrick Buchanan made the idea of the culture wars the staple diet of American Republicanism. Their echoes have been clear in every election since that time. The church is, once again, active in politics. It seems determined to build the "city set on a hill" envisioned by the Puritan founders. It is not surprising that the same spokespersons supported the controversial nominations of Robert Bork and Clarence Thomas to the Supreme Court. They warn that the United States is becoming a land of quotas and special interests. These are clear code words for people who are unlike themselves. Rigidity of ideas leads to automatic statements that advocate the non-inclusive solutions. This new racism makes ahistorical what is historical. It makes symmetrical what is asymmetrical. We must educate for change at the grass-roots level to combat the new, subtle racism increasingly common in American society.

Chapter Four, Racism—Questions for consideration and discussion:

1. If it is true that African-Americans often view racism as pervasive and Euro-Americans often view it as nonexistent, how can the two cultures have a meaningful dialogue about these issues?

2. What is the relationship between Eurocentric understandings of individualism and society and the problems of racism in contemporary America?

3. Why are terms such as "liberal" and "conservative" not very helpful in discussing the nature of contemporary American racism? Did this chapter make you rethink your use and understanding of those two categories?

Chapter Five
Sankofa and Ujima: Self-Understanding and Anger

Self-determination is a natural by-product of
self-awareness, and together the form the mental and
spiritual cornerstones of freedom.
—ANTHONY BROWDER

As human beings, our limitations rest only in our ignorance. We
are ignorant of who we are and what we can do. We have a need
to gain a consciousness (awareness) and only in consciousness is
our true human capacity opened to us.
—NAI'M AKBAR

We are a people who have flourished since the dawn of human civilization. God fashioned humanity in His image and placed them in Africa's Eden. The Bible describes Africans as a noble people and that caliber of greatness has endured. Incredible obstacles have been thrown against us. Bob Marley sings that:

> We're the survivors.
> The Black survivors.
> Like Daniel out of the lion's den, survivors....
> Like Shadrach, Mesech and Abendego
> Thrown into the fire but never get burned.

The fact that we have been able to withstand adversity speaks volumes about the determination that God has put within our collective consciousness. Once our ancestors survived the Maafa, they faced decade after decade of slavery; lynching; systematic racism and the segregation of the Jim Crow era. Even today, the larger society would stuff us into cargo ships of conformity to their expectations and plans for us. They would try to chain us into certain neighborhoods, careers or colleges and hold us, against our will, on their plantations.

We have not been defeated. We are not victims and ask for no sympathy. We are a people who have survived because God had invested in us His loving mercy and strength. God has always been on the side of oppressed people. The god of three-fifths theology is a god of domination, exploitation and the build-up of the military complex. He is a different god than the God of our ancestors. Our God liberates from slavery and brings wholeness where there is dichotomy. I (Lewis Tait) remember how the choir used to sing at my Daddy's church in Washington, D.C.: "We've come this far by faith, leaning on the Lord. Trusting in His holy word, He's never failed us yet." We, as an African people, have come this far by faith in God, our Great Emancipator. This "imani" (belief), which guides our lives, is not some idle "pie-in-the-sky" faith. It is a faith deeply rooted in the teachings of the African Messiah, Jesus Christ, Son of the Living God who brought a revolutionary message that disturbed the status-quo. Christ was never co-opted by either the political power of the Roman Empire or the religious elite of His day.

The long shadow of the Maafa looms, consciously and unconsciously, over our lives as Africans in the United States. It fills us with an intoxicating anger that affects our hearts and souls. Boiling inside of us are seething rivers of molten volcanic fire. We often feel like we will erupt at any moment. We must confront this anger and not deny it. Each of us, on a visceral level, must get in touch with that lava-indignation. The question is not whether we should be vehemently passionate, but how should we embrace our righteous, boiling anger and translate it into the fabric of our lives and our dreams of making this world a better place. How can our anger be constructive instead of destructive to ourselves and to those around us whom we love?

How can we guard inner resources of peacefulness in the stormy torrent of all the "noise" that is being thrown at us in our daily lives? Gil-Scott

Heron said that looking all around him made him want to shout. Anger. Rage. Fury. That is what we feel when we realize that day in and day out, America is trying to force-feed us with a steady diet of liberal and conservative notions, religious and secular mandates, regulations, orders, directions, instructions, controls, restraints; chains.

What is our hope?

"Sankofa" is a potent word from the West African Akkan language that means "to retrieve" or to "return and recover." We must go back across the North Atlantic and retrieve from Africa what has been stolen from us: our identity. We must "fetch" our own healing. We must return and rebuild inner lives of wholeness and stability.

To go forward we must reach back. We must travel back into the holds of the cargo ships and recognize ourselves, not as slaves, but as prisoners of war exiled from our homeland. We must reject the internalization of our European captors twisted logic and their three-fifths religion that tears ethics and love from spirituality. We must awaken from the stupor of deceptions. Millions were murdered to bring us to this day of spiritual insight and intellectual fortitude. We must salvage redemption from their sacrifice with militant dedication. Going back through the Maafa and across the stormy ocean waves will bring us back to a wise and ancient Mother Africa. We will learn again the stories that our grand-ancestors taught our ancestors. We will live in confidence again.

Our enemies have tried to take this from us. DuBois said, "We have lost something brothers wandering in this strange land-we have lost our ideals." [Butler, 1] Malcolm X, at a speech at Harvard University, said that when he was younger his perceptions of Africa were skewered by false perceptions:

Africa was a jungle, a wild place where people were savage cannibals who ran naked through a countryside overrun with dangerous animals. Such an image of Africa was so hateful to Blacks that they have refused to identify with Africa. We did not realize that in hating Africa and the Africans we were hating ourselves. You cannot hate the roots of a tree and not hate the tree itself. [Epps, 168]

Thus, our greatest battle is not with petty, malformed racist souls but with, as both Martin and Malcolm reminded us, ourselves. The tentacled brute force of America's systematic deceptions is not nearly as firm as the resolve that is within us that has been given to us by our Creator. He has a Nija for us, the path of self-determination. We will write our own Declaration of Independence on our hearts and announce our own freedom from the slave shackles of Eurocentrism. The battle within us asks if we are brave enough to define and to construct reality for ourselves. No longer will we allow any group of people to have dominion over us. We are greater than bitterness. We do not have any time to waste being small-minded or vindictive. We refuse to squander even one moment of our lives with the poison of hate. Taking on their hatred would change us and cause us to fall to their domination. The slave masters are nothing to us. We are moving forward.

In the movie *Hurricane,* based on the life of New Jersey boxer Rueben "Hurricane" Carter, the protagonist says of his prison that "hate brought me here, but love is going to break me out!" Hateful horror brought us to these shores, but it is love that is going to break us back out into the world where we are at home and where we have confidence. Some may look at the United States as a beacon of freedom in the world, but for African peoples it has been a bottomless pit of betrayal, suffering, exhaustion, distrust, and abuse, rape, torture, theft and injustice: hell. Our power enables us to transform present challenges into future victories. We have acclimatized from West African tropical warmth to frigid North American cold, and we will continue to sketch patterns in the snow that reflect the warmth of our creativity and ingenuity.

African-Americans are bicultural. Instead of allowing the reality of our two-world lives to lead to a deteriorating schizophrenia, it should become for us a well-spring of prescience. Necessity has forced us to understand the nature of this country through Euro-American eyes. We have learned their technology and their Teutonic discipline. We need not either accept or reject the strengths of their culture. By being bi-cultural, however, we have a flexibility that makes us uniquely strong in the world that we live in. We are gifted with an incredible dexterity that adds something new to our story as Africans. As Carlyle Fielding Stewart has said this enables us to "actualize ourselves in this society" [Stewart, 15] without needing to go to another continent to live lives of balance.

As Sankofa takes root in our lives, our world will come into greater focus. We will find strength inside ourselves to immunize ourselves against the murky waters of American racism. Sankofa will anchor us as an African diaspora people who live in America. Sankofa will bring us back into relationship with our ancestors and they will be able to find their healing and peace in us. The clarity that Sankofa brings us will make us more aware that those who claimed that they were trying to help us and interpret the world for us were actually trying to manipulate us. We can begin to scrutinize their world view assumptions, recognizing that they are not universal verities. Without this perspective we will question our own competence. Anthony Browder explains,

> The way that we interpret the world determines the our perceptions of reality and dictates how we will now function in the world. Since the world of the contemporary African has been shaped by racist ideologies formulated long ago, it is necessary to understand the roots of racism and white supremacy, in order to correctly interpret current events and formulate meaningful plans for the future." [Browder, 3]

Sankofa means that we will begin to know ourselves. Knowledge of self is the basis for our confidence. Without this knowledge one will forever be lost in a haze of limited of distorted vision. The corrective lenses of Sankofa must change the faulty vision of Eurocentric interpretations of the African experience. This is what God intends for us; that we see the world we live in through the perspective that God created us to use, free of fragmentation.

It is this contemporary distortion, and not only the tragedies of the past, that steel in us the on-going anger lodged in the "souls of black folk." No one can tell us to ignore this anger. No one else can tell us about the pain that we feel or, how as Christians, we should not feel it. For us, the United States is a daily battlefield where we go on in the face of petty slights as well as significant, systematic social problems. In America, we need to teach our contemporaries to "fear" the police because it is a possibility that they might end up dead just because they are "black."

Being African-American in this country means that we have to transform our anger into righteous indignation. Jesus was angry as he cleared the temple in Jerusalem. Love expressed in anger drove Christ to action. If it is true that the opposite of love is not hate but indifference, then the lack of anger that many people exhibit in light of the injustices in America today is lamentable. Many of us are fatalistic about the events that are pressing against our communities. Many of us would rather pass the buck to someone else than channel the wrath of God's Holy Spirit in us to bring change to our communities.

Anger must also be directed at those African-Americans who sacrifice our corporate dreams for progress for their own self-interests. An amazing character in African-American life today is Supreme Court Justice Clarence Thomas. President Reagan appointed Thomas to be the Assistant Secretary for Civil Rights in the Department of Education only three months after his inauguration. A year after that, Thomas was appointed chairman of the Equal Employment Opportunity Commission, a position that he held until George Bush appointed him to the Court of Appeals and then nominated Thomas for the United States Supreme Court. When his confirmation seemed doomed he used the term "high-tech lynching" to describe the stratagems of his opponents. This use of language struck such a memory chord among his Euro-American opponents who were forced to confront the memory of their own deplorable history. Thomas, who it seemed had lost any sense of cultural memory, regained it for the purpose of self-promotion.

What explains Thomas' meteoric climb? Consider accomodationalist opinions; e.g. that it would be "just as insane for blacks to expect relief from the federal government for years of discrimination as it would be for a mugger to nurse his victim back to health." [John Hope Franklin, 15]

Judge Thomas is, sadly, a man who has lost his way. Thomas is typical of many who opt for assimilation into the dominant culture instead of choosing the way of Sankofa. They want desperately to be accepted by "the master." This comes at a very high price. One isolates oneself from oneself and from one's own community. Some college students criticize other students who accommodate Euro-American preferences by calling them "incog-Negroes." Other well-known jibes are "Uncle Tom's", "Oreo's" or "Afro-Saxons." The charge against some is that they are not comfortable with their own culture. Students substitute dialects, workers adjust their clothes, people do not say what they are thinking. They pursue their dreams in a "white" dominated territory and in a "white sky." Parents and teachers tell us that to succeed we have to learn the nuances of the "white world" while others challenge this as "fronting" or pretending. A cultural "strip-mining" brutally wears away at our identity.

In whatever setting, Sankofa teaches that one must know one's self. American racism has put African-American self-esteem under siege. We have been attacked from all directions, but we have an obligation to ourselves to protest injustice against our dignity. We have an obligation to reject lies and half-truths about ourselves. Melden has defined dignity as "displaying an expectation that rights will be honored"[Boxill, 195] whether they are honored or not. We are not "displaying" something that we do not already possess as a gift from God.

The "X" that Malcolm substituted for the "Little" that the slave-masters had given him needs to return to center stage. The idea of Sankofa is that our names have been forgotten and something else has been imposed on us. Malcolm's "X" is contrasted with the St. Andrew's "X" of the Confederate flag. The potential for peaceful non-violence is in all of us. Sankofa means that we must resist falling into the trap of internalizing Euro-American expectations of our experience so that their standards become our standards. Sankofa is a way of balance.

Chapter Five—Sankofa. Questions for consideration and discussion.

1. Why is it that individuals have not stressed the importance of Sankofa? When and how did you first come to see that Afrocentricity could be a tool for your own empowerment?

2. What are the nature and the motivation of the criticisms of anti-Afrocentric perspectives? Why would African-Americans accept these criticisms?

3. How can we spread Afrocentric ideas in our communities? What is the role of the church and the school? How could these two spheres of influence intersect in some ways? How do Eurocentric characteristics of churches and schools need to be adapted? Can you cite some examples?

4. What is most empowering about an Afrocentric perspective to you? Describe your own process of Sankofa.

Chapter Six
The "Rip van Winkle Syndrome"
What Americans of European Ancestry Need

*White privilege is like an invisible weightless knapsack of special
provisions, assurances, tools, maps, guides, code-books, passports,
visas, clothes, compass, emergency gear and blank checks.*
—PEGGY MACINTOSH

*They lived on the surface of their days; their smiles were surface
smiles, and their tears were surface tears. How far apart in culture
we stood! All my life I had done nothing but feel and cultivate my
feelings; all their lives they had done nothing but strive for petty
goals, the trivial material prizes of American life. We share a common language, but my language was a different language from
theirs. It was in the psychological distance that separated the races
that the deepest meaning of the problem of the Negro lay for me.
For these poor, ignorant white girls to understand my life would
have meant nothing short of a vast revolution in theirs. And I was
convinced that what they needed to make them complete was the
inclusion in their personalities of a knowledge of lives such as I have
lived and suffered constrainedly....As I think back upon the memory of those girls I feel that for white America to understand the
significance of the problem of the Negro will take a bigger and
tougher America than any we have yet known. I feel that Ameri-*

ca's past is too shallow, her national character too superficially optimistic, her very morality too suffused with color hate to accomplish so vast and complex a task.
—RICHARD WRIGHT, **American Hunger** (1977), 12-13.

A Personal Journey Towards Satori

Buddhism is a great spirituality tradition that begins with a story about protective parents and an ominous prophecy. The legend goes that before the Buddha was born, his father received a prophecy from a holy man that his son would either be a wealthy ruler or a poor teacher. The aristocratic father was determined to protect his son from the fate of being a teacher outside of the opportunities for status and wealth, so he strove to shield his son from all things alien. The protective patriarch filled the boy's life with comfort and privilege. Reality broke through the cracks, however, and soon the young Siddhartha Gautama renounced his life of ease and determined to seek enlightenment.

What does this narrative have to do with what Euro-Americans need in confronting racism in the United States? Many of us are born into homogenous, safe bubbles called suburbia and, like the Buddha, grow up in islands of ignorance upheld by privilege. Like the Buddha, this neat little world of illusion is pierced at times by the intrusion of aliens, often African-Americans, into the mix. I (van Gorder) first remember hearing about "black people" from my grandfather when he complained how some of "them" had moved into "his" neighborhood in Florida and driven down property values just by living there. This mystified me. Who were these powerful people who could change things so radically just by being in the situation? What was the source of their power?

On the plus side, my father decided that our family vacation of 1967 should include stops in Montgomery, Birmingham, and Selma, Alabama to "see what was going on." This kind of "drive-by education" is typical for children of liberal Euro-Americans, and does more harm than good in children's minds in that it underscores the idea that African-Americans are "other than" themselves and in dire need of benevolent, paternal care.

The Christianity I was taught told me that Jesus loved all people: "red or yellow, black or white" and that He shed his blood and died for everyone. Curiously, however, I saw no "red or yellow or black" recipients of His love at the local Methodist church. Christianity, I learned by observation, is more about perception, image, appearance and rhetoric than about the hard realities of every day life. The gap between reality and the ideal began to grow in the tutelage of this typically segregated church.

White liberalism visited my horizon again when I went to work for Mr. Elton Hickman, a landscape architect who was determined to hire African-Americans as both a way to empower them and as a way to educate his Euro-American student workforce. I do not doubt the sincerity of this man who spent his life as a Latin teacher in the Pittsburgh inner-city school district. When the boss was gone, however, cultural cliques kicked into gear in his grand experiment and "we" complained about how "they" did not work as diligently as "we" did. No doubt, the memorable experience of being beaten up a few times by Sam Richardson also helped to support stereotypes that were painfully beginning to take shape. At age sixteen, I was given a driver's license and warned that I should avoid driving through inner-city at night. I was taught to use "common sense" and lock up when driving through the Homewood-Brushton area of Pittsburgh. Better yet, it was suggested that when I drove long distances, I used the conveniently segregating highways around America's dangerous cities.

At age eighteen, I was off to a Christian college, where it seemed to me that most African-Americans were either basketball players or musicians. All of us were "united" as Christian brothers and sisters but it was a very theoretical and amorphous unity. I never remember, for example, ever considering dating an African-American "sister" or spending time socially with an African-American "brother." The segregating line between rhetoric and reality grew stronger day by day.

After college and graduate school, I had little contact with African-Americans for another decade in my life while I lived in Asia as a teacher. I do remember being asked by Chinese friends to explain the nature of racism in the United States. Each time I would describe, with disdain, how uneducated "white people" lived lives of racism. I certainly was not a racist. The very idea was ridiculous. Why, I even cried when I heard tapes of Martin Luther King, Jr. talk about his dream. I was a very enlightened, charitable Christian.

However, the nagging questions of my Chinese students planted a seed in my heart. I knew that, although I spoke with authority to my Chinese students, I really didn't have any idea of what I was talking about. Sometimes I felt, when I talked to them about African-Americans, I was talking about people from another world.

Perhaps this made me more alert than I would ordinarily have been. Upon my return to the United States, however, I was confronted with the segregation of the American church and culture. I realized what I didn't know about African-Americans, which was almost everything. As a Christian, I began to see the fruits of racism all around me and see the vestiges of racism in my own life. I began to see, with the help of new friends, how my parents had made many decisions to protect me in a segregated society. I began to look at these facts from God's perspective. I saw injustice and racism everywhere I turned. It was as if a light had gone on in my mind. It was amazing; the best way to describe it would be to call it a conversion of sorts. Now, I am seeking to become a "recovering racist." I am working to change myself and educate my family.

When I talk with my friends who have not had the same discoveries, however, they are often offended at even the hint that they are in some way indictable. I have come to see this defensiveness as a major part of the problem. The problem perpetrates itself because people do not want to offend each other. Difficult questions are seen as hostile and insensitive. Coming to grips with our own levels of misinformation and isolation and acknowledging our corporate and individual sin is very difficult for Euro-Americans. Racism is almost always someone else's problem. I get the clear impression that most people would like to address racism in themselves for only a brief while before turning to other, more comforting concerns. It would be best if, ultimately, the whole issue would somehow magically go away.

Euro-Americans are stricken with the "Rip van Winkle Syndrome." In March of 1968, Dr. Martin Luther King, Jr. preached a sermon about Washington Irving's rendering of a Dutch fairy tale character named Rip van Winkle. In the story, Rip van Winkle falls asleep and does not wake up until twenty years later. While he was asleep, the American revolutionary war took place so that the painting on the wall of the tavern where he frequented changed from a portrait of King George of England to President George Washington. This different "George" was the subtle way that the Dutchman discovered he had been sleeping (One could say that while many Christians were asleep God also placed a portrait of a different

"Martin Luther" over their heads.) Dr. King challenged his audience not to sleep through the revolution going on in the United States in his day.

It is an apt warning for Americans today. De-facto segregation seems to be increasing instead of evaporating inevitably as some predicted that it would. This fact raises new challenges for all Americans. While problems grow, however, the Rip van Winkle's in our midst are just now hearing for the first time Dr. King's 1968 call for equality, while still others just seem to be awakening to Frederick Douglass' 1858 call for justice. Some people seem still to be asleep, as they question the need for Affirmative action. Meanwhile, the number of white supremacists, those locked in another century (with another President George) grows.

Stereotypes

My father taught us that the men who burned down our farm were not three white men. They were three individuals with hatred and jealousy in their hearts. He implored us no to label or stereotype anyone based on the color of their skin. My father warned us not to become embittered by other people's hatred because it would poison our lives as it had the lives of those three men.
—ARMSTRONG WILLIAMS, 1997

Awaking from the Rip van Winkle syndrome means coming to grips with the fact that many Euro-American understandings of African-Americans are rife with a host of stereotypes. This is common. African-Americans have many stereotypes about Euro-Americans as well. They are lazy. A few songs from the depression capture this "fact:"

White man in a starched shirt settin' in the shade. Laziest man that God ever made.

The bee flies high and the little bee makes honey. The black folks make the cotton and the white folks get the money. [Bays,167]

People often rely on generalizations to make sense of those around them who are different from themselves. What are some of these stereotypes? One common idea is that African-American men are threatening. This causes people to clutch their purse tightly to their chest when the see Denzell Washington or Blair Underwood walking towards them. Remember the face of New Yorker Colin Ferguson in 1997? He was the deranged lunatic with the glazed protruding eyes and flaring nostrils who sat on the commuter train until it got into the green suburbs. Only then did he open fire and kill six Euro-suburbanites at random.

What about the face of O.J. Simpson staring out from the cover of *Time* magazine? Another periodical printed mug-shots of Simpson with his face artificially darkened to accentuate the threat he posed. The spectacle surrounding his trial was aptly called, "The Greatest Story Ever Sold." Simpson, a former athlete, was described by his detractors as an archetype of almost inevitable savagery. How could he have supposedly killed Nicole Brown Simpson? Was it in him all along just waiting to explode from deep within his primitive self? Interestingly enough, the Simpson case saw the credibility of an African-American male "pitted against the integrity of a white police investigator" from the Los Angeles Police Department. [Griffin, 117] Mike Tyson is another man who knows no boundaries. Are these people individuals who are seen as themselves or are they somehow representatives who confirm stereotypes?

Another common stereotype of the African-American man is the mysterious enigma. The tall, godlike Michael Jordan, the sexually enigmatic Michael Jackson, the half-man, half-woman Dionysian Dennis Rodman or Little Richard or Prince are all characters who convey to Euro-Americans the fact that they are beyond understanding. They are mysterious, ambiguous entertainers available for our bemusement and discussion. Their entire lives are performances. Why, in the wealthiest nation in the world, would such people fixate the attention of so many? Do both the good and the evil have something in common? These men are either angels or demons but they are not like "us"; they are minstrels.

The Minstrel Show as the way to Promote Modern Segregation (Or, There were no African-Americans on Gilligan's Island)

Clowns are best with other clowns.
Gentlemen are welcome everywhere.
— English Proverb

120

In the midst of America's 270 million people there are more than 37 million Americans of African descent. While most of them have nothing in common with the caricatures described. Yet, they are held in strange regard for the over 210 million Americans of European descent. An odd relationship has developed between the two groups that is clearly rooted in the three centuries of the savagery, rape, repression, economic exploitation, lynching, and all of the perversities of slavery, and "Jim Crow." It could also be said that Euro-Americans understand their own culture in relation to African-Americans? Ralph Ellison described the African in America as a sort of giant Gulliver whose body is pinned down for the bemusement of the tiny Lilliputians.

It is a process of contemporary minstrelizing. Loewen writes that from the 1850s through the 1930s "minstrel shows, which derived in a perverse way from plantation slavery, were the dominant form of popular entertainment in America [Loewen, 139]. *Uncle Tom's Cabin* was the longest running play of the period; the first epic motion picture was *Birth of a Nation;* the first block-buster novel was *Gone With the Wind,* and the first talkie was *the Jazz Singer.* Loewen goes on to note that the most popular radio program of all time was *Amos n' Andy* while the most popular television miniseries was *Roots* [Loewen, 139].

The minstrel shows emerged after slavery ended in the American South, creating a new way to "put them in their place." It goes without saying that very few African-American men are criminals, athletic stars or musicians. Racism, however, cannot leave people as people; they must become "other people."

The idea of American democracy, that all people are equal and have levels of commonness that provide a foundation for a civil society, was forged by people who held the idea of the "other;" which excluded African-Americans from their utopian visions. They excluded them by ignoring them on one hand and by making them "three-fifths citizens" on the other. In a country where everyone is the same, the only way to become a hero is to be dead or to be, in some ways, a non-American. It was Will Rogers who said that if an American wants to become a hero (e.g., Lincoln, and Kennedy), they have to "learn the right time to die."

These observations shed light on how African-American men like Jordan and Jackson can be hailed as heroes even while they are segregated and thus marginalized. In the relational world of most Euro-Americans there is a sense that African-American men are already "dead" or, more accurately, nonexistent outside of the scope of their stereotypes. They live somewhere beyond the ordinary world of the known and acceptable.

Think again about the rise of the minstrel shows in the United States immediately after the Civil War. Is there any insight to be gained by this timing? Black face and song and dance were all about the creation of caricatures. Slavery's abolition meant that the legal "use" of African people was no longer possible but now Africans could be used in another way. They could entertain Euro-America while Euro-Americans played the black-faced caricatures that focused on debasing Africans in America.

Minstrel Millionaires: "We Treat Our Negroes Just Fine"

Bribery can split a stone.
—Irish Proverb

There is something safe about viewing people through the distant worlds of sports and entertainment; it is non threatening. When people (especially men) of different cultures get together in America and have nothing in common, they will often begin to talk about sports.

But the world of sports in the United States is firmly rooted in the plantation system. In 1995, 80 percent of the players in the National Basketball Association, 67 percent of the players in the National Football League, and 37 percent of Major League Baseball were African Americans. Athletics is both a promise and a prison. The Faustian bargain of American athletics is that a huge amount of money can be earned quickly and with relative ease, but a host of dynamics often conspire to destroy athletes in the process. Athletics promises "a level playing field," but some coaches still talk about some positions such as running back, defensive end, and wide receiver as "black positions" in contrast to the "white positions" of center, guard, and quarterback. [Shipler, 271]. Commentators sometimes laud African-American athletes for an "athletic move" and European-American athletes for a "smart" or "gritty" play. The way that sports boxes people in to stereotypes is well illustrated by a story a college student related. When he arrived on campus for the first time, someone asked him "what position do you play" instead of asking his name or academic major. He was not an athlete.

Real integration of power has not occurred outside of the safe zones of entertainment and athletics. In 1999 only 4 percent of America's doctors, 3.4 percent of its engineers, 3.3 percent of its lawyers, 1.4 percent of its architects and 6.5 percent of its construction tradesmen were African-Americans. Only 0.6 percent of all senior managers were African-Americans, and these kinds of inequalities can be cited ad infinitum [Ansell, 213-215].

In the world of sports, wealthy corporate businessmen sit in their plush seats and watch a predominantly large number of African-American gladiators of boxing, football, basketball and baseball attack each other to symbolic deaths. These athletes are not people. They are commodities to be bought and sold or traded. Their careers are interchangeable and disposable. They are heroes but not role models. In fact, what do their public failings accomplish but write large on the billboard of culture the image of the unmanageable, irresponsible savage?

Today's minstrels of sport and entertainment are about as far as many people see "race relations" have progressed. Denzell Washington and Oprah Winfrey and others have made their money, and they are accepted but their acceptance is always the acceptance of the other. Separateness, distance, and isolation define the nature of the interaction.

Beyond a few celebrities, most African Americans do not exist in the consciousness of European-Americans. Only two extremes in the society seemed concerned about African-Americans; the extreme right and the extreme left. Both these groups relate to African-Americans out of a posture of either critique or advice, but both are paternalistic and, as such, perpetrators of racist assumptions. Visitors do parachute into the leper colony America's urban communities from time to time but mostly they are suburbanized Christians armed with a "do-gooding suburban Christianity" that comes to change the bandages on the lepers and provide a few warm meals along the way. They usually "get out" (or retreat to their neo-religious houses of refuge) by nightfall.

In another fascinating reflection of the modern minstrel show it is interesting to see Euro-American teenagers getting their entertainment from gangsta-rap hip-hopping musicians who lace their music with violent and sexual themes. What do these lyrics do but reinforce stereotypes while saying nothing about the reality of most African-American lives? It is a spectacle. Young males who are not criminals posing as such to Euro-Americans in order to make some money; hip-hop black face. The Euro-American teens, meanwhile flirt with images of the happy 'hood and take cocaine in luxury powdered form, while progressive the stereotypes become more entrenched. Stereotypes endure while most corporate images (with the exception of Aunt Jemima's syrup and Uncle Ben's Rice) adhere to new social courtesies. Advertisers do continue to present the country with images of sensual and non-intellectual minstrels. It is the modern variation on the old minstrel show.

"Would You Like to Be White, Brother?" The Euro-American Imperative

He has understood the system
so well because he felt it first as his own contradiction.
—JEAN PAUL SARTRE in Albert Memmi's,
The Colonizer and the Colonized

The one who is guilty is usually the one who talks the most.
—Ashanti Proverb

Sterling Tucker asked the following question of African-Americans: "Would you like to be white, brother?" [Tucker, 110] Can you imagine recognizing that it was your culture that sponsored centuries of brutal slavery and continues to avoid confronting its responsibilities before God and man? Euro-Americans might well be tempted to move out of the country, but the whole world knows the story. It would seem that everyone in the world (except many European-Americans themselves), knows all about European-American relationships with Native Americans and with African-Americans through history.

The Ku Klux Klan is allowed to continue to march in the United States along with neo-Nazis. What definition of civility allows some the freedom to speak up in such provably hateful and destructive ways? No one is advocating an end to freedom of speech. What about rethinking the dynamics of that freedom, however, in light of the need for civility and mutual respect. How far is too far? To be Euro-American is to wish the whole thing away. America is trying to live a lie.

Our focus has been on education. We are not clamoring for quick solutions or happy gloss-overs as long as serious surgery on the body politic is required.

One of our convictions is that it is the burden of Euro-Americans, and not African-Americans, to address the issue of racism. Why? The problem may be experienced primarily by African-Americans and certainly affects all Americans but it is primarily the creation of the Euro-American community. Because Euro-Americans have diminished diasporic Africans to a three-fifths status it must also be Euro-Americans who must do the hard work of making reparations for what has been stolen. Identity and power are at the heart of these issues. College administrators and church leaders love to compete with each other and share all that "they are doing to level the playing field" of social injustice. The reality is that these same administrators and pastors have been, for most if not all of their professional lives, silent about these problems and have done little or nothing to solve the problems of de-facto segregation and racism.

African-Americans, in contrast, must work to restore a strong sense of self-identity and to put an end to the dynamics at work at the heart of America's prostituting minstrel shows. In American colleges, African-American students must not serve as the "minstrels" to "educate" Euro-American students about "what it means to be black in the United States" or any other topic of amusement. Those students must focus on being all that they can be and on getting full value from their education so that they can succeed in their lives.

Why is it not obvious to Euro-Americans that the judge of whether or not progress is taking place in these areas should come from the African-American community? This does not happen, because it really is about control. The kind of accountability we are calling for demands a transfer of control. Today's quality control experts are the same people who have a 400-year track record of abuse and neglect. Euro-Americans must submit to the judgment of African-American colleagues and not to themselves to be the judge of whatever progress is substantive, and what progress is merely symbolic, and thus, inadequate.

Change in church and college must begin with the recognition that the present power structures are uniformly Eurocentric. They carry with them assumptions and an air of condescension in their methodologies. If one culture seeks to promote lively discussion by introducing controversial ideas but another culture sees that strategy as being uncivil, who will have to concede? Obviously, those with the power have been the ones who have written the rules of the games and the codes of conduct. On this topic, Thomas Kochman's book *Black and White Styles in Conflict* serves to illustrate how Eurocentric most business and academic forums are in conforming to and supporting Euro-American comfort zones and expectations.

Beyond the obvious and visible we must confront the subtle and the insidious. Most American student curriculums and church formats are so Eurocentric that there is little room for African-American students or church-goers to feel appropriately proud of their philosophic, religious, and literary heritage as Euro-Americans are encouraged to feel. Eurocentric anthropological assumptions, for example, elevate the literate and downgrade the oracular. Structured European classical music is seen as greater than the creativity of jazz improvisational music. The lecture or the sermon is better than fable or personal narrative. Rational calm is better than emotion and passion. The individual is better than the community. The list is endless.

When it comes to teaching American history and the terror of slavery, the subject remains bracketed into a specific time and framed in a specific, limiting context. Even slavery is presented in such a harmless way that saccharin assumptions can emerge to blunt hard realities. What do we mean? Lincoln becomes the great Odysseus and the "Southern rebels" become the villains. When the educator turns to the larger world there must be clear explication of how, even Euro-American students, are of African descent. Youth must be taught that Mother Africa's great Nile River civilization and Egypt's great thinkers were not somehow pseudo-Europeans. While visiting Addis Ababa, Ethiopia, a European whom we encountered explained to us that the great treasures of Ethiopian history were actually created by "Semitic" peoples and not "Africans." President George W. Bush, you will notice, refers to Egypt as being part of the "Middle East" and not as part of Africa.

A vast paradigm shift needs to take place. Euro-Americans must undergo some kind of spiritual conversion from impotent spiritualized pabulum about reconciliation and begin to participate in waves of change that can be measured with concrete, economically verifiable, and relationally accountable choices. It is all about the choices that are made and are not made. Uncomfortable choices will become requisite for meaningful change to take place. Because of the inevitability of inertia, Euro-American educators and religious leaders must begin to take risky initiatives into uncharted territory. Senator Bill Bradley said, responding to the question of why he had decided to make racism a major theme of his failed 2000 bid for the Presidency, "As long as white Americans resist relinquishing the sense of entitlement that skin color has given them...." then there will be no major progress in the area of confronting racism.

Personal and institutional micro-cultures need to be aerated so they are welcoming bridges to integration instead of stifling boxes for segregation. In the church, Euro-Americans need to come to grips with the facts that they are actually preaching a three-fifths theology made in their own image instead of what St. Paul called the "whole counsel of God" who requires justice, not sentimentality.

Original thinking needs to be developed. Old assumptions need to be challenged. Power roles need to be reversed so that minstrelsy in all of its diverse forms can be unmasked. In actual fact, Euro-Americans themselves are minorities in the world that they live in and, it will not be all that long (perhaps by about 2030) until Euro-Americans will become the minority ethnic population in the United States. This is already true in many cities and even states. The long held notion of being a majority feeds a sense of entitlement that often support racist assumptions. Euro Americans need to stop talking to African-Americans about racism and begin to talk to other Euro-Americans about their own myopia. In interethnic issues this will mean, among other things, not being quick to offer Euro-centric solutions to problems in other cultural communities. Listening and learning will go far towards addressing the chronic deafness that has so often defined the history of the African and European encounter in the United States.

From a Christian perspective, it is one's security of the power of God in Christ that enables the scholar and the pastor to press through pessimism and complex problems with a sense of faith and expectation. Perhaps Rip van Winkle cannot do much about the years that had already been lost to sleep but it certainly is not too late for us to awaken from a stupor and contribute to the next steps toward genuine justice. What do Euro-American Christians need to do in relationship to African-Americans?: Educate, inform, confront, motivate, train, and equip.

Even when racism goes unmentioned, Euro-Americans often interact with African-Americans in tense, unnatural ways, perhaps to avoid making a mistake or causing offense. Some Euro-Americans are provoked, while others are awkward or fall into an eager friendliness in unnatural dialogue. This tension underscores relational isolation and alienation. These interactions are impersonal and fleeting, that is, the way a customer relates to a sales-person. Lacking personal interrelationships many well-meaning Euro-Americans revert to symbolism and statement. It is the appeal of symbolism that led Paul Ricoeur to note that our symbols are more important to us than our philosophies. We rely on the emotive instead of the substantive. This leads to scenes where Euro-Americans ask to hold hands with African-Americans and sing songs like *Black and White Together, Black and White Together. We Shall Overcome Some Day.* Tokenism and symbolism are not enough. Not only are they not helpful; they are cruelly misleading and retrogressive.

The long history of such gestures combined with subsequent betrayal litter the horizon. Four hundred years have given no reason for African-Americans to trust Euro-Americans in their words or promises. Stories of well-intentioned Europeans "abandoning ship" when the pressure came are too numerous to document. The Methodists may have preached against slavery in the 1780s, but there was a quick retreat to the safe confines of justice in the world to come when the church wanted to grow. Prudence has often trumped conviction. Repentance followed by action is the appropriate way to proceed. When the athlete in the 1996 film *Jerry Maguire* states "Show me the money!" he could have been speaking for any number of interethnic relationships as well as his own professional situation.

Action cannot be delayed. The Bible reminds us that "hope deferred makes the heart sick." Euro-Americans are often as slow to act as they are quick to acknowledge the problems of injustice. In 1963, eight clergy cautioned Dr. King to slow down and take a broader view of things. They agreed with him in principle but felt that his tactics were too extreme and untimely. King's response to their request needs to be revisited today in light of the relation that caution and inertia tend to have on each other. It is much easier and safer to stay on the sidelines. Euro-American Christians need to know that following Christ means that there is no sideline to stand on, and that obedience in faith will mean working proactively for justice.

It may be the luxury of those who (think that they) are in the majority to be oblivious. They may chose a life of harmony and sameness, pillowed in comforts that lull the conscience to sleep and drown ideals in self-satisfaction. This is the sleep of one in a carbon monoxide cloud. The poison of obliviousness dulls and makes Euro-Americans deaf. Noone considers himself or herself a racist. Everyone wants to think of the problem in individual terms and, by inference, someone else's problem. Impersonalize it, and detoxify it. Even if they do not wear a hood and burn crosses in Alabama, they are still racists. They are not guilty because they did not own slaves. In fact, their ancestors fought in the Civil War or came over on the boat long after slavery. Those who are recent immigrants may have forgotten that it was in Europe that the slave trade originated and was long propagated. They are too quick to give their ancestry the benefit of the doubt.

Today, the most blatant forms of racist anti African-American behavior are not common in the United States. Segregation is now more subtle, but it is just as potent. Power is still maintained but not with whips and bullhorns. It is cloaked in the camouflage of legitimacy.

It is one thing to acknowledge these facts, but another to act on them. Inaction is a form of action. Subtle racism is much less dramatic and much more pervasive than blatant racism. The power to be racist is directly related to the power to control. It is easy to understand why people sneak around the problems and wish they would go away. It is easy to understand why people would rather to complain or to argue than begin to learn and to talk about these issues. It is easy to understand why most are silent and prefer sleep in safe harbors than to engage in a battle that often feels like it is being waged on a minefield. Confrontation is hard. The alternative to confrontation, however, is for America's "Rip van Winkles" to sleep for another thirty or forty years.

Chapter Six—Rip van Winkle. Questions for consideration and discussion:

1. Have your good intentions ever been sidetracked by your desire to maintain your comfort zones? Explain. Describe the situation.

2. If you are a Euro-American, are you very aware of your own ethnicity? Explain. How is your ethnicity expressed and talked about?

3. How and when did you become aware of your own ethnicity and the ethnicity of other people?

4. What kind of stereotypes did you confront growing up in your family? How have you shed these stereotypes from your life?

5. How is racial knowledge 'taught' or is it 'caught?' Respond to this quote: "Most white adults, including many scholars, believe that very young children are incapable of seriously understanding the implications of race and racism. In contrast, most Black adults and other adults of color are of necessity much more aware that their children do employ racial concepts" [van Ausdale and Feagen, 2].

Chapter Seven
Burning Down the Big House: Desegregating Reality with Respect

Taking The First Steps

*I know someone had to take the first step and I
made up my mind not to move*
—ROSA PARKS

*You must **be** the solution to the problem that you face.*
—MAHATMA GANDHI

An emphasis on respect is essential in order to advance the cause of justice and an end to racism in America. Respect is the recognition of one's God-given value. It is accepting people for who they are. Any assumption of inequality; any perception of three-fifths incompleteness will inevitably result in fractured relationships.

Respecting someone does not mean that one grovels or "Toms" at another persons feet in servile sycophancy. African-Americans are in no way beholden to Euro-Americans for their self-worth. Inversely, there is no need for further "feel-good" campaigns designed to make Euro-Americans realize how worthy African-Americans are of high regard. The focus of these contrivances results in a perilous trap where some people are recognized and others are ignored because they are not co-operative. One of the "final" lessons of the Civil Rights movement is that a sense of wholeness in a culture is not contingent upon the imprimatur of another culture. When the civil rights "party" was over, most of the "friends" of the movement retreated homeward without warning. Efforts had been focused on enlisting Euro-Americans support. Interest waned, and most Euro-American opted out of the issues and the lives of their compatriots; fleeing back into secure suburban fortresses.

African-Americans may well be the holders of the American dream and the keepers of freedom's flame in this country. Future hope may well come from people rooted in the multi-dimensional realities of the United States and not in "patriotic" mono-cultural fantasies about what the country can become. W.D. Wright's position is that,

> Blacks usually know better than whites what America is and what it stands for. They know better than most Americans when America is at its best. Blacks have to contribute significantly to the direction that the country takes in the future. There has to be an effective black participation to keep white racist America, the antithesis and negation of America at its best, from monopolizing contributions to direction and content. [Wright, 178]

Leadership in both communities must concentrate on the implementation of change. During wartime, what would you expect from a general who said that there were no enemies when, in fact, the troops were under attack? Today, America spawns countless politicians who passively act as if our primary concern should be the threat of foreign terror. There are no major domestic problems. This may well be the case in their gated communities or on their golf courses, but it is not true across the country. If Euro-Americans benefit in a system designed by Euro-Americans for Euro-Americans and that system is corrupt and "un-American," who is to blame? Many are content to bestow charity but not to share power. Sadly, some African-Americans have themselves come into the "big house" of self-centered moral compromise. They have lost their cultural identity. This is not a new story. Some African-American youth have learned to "play the game" of assimilation and make it work for them. That is why so few are working for concrete social, political, and economic change. Young people must refuse to be co-opted by a "master's plan" that calls for monocultural social conformity.

Reconcile to What? When? Where?

By going and coming a bird needs to rest.
—Ashanti Proverb

Some Christians are quick to talk about reconciliation. James Cone warns that much of this "seldom gets to the core of the issue." [Cone, 1975, 215] Christians are willing to hold religious crusades at football stadiums, to go on "unity" marches, to visit each other's churches or, hold hands and sing together. These gestures are hollow if not linked to the real problems in the United States. It is popular to discuss reconciliation. What does the term "reconciliation" mean? It implies that there was, at some point in time, some "conciliation," which the *American Heritage Dictionary* defines as the process of placating someone. It has often meant placating Euro-American guilt and keeping African-Americans working in the steaming "cotton fields" of assimilation.

The prefix "re-" means to go back to something that already exists. To what point in time in the relationship between European and African-Americans are these "re-concilers" asking us to revisit? The only possible answer is to return to, at least, the early fifteenth-century at least before racist slavery emerges as one of the dominant characteristics of African-European relations. People should not be pre-occupied with reconciliation until they work for transformative justice first. African-Americans do not call for retaliation nor is there interest in "cheap reconciliation." Inspired by a shallow understanding of scriptural mandates, shallow pantomimes will never foster mutual respect. In Matthew 25:31, some are described as surprised that they are "goats" when they expected to be categorized as God's "sheep." Three-fifths theology led them to some traumatic "species-confusion!" The Bible explains that the final judgement of God will be a time of reckoning when people will be divided, to the right and to the left, not for any other measure but their service to God on behalf of the oppressed poor, imprisoned, and infirm.

Corporate Respect and Mutual Recognition Remain Elusive

To love is to make one's heart a swinging door.
—HOWARD THURMAN

Before meaningful affinity can evolve among different cultures it is necessary to have mutual respect. The myth of the melting pot has always meant that non-Europeans were expected to become "Europeanized." Sanitized scripts calling for reconciliation are often simply abstract morality plays. Talk of politically-correct multiculturalism and reconciliation often sidesteps the difficult task of addressing structural issues of power.

Americans of the African diaspora should claim the rich blessings of an African birthright and draw from the deep wells of African cultural identity. One should be proud of one's cultural heritage and not be, as Toni Morrison suggests someone who is "un-raced." To deny one's African or European roots is to deny one's personhood. A person is born into an African or a European cultural context before making the decision to become a Christian. Our ancestry informs everything we do. To continue to deny our ancestral heritages will lead to further social alienation and fragmentation.

Self-defining respect is nurtured by education and community "re-tooling." It is both personal and corporate and has specific, concrete applications. One specific, personal example is the slight that many Euro-Americans visit on African-Americans when they refer to people informally without the relational permission for that informality. During centuries of slavery, the master only called the slaves by their first name and gave them their own last name as a way to stress their role as property. In contrast, many contemporary Euro-Americans see the use of the first name as a "bridge to intimacy" and not of dismissive disrespect. It is incumbent on the one who offends, however, to recognize cultural faux-pas and not to demand that those of are offended comply with their standards of social etiquette.

Confronting Simplistic Segregating Fantasies

Being a Negro in America is not a comfortable existence. It means being part of the company of the bruised and the battered and the scarred and the defeated. Being a Negro in America means trying

to smile when you want to cry. It means trying to hold on to physical life amid psychological death. It means the pain of watching your children grow up with clouds of inferiority in their mental skies. It means having your legs cut off and then being condemned for being a cripple. It means seeing your father and mother spiritually murdered by the slings and arrows of daily exploitation and then being hated for being an orphan. Being a Negro in America means being harried by day and haunted by night by a nagging sense of nobody-ness and constantly fighting to be saved from the poison of bitterness. It means the ache and anguish of living in so many situations where hopes unborn have died.
—MARTIN LUTHER KING, JR.

Dear reader, is the above quote from Dr. King shocking to you? The way you respond to it says much about the world you live in. Many Euro-Americans are living in a country where they have little or no interaction with African-Americans on a daily basis. What is often between the two ethnic groups is a vast sea of ignorance. What is needed are voyagers who will launch out into that sea and encourage mutual appreciation. While misunderstanding can never be an excuse for inertia, action will be ineffectual if not rooted in awareness.

What do Euro-Americans need to recognize in today's segregated society? First of all, they need to understand their ethnicity and recognize that culture, not race, is what is at play in contemporary America. These cultures are not static but complex, changing, and are as variegated as are Euro-American cultures.

Second, It must be acknowledged that the American story has never been a Euro-American story alone; one that begins with Columbus or the Mayflower. Euro-Americans are late-comers on an ancient land that Native Americans called Turtle Island which has hosted immigrants from all over the world. The history of the United States is one story of many cultures. Who is to determine which of these is the most significant? European influence on the American continent is quite recent and has often imposed itself violently at the expense of other cultures.

Third, Euro-American fantasies of inevitable social progress and the myth of the "happy hood" need to be put to rest. Clark writes that the "pathologies of the ghetto perpetrate themselves through cumulative ugliness, deterioration and isolation and strengthen a black sense of worthlessness." [Clark, 131] Malcolm X reminded African-Americans that, "We live in the poorest houses and pay the highest rents, eat the poorest food and wear the poorest clothing at the highest prices." [in Epps, 65] The reality is that many social ills grow worse in African-American communities. Serious economic, social, physiological, and psychological problems are snowballing at the very same time that much of the country is enjoying increased economic wealth.

There is an emerging middle class among African-Americans. It is far smaller however, than most people perceive it to be; and an astounding one-fourth of its constituents are employees of the government. Lynn Burbridge's article in the *1999 State of Black America* (published by the National Urban League) stated that "between 1970 and 1990, the reliance of African-Americans on government employment continued to increase, despite overall reductions in the government sector and the number of African-Americans in for-profit sectors continued to decline" [187]. Much of this growth is a result of African-American men joining the armed services. The most important fact is that there is an undue reliance on one sector of the economy with little participation or leadership of the private sector. According to Stephen Steinberg many African-Americans in management,

> serve in personnel functions often administering affirmative action programs. Others function as intermediaries between white corporations and the black community....Cut off from the corporate mainstream, these black executives often find themselves in dead-end jobs with little job security. [Steinberg, 196]

This is de-facto segregation in the workplace. Many tenth-to fifteenth (ca. 1650-1800) generation African-Americans are consigned to "lives of poverty in a sea of prosperity." (King) Historically, the major incentive for the propagation of "the peculiar institution" of slavery was wealth-building. These trends continue. African-Americans are beginning to confront these economic disparities. Many who benefit from the massive amounts of money that African-Americans spend are not interested in the economic well-being and independence of the very communities where they are making their money.

Another social issue is an emerging family crisis among African-Americans. "Afro-Americans are the most un-partnered and isolated group of people in America and quite possibly the world" with 60 percent of all African-American children living in a home without a father [Patterson, 4]. These problems are deeply rooted in the legacies of slavery, where African-American male slaves were forced to breed and not father, where the role of a viable father did not often exist.

The new American racism subtly advances a divide-and-conquer mentality between the women and men of the African-American community. "Only 34 percent of African-American men and 26 percent of African-American women disagreed with the statement that there is distrust and often hatred between black men and women." [Patterson, 5] For a host of reasons it would seem that African-American women are seen as less threatening to Euro-Americans, and thus their status is improving in the larger social setting. African-American women are gaining economic and academic status far in excess of their male counterparts. Patterson reports that "Afro-Americans are the only ethnic group in the country where women outperform men in hard sciences including computer sciences, math, and physics." [Patterson,17] There are increasingly many more African-American women doctorates than men.

Another enemy of the African American community is the "kidnaping" of children into the prison system. Adult sentencing for minors is increasing. Other youth who enter the prison system come out only to be "rescued" by enlisting in the military establishment. A high crime rate is exacerbated by the fact that certain drugs (i.e. "crack" cocaine)are not only used more by African-American youth than other varieties (the so-called "designer" cocaine which is both more refined and more expensive) but these drugs also face stiffer drug sentencing than do the others. The extensive criminalization of African-American young men confirm stereotypes about their ability to contribute to society. It may also explain the high incidences of racist attacks against them. Because they are "demonized" as being threatening and free of moral constraints, African-American men are often racially profiled and often followed through businesses simply because of the color of their skin.

In most instances, people cannot be manipulated unless they allow themselves to be manipulated. Conscious submission to pervasive misconceptions brings a kind of emotional and spiritual disease which is increasingly rampant in American schools and churches. People feel that they will be crushed if they do not submit to demands of society. The solution is to not allow people to handle you like merchandise, to distort who you are and brand your skin with symbols of their corporate logo. Heed the warning from Lerone Bennett (ca. 1960):

> From birth to death, the Negro is handled, distorted and violated by the symbols and tentacles of white power; tentacles that worm their way into his neurons and invade the gray cells of his cortex....The Negro must not only don a mask; he becomes, in many instances, the mask he dons. [Mazel, 68]"

Recognizing Contemporary American Social Apartheid

Housing residential segregation has proved to be the most resistant to change of all social realms. Perhaps this is because, in general, most racial change has been artificial
—THOMAS PETTYGROVE

Where does a Black soul go to rest?
—RANDALL ROBINSON

It does not take a social scientist to notice that African-Americans are the most residentially segregated cultural group in the United States. People should have the freedom to live wherever they want to live. It is one thing for African-Americans to choose to live in an urban environment because that is their wish. However, when zoning decisions, bank loan programs, insurance policies and real estate practices are racist; that freedom of choice is under serious threat. There has not been a time when de-jure as well as de-facto segregation were not resident in the United States. People are forced to live only where others determine that they should live.

The United States government relocated First Nations people onto reservations where they could be monitored. After the Civil War, the American government began to undertake a similar initiative to isolate African-Americans. It was to be administered by General William Tecumseh Sherman, with the aid of the Freedman's Bureau but it was disbanded because it was not in the best economic interests of those Euro-Americans who relied on cheap African-American labor.

Today, however, Sherman's plan seems to be in effect on a large scale. Many American inner city communities function as "reservations" of a sort. The spatial and social isolation of African-Americans is phenomenal when one considers that Africans have been resident in the country for over four centuries. Watch who gets off where, or who rides which commuter lines in America's urban public transportation networks. Our separateness is seen in our equally segregated comfort zones.

What does this isolation do to African-Americans? It makes them "invisible" to many Euro-Americans. Small children learn that only people who look like them will attend birthday parties or worship services. While some social analysts describe the United States as being at the center of an "information age," social networks, the key to getting information about jobs or friends or spouses, remain segregated. What do many Euro-American politicians suggest? Improving the ghetto with Euro-generated empowerment zones and development programs. Welfare programs are the most common solution and may be needed, but they also create troubling dynamics. Wright states:

> Welfare is a substitution for educating the masses of Black people. Without the educational, financial, or occupational opportunities needed, most people will have to stay put in the ghetto. Welfare programs have never failed in America. They have succeeded in providing jobs to middle class Whites, kept Blacks at subsistence level and out of the skilled labor market with its high paying jobs, allowed Blacks to remain a vast source of cheap labor and a readily available political scapegoat. [Wright, 123]

Urban ghettos must not only be improved. They must be eliminated. They were racist "reservations" in their origin and in their development and keep people in "their place" in their propagation. Some politicians benefit from their existence. All the while, other cultural groups move in and out of the cities and into the suburbs. This hollowing out of the city's central core has been called the "donut effect" of American urbanization patterns. Slumlords become wealthy. Management of these ghettos is in the hands of those who make their livelihood off the backs of those in the community. As true

as it is that European greed perpetrated the slave system, it was also supported by African greed. Unscrupulous African leaders made their livelihood
surrendering their citizens to the slavers. This backfired, and many of them
were betrayed and also sold into slavery. Perhaps it is the ancestors of these
vultures who are once again working with those who keep people bound in
the dank cargo ships of America's crumbling cities.

Contemporary Apartheid in Church and College

*Education? How much faith in education can be clung to
by people whose minds have been raped. For three centuries, Blacks
have been told by Whites that they were intellectually
inferior —and generations of Blacks have
believed it and acted accordingly.*
—CARL T. ROWAN

Segregation is a fact in America's churches. It was true forty years ago.
It remains true today: 11 o'clock on Sunday morning is the most segregated hour in America. Historically, these segregated churches were initiated by Euro-Americans. On 12, April 1792, Absalom Jones and Richard
Allen were compelled to organize the "Free African Society" (and then,
the African Methodist Episcopal Church) after they were literally lifted off
their knees by Euro-American Trustee while they were trying to pray at St.
Gregory's Methodist Church in Philadelphia.

American churches are more homogenous than they have ever been. In
fact, more Christians worshiped across cultural boundaries a hundred years
ago than they do today. The situation is actually devolving. Why is this?
Where do we go with these facts? African-Americans, forced to relate to
Euro-Americans in every other dimension of American culture, have found
in the church a haven away from all of the hassles of racism. For this reason,
Euro-Americans should not invite African-Americans to leave their churches and join them. Instead, Euro-Americans should ask if it is possible for
them to participate or contribute non-intrusively in the African-American
church in a way that does not dominate or disrespect. Then, after a few
decades, a few catechism classes from some African-American churches
might call upon a Euro-American church, asking whether if they could par-

ticipate in a Sunday morning service. Euro-Americans love "African-American music," but they do not like the indictment of injustice that the African-American church, even in its very existence, brings to their attention. At the Harambee Church of Harrisburg, many Euro-American churches telephone the church office and ask if they can "come down" and visit to experience "African-American Christianity."

Why is it that African-American churches are not usually interested in reciprocating these types of initiatives? Christian colleges offer courses entitled "African-American Theology" but do not offer parallel courses entitled, "European-American Theology," because that is seen as normative theology. One-way initiatives should give way to mutually developed partnerships rooted in respect. It is not an issue of shared worship experiences. These do nothing to challenge the ugly stains of racism in this country. What is required is a genuine effort on the part of Euro-American churches to work against white privilege, white supremacy and for a thorough attack against systematic racism. The call for restitution must also be clear otherwise all other efforts are only "clanging brass" (I Corinthians 13:1).

Segregation is also the de-facto reality of the American educational academy. In many integrated high schools, honors courses serve as a sort of filter where African-Americans who have conformed in certain speech patterns, attitudes, and achievements are deemed worthy enough to enter the hallowed halls of knowledge that are otherwise reserved for the elite. Integration in this form is only another way to maintain the status-quo. The threat is "integrate or be marginalized." This is a one-way, one-directional integration that invites people to be assimilated.

Legal initiatives to promote African-American integration in society have often indirectly advanced the causes of other social and cultural groups. Euro-American women have made tremendous strides in the legal and medical professions and in the Academy. [Griffin, 100] A gap has grown, however, between the advancement of civil rights for Euro-American women and civil rights for African-Americans since the early 1970s. Although both groups began at about the same place they have benefitted in dramatically different ways. African-American women earn, "58 cents on every dollar that is earned by Euro-American women who, themselves, only earn a portion of what white men earn." [Griffin, 111]

In 1993, Euro-American women comprised over 30 percent of all employees at America's colleges. These women need to ask themselves if they have been co-conspirators in emerging arrangements that have advanced their interests at the expense of African-Americans. In 1994 only 4.7 percent of all college faculty members were African-Americans. In that same year only 4 percent of all applicants for doctorates were African-Americans. In 1990, not one African-American was receiving a doctorate in applied mathematics, molecular biology, particle physics, oceanography, philosophy, ecology, geology or biophysics. [Shipler, 16]

College is an important context for this discussion, because it provides an opportunity for society to foster forward-looking solutions as well as corrective ideas about the problems of racism. Colleges can initiate programs which are consequentialist in nature such as proactive mentoring and generous funding for scholarships. In Michigan, Calvin College, brings area-urban high school students to the campus for pre-college courses. These kinds of initiatives should be encouraged. The college campus should not be a racially charged environment. Yet, this is exactly what happens in many college communities. Problem often arise when African-American students, celebrating their culture in a context where they are the minority, are often mistakenly accused of racializing the situation. At colleges and universities, African-Americans are accused of separatism:

> Many whites seem captivated by an optical illusion. As they gaze out over a vast dining hall of all-white tables, their eyes are drawn to a black group sitting together. They see the blacks separating themselves; they rarely see that the whites have separated themselves as well. When whites ask why no black comes to sit with them, some blacks reply why do not any whites come sit with blacks? Does one have to be invited to sit with someone in the lunchroom? [Shipler, 27]

A basic question must be asked: What do the decisions that promote the de-facto segregation in the United States say about what African-Americans and Euro-Americans think of each other's churches and schools. In this segregation by choice is there not an implicit rejection, on some level, of those institutions and their cultures?

Mutual Respect Christianity: Shifting Out of the Mud

*There was not, no matter where one turned, any acceptable
image of one's self, no proof of ones existence. One had the choice,
either of "acting just like a nigger" or of not acting just like a
"nigger" and only those who have tried it know
how impossible it is to tell the difference.*
—JAMES BALDWIN

How can these inequities be addressed? "Mental plaque has to be
scraped away from our thinking." [Griffin, 103] People do little meaningful thinking across the color-line. Instead, preference is evoked as the
prime alibi for the ongoing dynamics of America's de-facto segregation.
People worship where they are comfortable and evidently most are not
comfortable in inter-ethnic contexts. People lack the will to work to
change unequal structures. Instead, they have used power and privilege
for themselves. They have been "Rip van Winkles" at a time of need. The
onus is on those with resources to give them away and see what Jesus
meant when he said, "Whoever wants to gain his life will have to lose it."

Christians have been far too cavalier about this issue. There is no foundation for mutual worship without a mutually conscious effort to value
the dignity of all peoples and their cultures. What does God think about
His divided church? American Christians do not worship together, and we
are also predominantly divided culturally, politically and economically. If
this is God's plan, what does that say about God's character? If injustice
and inequality are not God's will for the church, then what does their existence say about the nature of the American church?

Has American Christianity given thought in this context to its standing
among world Christianity? Throughout the globe, people of other traditions meet Euro-American missionaries and hear from them how much
God loves them and how they need to become Christians. These same
people ask (or at least think to ask) the obvious question: If true, is it true
in your life? If Christianity is what my country needs and if it is so inclusive
in creating a sense of community, then why are their deep racial divides in
your churches? Chinese citizens, as part of their "political education"
often learn about the Ku Klux Klan and their cross-burnings. They learn
about slavery. They know about the present inequities in American

society. What kind of credible witness does the American church have in the eyes of the world without addressing these realities?

Confronting the New "Uncle Tom-maker": Passive Multiculturalism

The problem of the twentieth-century is the problem
of civilizing White people.
—NIKKI GIOVANNI

Integration is not enough. Integration has never resolved racism. Attempts at integration have even caused rifts in the African-American community. Perhaps this fostered a "white is right" mentality which has led to people seeking to disconnect with their own culture and seeking to become like those of the dominating culture. African-Americans have often been integrated away from their own core cultural values and spiritual selves.

The American South was integrated in many ways even while it was segregated and while people were being lynched and abused. Even among rabid segregationists one could find some levels of "friendship" or relationship. The lyncher and the lynched often knew each other's names and each other's families. For decades, African-American servants wet-nursed Euro-American children. Some racists even admitted to "loving their Negroes," while looking down on African-Americans in general. It is a romantic notion that says the problems will simply fade away when Euro-Americans and African-Americans get to know one another better.

Proximity is not affinity. Contact is not enough. Sharing lunch counters is nothing compared with sharing power and wealth. Sadly, contemporary efforts at multiculturalism are often passive and only about "sharing cultures." They are not often enough about sharing resources. It is a tinkering process that makes only superficial adjustments on dysfunctional structural injustices. In this way, moves toward multiculturalism can serve as a form of respectable subterfuge. Passive multiculturalism often only promotes the romanticization of each other's worlds. It can lead to the idea that whatever one culture lacks another culture may have in abundance. Essentialist stereotypes results are as familiar as they are infuriating: African-Americans are more friendly and communal while European-Americans are more organized and intellectual. Essentialist stereotyping enforced by passive multiculturalism means that one goes to the smorgasbord of multi-cultural values and picks out whatever one wants to appropriate.

It should not be surprising that the initial advocates of contemporary passive multiculturalism were not African-Americans. The people who brought you passive multiculturalism were the clergy and the scholars of the Euro-American community who fought against segregation and worked to pass the Civil Rights Act. Before it was called multiculturalism it was known as diversity or pluralism.

At its best, passive multiculturalism is a response to the fantasy of American monoculturalism and is a step in the right direction. One should not doubt that these phrases speak of a sincere effort on the part of Euro-Americans. That is not the issue. Does the vehicle of multiculturalism in some way actually uphold feelings of superiority and privilege by Euro-Americans? Can it become a way to concretize stereotypes and "keep people in their place?" "Multiculturalism is primarily a white thing" [Griffin, 96] The danger is that monocultural filters of Euro-American power-brokers can aristocratically determine the role of multi-cultural realities. People are put in boxes and controlled.

If passive multiculturalism is steered by a Eurocentric institution, it will become a mode of corporate instrumentality. Euro-American conjurers of their mono-lingual multi-cultural programs can feel good about providing lip service to the notion of equality. Diversity is a pleasant flair or "add-on to the dominant United States' host culture." [McLaren, in Goldberg, 49] It says to the deracinated and culturally stripped: "Welcome to our club!" Passive multiculturalism can be used as a method to "keep people happy" and not to lift constraints of injustice or to provide power. It can become a way to keep the peace and entertain instead of working to forge a meaningful sharing of control. Waters offers this warning:

> Pluralism and multiculturalism are wonderful pursuits, if only we were sincere in our efforts, if only we were aiming for genuine pluralism or multiculturalism. But usually when people speak of multiculturalism, what they really mean is "Yes, let's all get together but on white terms." This especially happens in church worship settings: We can write the prayer in Spanish, lets do a responsive reading in Cherokee or Korean, and lets throw

in a 'Negro' spiritual and have someone perform a Japanese dance. But when it is all said and done, all we have is a white worship service with ethnic trappings. [Waters, 71]

What does passive multiculturalism often offer in return for its services? Often, not very much. The Mormon Tabernacle Choir might sing an occasional "Negro Spiritual" or children might celebrate Martin King's birthday, but that is hardly being in touch with the experience of African-America. This kind of multiculturalism continues to promote ignorance and essentialist role stereotypes, where African-Americans remain the athletes and the entertainers. If you doubt that is how these role stereotypes function in "multi-cultural America" today, just ask a Euro-American to name ten living African-American males (from among the 18 million) who are not entertainers, athletes, or politicians.

Instead of pallid universalistic humanism, the solution is genuine recognition that will lead to mutual respect. Theologian Jurgen Moltmann, in his book *Experiences in Theology,* told about his experience of coming to America from Germany and coming to recognize that only African-American theology was representitive of the interrelation between faith and American culture. His call, was to encourage all Americans, whatever their cultural heritage, to fully embrace the social issues and theological questions embedded in African-American Christianity. Authentic theological expression must be relevant to its *Sitz im Leben* ("situation in life') and express itself through the vehicle of culture. This truth is expressed in the Christian doctrine of the incarnational revelation of God in Christ in a specific cultural context.

The extent of recognition must also be self-determined and not externally imposed. Often, the condescending patronizing of multi-cultural initiatives is readily apparent. At colleges, students may invariably sing the "Lift Every Voice" at the time of yearly Martin Luther King Day celebrations. Meanwhile, college faculty hiring remain lopsidedly non African-American. Genuine recognition is much more than bringing ethnic food to the national table and allowing Scottish Highland dancing followed by a display of fierce Zulu war-threatening reels. Adding Martin Luther King Day to Saint Patrick's Day and Oktoberfest and Cinco de Mayo [Griffin, 85] does not determine genuine recognition and mutual respect. When Chinese chefs want to kill a frog, they do it by placing the frog in cold water and then, ever so gradually turning up the temperature so the frog does not notice that it is slowly dying. Placating real social issues with symbolic passive multiculturalism may fool a few "frogs" but those who settle for comfort may find themselves in "hot water" where genuine respect is absent.

Genuine recognition will reverse the trend that marginalizes Afrocentric studies by ghettoizing them into a specific course (or series of courses) away from the mainstream curriculum in our colleges. Why shouldn't every American take a course in Afrocentric studies or in the history of African civilization? They are required, at some point in their education, to take a course in European history, a topic that conservatives call "Western" history or civilization. Dynamic multiculturalism, a by-product of justice and equality, is the goal. Genuine recognition that shares power is the goal of what Giroux calls "insurgent multiculturalism"

Confronting "Disneyfied"Optimism

Sticks in a bundle are unbreakable.
—Bondei (Kenyan) Proverb

You want to integrate me into your anonymity because it is my right you think to be like you. I want your right to be like yourself.
—GERALD W. BARRAX, **Black Narcissus**

Lift every voice, and sing America! Lift every voice of disagreement and insight and let it be added to the board rooms of American companies; to the President's Cabinet; to the staff meetings of our churches; and to the department meetings of our colleges. Euro-Americans do not need to "bring in" (the house servant paradigm) African-Americans to their churches and their schools to talk about the Underground Railway or the Reverend Dr. Martin Luther King. We need to get together on equal ground and talk together about the business of our shared country; the function of our government; and the strengthening of our common commitment to Christianity, etc. Fear and genuine power inequities keep this from happening in colleges, schools and businesses while inauthentic, three-fifths theology keeps this from happening in America's segregated churches.

Many Euro-Americans are schooled in a world-view of perennial, hopeful, bright optimism. A distorted sense of justice at home has allowed Americans to trek all over the world decrying the injustices of other countries and offering American solutions to their problems. American hagiography proclaims that we are a "can-do country," founded by pioneers who carved a "new world" out of the savage, godless wilderness. A more accurate history notes that a significant percentage of the early European settlers came to the American colonies because they had failed in their businesses and were marginalized or even criminalized in Europe. These facts are rarely presented in America's grand-eloquent re-creation narratives. Instead, Euro-Americans preach a confident Emersonian transcendentalist message that any problem can be solved. Nevertheless, the desire to cling to icons and dreams often means that Euro-Americans resort to "quick fixes" and easy solutions (such as legislating problems away)instead of substantive changes. Issues become "Disneyfied." This kind of utopian optimism may help people to feel better, but how can they touch America's deeply rooted social problems?

This brand of optimism can even keep racism "off the radar screen" because it is so complex and unpleasant. Many Euro-Americans have given little thought to the issues surrounding racism. Their parents do not usually give them advice about how to cope with racism or how to decipher hidden agendas. Euro-Americans do not have to cull their history and literature textbooks to find themselves. Euro-Americans do not have to swallow the mockery of their slang or ignorant statements and do not usually have to "translate" what people of other cultures are saying.

It is almost unheard of to ask a Euro-American to speak as representatives of their ethnicity. In contrast, many African-Americans feel as if "being black is a twenty-four hour a day, lifetime job!" [Shipler, 236] Few Euro-Americans have struggled with the uncharted territory with which many African-Americans are so conversant. Many take on a posture of calm indifference to being confronted with these problems and foster a level of emotional distance from the issues so that they can avoid both intellectual and social discomfort. Otherwise, Euro-Americans will accuse them of reverse-racism. Some Euro-Americans take solace in the fact that they have African-American friends, all the while oblivious to the fact that the entire system demonizes and marginalizes those same acquaintances.

Perhaps most telling of all is that many Euro-Americans do not know how to answer the question of whether racism is getting better or worse in

America. George Wallace hurled an unambiguous insult at African-Americans that they probably not only didn't know where Alabama was, but that they probably also did not know what country they themselves were in. This accusation of obliviousness could be leveled against many Euro-Americans who talk about issues of racism in the same way that one might talk about problems going on in Senegal or Burma or some other distant corner of the world. They do not understand their own country.

**Chapter Seven — Burning Down the Big House
Questions for consideration and discussion:**

1. Why is the African-American church such an ideal vessel to confront injustice and inequality in America today? What other agencies can be allies in this cause?

2. If the African-American church has this potential to be an agent for change, why is it not more of one? What specific steps should Euro-American church congregations take to become agents of change in the society? How should these churches confront de facto segregation.

3. What is the opposite of mutual recognition and mutual respect? Describe the ways that you have experienced these problems in your own life or in the life of your community?

4. How do children and young people begin to falter in respect for others? How can we teach people to be more sensitive to one anothers particular needs in society?

Chapter Eight
Incarnational Resurrection Christianity:
"When Justice Flows Down Like Rivers!"

Rolling Away the Heavy Stones at Christianity's Tomb

No social advance rolls on the wheels of inevitability.
Each and every step toward the goal of justice requires sacrifice,
suffering and struggle; the tireless exertions and passionate
concern of dedicated individuals."
— MARTIN LUTHER KING, JR.

For Christians, the incarnation of Christ offers direction as to how we understand our relation to culture. The incarnation comes into a specific human context and, in so doing, reveals that every culture is equally capable of receiving divine revelation. The God of Christ becomes the Jesus of humanity; this transformation mirrors the belief that individual human worth originates in our initial creation fashioned in God's divine image (Genesis 1:26-27) and in our on-going specific generation inside of a specific cultural context. Afrocentric Christianity, founded on cultural values that have been forged by millennia of experience of knowing God, is motivated to resolve cultural injustices because of its conviction that cultures are created by God. This "Imago Dei potential" within culture is why each

Christian should cherish a clear sense of their own cultural identity. It is a perspective that confronts what Mark Chapman calls "oppressive Christianity" that seeks to preserve tradition for traditions sake and is "inflexible and dictatorial and teaches believers to serve out of fear and love." [Chapman, 175] Oppressive three-fifths Christianity is an enemy to the celebration of culture in faith; because it sees Jesus only as a universal source for personal emotional comfort and salvation instead of seeing His Lordship of a corporate, multi-cultural kingdom of God's justice; the church.

The once-and-for-all-time event of the incarnation has an on-going expression in the life of the church through the agency of the Holy Spirit. It is this presence of God in the world that is a constant protective against the worship of false idols and supremicist ideas of race, culture, materialism, and self. In the same way that the incarnation of Christ models Christian engagement with the world, the resurrection of Christ offers the church the hope needed to deal with the vast challenges that incarnational participation within society demands.

Greek mythology portrays a character named Sisyphus, the ruler of Corinth whom the god Tartarus punished in a cruel and unusual way: Each day he is called upon to roll a huge stone up a mountain. It takes all of his energies, and all of his time. At the end of the day, the weight of the stone escapes Sisyphus and the stone rolls back down to the bottom of the mountain. All his labors come to nothing; it is a futile task. The next day he has to start over again at the bottom of the mountain. Sometimes workers for justice feel they have also been afflicted by the curse of Sisyphus. But the Bible tells us about some stones that have been rolled away. Jesus called on his friends to remove the stone in front of the tomb of Lazarus, dead for four days. Later, Jesus was buried in a similar tomb blocked by a huge stone. Angels had to push that stone aside to let the resurrected Christ present himself alive again to the world.

A heavy stone of injustice stands in the way of the power of Christ and dead American Lazarus Christianity. The stone must be removed before our churches can reflect the power of God's love. Jesus, through the Holy Spirit, is calling His friends to roll away the stone so that, once again, a "Lazarus church" can be resurrected to life. Rolling away this stone will be hard work. It will not be Sisyphean; although at times it may seem overwhelming. The Christian life is a difficult one. It calls for commitment and persistence. We are following a Christ who tells us to share not only, "the power of His resurrection but also the fellowship of His sufferings and becoming like Him in His death." This kind of Christianity is opposed both in history and in the contemporary world by a form of gnostic dualism that separates the demands of this earth from the spiritual life of the believer. In any expression, it lends itself to what can be called "easy-believe-ism,"or what Dietrich Bonhoffer called "cheap grace," i.e., where daily decisions have no bearing on the spiritual life of faith.

Has Christianity been "tried and found wanting?" It has often been found difficult and left untried. Are Christians caught up in some idealistic, delusional, and quixotic quest for the kingdom of God on the earth? Is our mission similar to some medieval search for a "holy grail" or some unattainable fantasy? Is the attainment of justice ever really possible?

Biblical revelation resounds with the call for people of faith to work for justice. Hosea called his people to follow a God who required "mercy and not sacrifice" (Hosea 6:6). Amos asked people to do away with idle praise songs and replace them with acts of justice (Amos 5:22-24). Habbakkuk (Habbakkuk 2: 2-9) Obadiah spoke against those who were drunk with the wine of pride and privilege (verses 2-5), when in fact God saw them as nothing more than thieves. God judged Nineveh because of its injustice and sent Nahum and Jonah to the people to preach repentance (Jonah 1:1). Micah challenged people to act justly (Micah 6:8). Zepheniah spoke of the Day of God's wrath as a day of accountability for the evil that had been done in the world (Zepheniah 1:14-18). Malachi promised that those who had robbed God and lived for themselves would one day stand in judgement before God (Malachi 3:8-4:3). The hope of the believer is that ultimately justice will be established and evils will be corrected.

It is with this faith that African-American Christians face their country. The American justice system is not a just system for African-Americans. In 1993, 89.5 percent of those convicted for crack cocaine were African-Americans while only 4.2 percent were Euro-Americans. [Shipler, 380] The American legal system is limited. Laws are in place, and material resources are available to set those laws into effect. Some communities, for example, enact and strictly enforce laws regarding prostitution and drug-sales, while these same offenses are "tolerated" in other communities. "What America lacks," in the words of Shirley Chisolm, "is the heart, the humanity, the Christian love that it would take to right injustice." [Mazel, 110] Violence against African-Americans is another injustice that is rampant. Many African-Americans are harassed by the police without cause. This "profiling" and has also affected Arab and Muslim-Americans. It is unjust in a society that claims to provide equality for all under the law. Making communities safer is just as important as addressing other injustices in society.

Segregationist state and local laws have been dismantled. The de-facto realities of segregation, remain in many of our neighborhoods, churches, schools, and businesses. The Apartheid system was a horrendous heresy inaugurated in the three-fifths church of South Africa that destroyed those who stood in its way. The system in the United States, while not nearly as blatant, also works to maintain the status-quo. It is a system that must be challenged with prophetic resolution. Only when Christians begin calling for justice can the national conversation shift from the present focus on fairness and merit and patronizingly limited multiculturalism. This will open up new horizons of possibility. Efforts in this direction will foster hope in our communities. An articulate Christian voice calling for action will serve as a much needed alternative to the many voices in our society of pessimism and despair.

For that to happen, the rules for Christian engagement with society need to be transformed. The church must be, as it was with Wilberforce and King, an authentic voice for social change. Christians must "become" Christians again. Many have worshiped at the troughs of Baal-ish materialism and hedonism long enough. American Christians must begin to follow Jesus's call to build the Kingdom of God instead of following Thomas Jefferson's call to forge a society based on individual rights and the pursuit of happiness. They must give up Jefferson's platitudes about human dignity in the context of moral inertia and embrace the prophetic mantle of incarnational Christianity. God's heart for justice is a major theme in the Bible. This is not, as some would suggest, a "liberal agenda"; it is a biblical mandate. American Christians must ask themselves if they are seeking justice or "the pursuit of happiness."

Justice is needed in America. One-fourth of America's children are born into poverty. A tiny minority of privileged people in the United States own a vast majority of the wealth. Capital punishment is on the increase. Proportionately more Americans are in jail than in any other industrialized country in the world. This explosion of incarceration has long-range implications for voting issues and many other social concerns. Guns have flooded society and are even in schools. The authors of this text both know of Christian pastors who own guns. American schools are imploding because of neglect. American prisons are now money-making businesses trading on the New York Stock Exchange. In a vicious cycle that ties punishment with profit, criminals mean more "cargo" for the prisons, which in turn means more profit for investors. The more tightly the cargo is packed into the prisons, the greater the profits for the stockholders.

A "Zacchaeus-Church" That Seeks to Effect Restitution

An intelligent thief does not steal in his own quarter of the town.
—Egyptian Proverb

Zacchaeus stood up and said to the Lord, Look Lord!
Here and now I give half of my possessions to the poor; and if I
have cheated anybody out of anything, I will pay back four times
the amount. Jesus said to him: Today salvation has come to this
house, because this man, too, is a son of Abraham.
—Luke 19:8-9

There is a powerful story in the Bible about a wealthy man who wanted to see Jesus. His small physical stature, as well as his selfishness, drove him into a tree of unresolved guilt that made him feel unworthy to stand with those in his community. Jesus saw him and called him to Himself. The calling was transformative. After inviting Jesus to dine with him, Zacchaeus responded with the true gladness of salvation expressed by a desire to make right past offenses. Maybe before Zacchaeus had met Jesus this tax-collector had not even seen his career as a form of theft. After all, he was doing what everyone else was doing. He was only "getting what was coming to him." It was his privilege because of his standing in society.

Meeting Jesus gave Zacchaeus the courage to confront his lifestyle as Jesus saw it and to leave it behind. Dietrich Bonhoffer thought that a clear sign of God's work in a person's life was the willingness born in the new believer to do the right thing in their society. Christian salvation is not merely a personal decision that is expressed in fervent rhetoric; it also has visible ramifications that serve as witness to the world that has seen us before we have met Christ. Salvation will lead to the life-long process of converting one's consciousness.

Zacchaeus announced that he would pay ample reparations for the wrongs he had committed. This expressed his salvation. The American "Zacchaeus-church" may only now be descending from the tree of its self-exaltation. Like Zacchaeus, they may have heard much about Him but they have yet to meet the liberating Christ. The transformation we experience within our hearts will invariably include a liberating "outward expression"; namely, restitution. This response to God's will on our part will cause us to see how God sees our past life of self-centeredness. It is easy to fire rhetoric at problems and to talk about the "upside-down kingdom of God." Zacchaeus had to make fair restitution. Fair restitution will come on the terms set by those who have been offended, not by those who have initiated the offense.

Zacchaeus' conversion forced him to re-examine his life. Meeting Jesus shook his world. One cannot meet Jesus and remain the way they were before the encounter. The presence of the liberating Christ will always exorcize the demons that are bringing destruction. This "exorcism" may be very traumatic. However, many Christians are in need of a "divine upheaval." They need Jesus to pass through their village. They have settled down into a Jericho of complacent, predictable patterns. Their lives are no longer charged with the energy of resurrection faith. Perhaps, these Zacchaeus's are mired in routines because of commitments that they have made through time. Perhaps, they have been worn down by the monotony of the daily routine and affected, ever so gradually, by their lives as "tax-collectors." Jesus can visit their tax-collecting stations and help them look again at life with the freshness and immediacy that resurrection faith promises to those who "seek first the Kingdom of God." Incarnational faith, not the three-fifths variety, will invariably foster social justice. When we confront injustices for which we are responsible, our restitution must be presented to Christ just as Zacchaeus professed the nature of his reparations to Jesus. They must not be geared to our own levels of comfort or to a partial sense of justice.

A classic example of partial reparations can be found in the way that America has responded to the First Nations peoples. In the Black Hills of South Dakota, a treaty was signed promising that non-Native Americans would not invade the sacred land of the Lakota Sioux. A few years later, when gold was discovered this covenant was broken and the land was stolen. Finally, after a hundred years of protest, the illegality of this theft was brought to the attention of the American government. The Lakota explained before the United States Supreme Court that the treaty they signed had been agreed to in perpetuity. The Lakota could not accept that ten years was synonymous with "in perpetuity."

The legality of the contracts could not be denied. It took a hundred years, but finally the Supreme Court admitted that a grave injustice had been done. While admitting this, the court also proposed a solution. Yes, the land had been stolen, and the government was sorry. But it would not be "realistic" to return the land. Instead, nine million dollars would be given to the Lakota nation for the cost of the land. The national leaders of the Lakota Sioux responded that they did not want the money. They wanted the land. They wanted justice. A resolution to this impasse has yet to come. The situation is once again, paralyzed between inertia and inconvenience. Unacceptable solutions will not correct unresolved injustices, and it is audacious to recognize liability but to refuse restitution.

Imagine that someone steals your automobile. After some time, they come and apologize to you for the theft. Then they tell you that to make reparations they will give you a year's worth of tokens for the public transportation system! Is that justice? Common sense says that restitution must take place and that the offended should have returned, as far as it is possible, what has been stolen. The time has come to move forward, but the thief should not set the terms for restitution.

Social injustices are not resolved by the "rich" condescendingly doing a favor on behalf of the "poor." Jesus, the liberator, said that the happiest among us are those who are "rich in the things of God." Mother Theresa of India echoed this redefinition when she first visited the United States. An interviewer shoved a microphone in her face and asked her what it was like to come to a "rich country like America" from a "poor country like India." Mother Theresa replied, "I have never been in a poorer country in my life than the United States." Our lives must be rooted in the biblical injunction that we live lives of compassion with a hunger and thirst for righteousness.

America's "King Ahab Church"and Elijah 's Call for Justice

The Devil does not destroy his own house.
—Egyptian Proverb

When Ahab met Elijah he said to him, is that you, you troubler of Israel? Elijah replied, I have not made trouble for Israel. But you and your father's family have. You have abandoned the Lord's commands and followed the Baals. Now summon the people from all over Israel to meet me on Mount Carmel....
—I Kings 18: 16-19

In the last section we talked about a "Zacchaeus church" that was will-ing to change. This is a positive model. History, in contrast, shows us a "King Ahab church" that is more troubled than motivated by calls for jus-tice. King Ahab, you recall, was the brooding despotic king, described in I Kings, who led his nation into a life of materialism and irresponsible hedo-nism. The righteous, however, suffered greatly during his despotic rule. Diasporan Africans have faced "King Ahab" more than they have faced "Zacchaeus." When one stops to consider all the atrocities committed against people of African ancestry, it is incredible that any African would even consider becoming a Christian. "King Ahab Christianity"captured slaves during the horrors of the Maafa and killed many of God's people by ritual sacrifices during the Jim Crow era. We can assume that Ahab will not go willingly to Ramoth-Gilead to confront God's prophet Elijah. But eventually he will come. We are aware of the very real possibility of little progress being made in the area of justice. As Christians, however, we believe in the eventual justice that will come to those who are offended and the eventual judgment against those who persist in presumptive pride.

Ahab's rule is not an authentic kingship. Elijah's vision of the kingdom of God was based on justice and not in power contests against Ahab's rule. The nation of Israel was offered two clear choices on Mount Carmel; between the way of Ahab and the way of Elijah. The same two choices are offered to American Christianity today. Patterson writes:

The tragic facts of slavery and Jim Crow show that there are real-ly two kinds of Christianity at the heart of the American experience; one that has largely neglected the radical relational and spiritual message of Jesus preached by King and completely focuses on the personal, sacrificial meaning of Christ's death and another which takes the life and teachings of Jesus seriously as a way of life and not just as a way to avoid punishment and death.... [Patterson, 201]

This schizophrenia in American Christianity must be uprooted. It promotes a theocentric theology that minimizes the significance of the incarnation of Christ as a guiding principle of Christian practice. It is, as Patterson says, a religion about Jesus which is fixated on His bloody, sacrificial death instead of a religion of Jesus which centers on His life and teaching; calling people to a path of daily discipleship. The power of the incarnation keeps Christians from seeing God only as, Islam does, as an authoritarian judge. It also keeps Christians from the personalized preoccupation of some Asian religious adherents (and sadly, among some Christians) that focuses on a Spirit of inward cultivation and enlightenment at the expense of social justice demands.

The incarnation roots Christians in this life. Christians will participate in the challenges of our era, but do not worship the physical at the expense of the moral. They do not choose aesthetic but inauthentic worship over genuine community. That was the religion of King Ahab. He was a king who promoted a religion that joined his personal and political ambitions with a gloss of religious authority. For the Christian, social religion and incarnational faith will always be separate. The political interests of an American Ahab must not be joined with the prophetic interests of God's Elijah remnant. Only when Americans come to see that there are two "Christianities" can the usurper be dethroned and the way of the liberating Jesus be established. King Ahab Christianity will never provide genuine partnerships in faith. It is opposed to power sharing, and committed to self-sustenance. The gap is so pronounced that we must meet at Mount Carmel and resolve the issue with clarity. It will be a traumatic encounter that will not have much to do with aesthetic symbolism and flourishing rhetoric.

Is the situation so polarized? Are most partnerships between Euro-Americans and African-American Christians only symbolic and not substantive? We respect voices like those of Chris Rice and (the late) Spencer Perkins who might suggest that we are not taking enough good initiatives into account. We would be happy to be proven wrong.

There have been a few instances where African-American Christians and Euro-American Christians joined together to bring social justice. The passage of the Civil Rights Acts of 1965 saw a handful of Euro-American churches in the Midwest, mobilized by the World Council of Churches, involved in a grass-roots effort to write letters and support legislation. Even this "partnership" ultimately dissolved after civil rights laws were passed. Why? African-American Civil Rights activists regarded civil rights legislation as a first step; a starting-point. Many Euro-American supporters, however, saw these same initiatives as a final step; an end-point of achievement. The thinking was that now that African-Americans could eat and study and work with Euro-Americans there was no further need for church-based activism and the confrontation of the "Ahab system."

Griffin calls this the divide between "first-step desegregationists" and "final-step whites." [Griffin, 86] Euro-Americans saw the lines of division as inevitable and, if they were honest, even desirable. Today, these views are resident in the new racism which blames African-Americans for their hapless inability to take hold of opportunities to advance. Euro-Americans, during the civil rights era, called for formal desegregation without top-down integration. The three-fifths theology that segregated America in the first place was never reframed. Church-based repentance, as well as efforts to make restitution, were never initiated to any significant degree. Attention to legal changes made personal repentance and personal responsibility for restitution somehow less pressing. The legislative solutions of the era allowed for a convenient escape from personal obligations.

The problem with this approach is that, ultimately, it did not work. Issues were not resolved. Three-fifths theology only provided a partial solution. Even as this type of "nocturnal-marsupial" Christianity (to draw an allusion from nature suggested by Lamin Sanneh) fled into the shadows at the first hints of social daybreak; the on-going racist structures that made the unjust laws in the first place continued to grind ahead unimpeded.

Superficial adjustments were made. Improvements were ascertainable. Deep wounds, however, remained even when covered over with the few bandages of white-liberal goodwill. The next step along the path toward justice requires a new level of commitment. The Bible tells an interesting story of Moabite raiders who hastily threw the body of one of their dead compatriots into a tomb that happened to house the bones of the prophet Elisha.

As soon as the corpse touched Elisha's bones, the story says, the dead man "came to life and sprung to his feet" (II Kings 13:20-21). Perhaps what we need today is to throw our efforts on the bones of Malcolm X, Medgar Evers, et.al. Perhaps we need to take Malcolm's words to heart and seek to bring change "by any means necessary." It is time to explore any and every avenue to see God's work come into existence "by any means godly."

We are following in the footsteps of all who have given their lives for the sake of justice. We need to fall on their bones and find ourselves alive in their commitment. We are also following Jesus. The murder of Jesus was an act of injustice done in the name of God. What would Jesus do if He lived today? Where would He live? Would He be murdered again today by religious leaders as He had two thousand years ago? Christ lives today in His church. Where is He in the United States?

Martin and Malcolm are dead. Elijah is dead. The Bible says that, "the word of the Lord came to Moses and told Joshua, Moses, my servant is dead: Now then, you and all of these people, get ready and cross the Jordan into the land that I am about to give them" (Joshua 1:2). This is a message of empowerment for us today. The torch of God's work has been passed in our relay race to a new generation of runners. That which has happened before can happen again, because God in heaven is unchanging. The God of Martin and Malcolm and Elijah and Moses lives and is able to live through us for the advancement of His glory and honor in contemporary times.

Co-existence or an Imposed Assimilation

Life's piano can only produce the melodies of brotherhood when it is recognized that the black keys are as basic, necessary and as beautiful as the white keys. The Negro, through self-acceptance and self-appreciation will one day cause white America to see that integration (Tait: co-existence) is not an obstacle, but an opportunity to participate in the beauty of diversity…Our movement does not seek to integrate the Negro into all of the existing values of American society. Let us be those creative dissenters who will call our beloved nation to a higher destiny, to a new plateau of compassion and to a more noble expression of humanness.
—MARTIN LUTHER KING, JR.

Jesus tells story of the Good Samaritan in Luke 10: 25-37. It is an oft-repeated parable about neighborliness. It is a message about caring for each other in a way that empowers people and keeps their dignity intact. In the American context, both African-Americans and European-Americans play at different times the various roles of the helping Samaritan and the needing recipient of this parable. Both communities need the mercy that the Samaritan provided. People should not focus on who is helping whom the most. God has called African-Americans and European-Americans to be each other's neighbor.

The parable of the Good Samaritan has interesting applications to the challenge of racism. Christians can envision a beloved community of mutuality more than any other group in society. Perhaps that is why many of the leaders of the civil rights movement came from the ranks of American churches. If this movement saw legislation as a first step, then what did they see as the next step or even as the final goal? This is a very important question for all of us mired in the ditch we find ourselves in beside this treacherous Jericho road. Some people envision a Jericho, the ultimate destination of our road, as a place of co-existence. What does co-existence really mean? To co-exist is to be together at the same time of place. The term "integration" has come to mean, for many African-Americans, the continued domination by Euro-Americans and the loss of identity. The Larousse dictionary definition of "integrate" is to make complete by adding parts into the unified whole. This kind of integration has never been the reality of American society, or the goal of Euro-American social power structures. Instead, the plantation system was based on a "divide and conquer" strategy for inter-relationships. Perhaps, thinking in terms of the concept of "co-existence" is a more honest and helpful goal for the immediate future.

Taking the road we have historically been on in the United States has found each of us lying in separate ditches. Segregation remains marked out by a line across our cities and our lives. Rivers and roads and railroad tracks have also marked this line. What will the just integration of "Jericho" look like? It will not mean assimilation. Integration does not mean a small cube of sugar joining with a large mug of coffee in order to loose its identity. This is a clear danger when "40 million sugars join 210 million coffee cups." This kind of assimilation has been going on since the first African stepped onto "Turtle Island" North America.

Genuine integration must be a marriage of equals. It is not inviting Africans to join the European club or be an "American," if that really means one being an "honorary" Euro-American. Our road must lead to a "parliamentary-democracy" society where everyone has a voice and not a simple "majority-rules"democracy that asks African-Americans to sanitize and "de-Africanize" their American-ness. The Jericho road Samaritan of African-American Christianity makes this kind of mutual co-existence possible. Without identity, without history, without Sankofa, there is no integration worthy of the name. Integration demands mutual recognition.

The envisaged integration is neither utopian nor vague. It will take time to unfold as people learn to trust one another. The Good Samaritan took a great deal of time and effort to resolve the situation. We find ourselves in a similarly difficult relationship. The Chinese say that "one who hurries cannot walk with dignity." Christ's parable pointed to the love that the Samaritan had for someone from another culture. It is a love rooted in a clear sense of equality. Unlike, those who passed the beaten victim, the Samaritan knew that he was not "better than" the person needing his assistance. His generosity was not patronizing. It was the logical conclusion of his belief that others had value as children of God made in divine image.

Integration and partnership without this assumption will fail. Three fifths theology promotes either condescension or patronization. Paul talks about preferring others to be better than yourself. The African-centered world-view teaches that strangers are regarded as elders. Elders are seen as mothers and fathers, people who can provide valuable wisdom. When there are no elders, a village is sure to be ruined. This attitude of respect is appropriate. We have much to learn from each other and contribute to each other's betterment. The music that we can make together is more beautiful than that which we can make by ourselves.

Perhaps that sounds too theoretical. Let us return to the application of the Good Samaritan parable for our daily lives. Probably one of the clearest ways that a sense of equality can be seen is in the dynamic of designated power in a given relationship. Who is in control and making the decisions? This is an easy way to separate sentimentality from genuine love. Those who do not share power do not love. Mutuality can never be about one group of people claiming to work on our behalf without our input. Co-existence that shares power has great creative potential for change.

Restitution Models Revisited: "An Individual Slavery Restitution Tax"?

As Malcolm X said "if you have had a knife in my back for four hundred years, am I supposed to thank you for pulling it out?" The very least of your responsibility now is to compensate me, however inadequately, for centuries of degradation and dis-enfranchisement by granting peacefully—before I take them forcefully— the same rights and opportunities for a decent life that you've taken for granted as an American birthright.
—ELDRIDGE CLEAVER

The first step is the admission that there is a problem between African and European-Americans. The next step is genuine repentance for offenses that have been caused. Once and for all, Euro-Americans must not take up the conservative mantra that African-Americans are complaining about being victims and recognize that African-Americans have been victims. That recognition, however, is not the end-point. Biblical justice demands restitution. It is not about relieving the guilt of the offender.

There is no real way to make amends to Africans in the United States for all that has been suffered. Larry Neal, a professor of economics at Illinois calculated that between 1619 and 1865 slaves in this country performed over 220 million unpaid man-hours. In 1983 he concluded that the value of this labor would be anywhere between two and four trillion dollars [Munford, 1996, 428]. Al Sharpton, in his book *The Black Agenda* called for 6.6 billion dollars to be paid by the government over ten years. Something must be done and it must be just. Perhaps what is needed is a sort of international "independent counsel" who would moderate between the self-interests of the government and the need for settlement to outstanding social debts. Perhaps it is time to move on Malcolm's agenda to place before the United Nations World Court the case for reparations.

Whatever steps a "Zacchaeus church" takes in this direction it must not be in terms of being tokenistic. As Clarence Munford says: Despite all our sacrifice we have been handed law-book freedom without make-right compensation." [Munford, 1996, 414]

Randall Robinson, the director of the organization Trans-Africa, has written a significant book called *The Debt: What America Owes African-*

Americans. Robinson contends that this issue will be a defining point in future inter-relationships between European and African-Americans. It has pervasive ramifications. Robinson noted that when visiting the White House and the Capitol building of the United States, he could find no reference to the slave labor that the government had used to construct these great monuments to American freedom.

Who should pay this restitution? The logical answer would be the American government. It was the government that legally sanctioned slavery at all levels until the Civil War. Wolfe-Devine notes that it is,

> Also the sort of transgenerational entity that is needed to bridge the gap between the wrongs done to the slaves and the present day black population. [Wolfe-Devine, 54]

Ancestors of those freed prior to the Civil War would also be eligible in that the issues of injustice, although initially an expression of slavery, have had wide-ranging and on-going expressions, not the least of them, the post-Civil War Jim Crow laws.

Economic restitution is what is appropriate. Today, America is spending billions worldwide to fight terrorism. In 1969, while the government was spending billions of dollars for the mission to the moon, James Forman and others drafted a "Black Manifesto" asking for financial remuneration. Once again, America is planning to spend billions on a mission to explore Mars while the mission to bring justice has yet to be properly funded. Economic restitution was appropriate when the proposal was to provide every freed slave "forty acres and a mule" was approved in 1865, and it is appropriate today. The disbursement of economic resources is not an act of charity; it is a duty that will generate significant social benefit and will foster greater equality. Restitution admits a dimension of fault and obligation. This would go a long way to countering the claims of those who believe that the plight of African-Americans in slavery and in their present status of inequality is of their own making. Genuine restitution must not only be distributed based on certain arbitrary criteria of wealth. The push for restitution could be modeled after similar programs for Jewish Holocaust survivors or with reference to programs arranged for Native Americans. Ideally, it should be a government led initiative. One suggestion is that African-Americans would be given an exemption in paying Federal

Income Tax or students would be exempted from paying college tuition. The options for government initiated models are endless.

Forman's 1969 "Black Manifesto" called for economic reparations in the amount of $500 million dollars to be paid by the American government to Americans of African descent. That is a small amount of money in contemporary terms. Compare that amount with the $400 million dollars that the Canadian Government gave to the much smaller Native American population by the Canadian Government in a settlement in 1998. On 10 August 1988 Ronald Reagan signed a bill giving reparations ($20,000 per internee) to the 60,000 Japanese-Americans alive at that time in recognition for the injustices they experienced during the Second World War. More than thirty years after Forman's call, the American government has not seriously considered the idea of reparations. One of the major exceptions is the yearly presentation that is made by members of Congress, led by John Conyers of Michigan, calling for reparations. To date, no significant action has been taken.

This kind of initiative, however, does not have to wait for federal support to take effect. Restitution could also be initiated on the state or the local level or even on the individual level. Americans do need to wait for a top-down action to begin the process. Why not launch initiatives at the grass-roots level that will bring positive change? Companies, colleges, businesses, community groups and even individuals can develop creative solutions that will foster a climate of reconciliation.

Consider the idea of an individual "slavery restitution tax" where Euro-Americans would voluntarily pay a set amount of money for the years of slavery in the United States (1619-1865). This would be appropriate if they felt that, as Euro-Americans, they had been direct beneficiaries of "white privilege" and if they could acknowledge the fact that slave labor built the country they now cherish. Each person could determine the amount that they feel would be appropriate to their ability to pay or to the size of their family. Perhaps a minimum suggested donation would be that each person would pay $4,000. Ten dollars per year for approximately four hundred years of slavery is clearly only a token gesture, but it would make an individual statement about being a direct beneficiary of injustice. This minimal amount, if given by two hundred million Euro-Americans, would total, not including interest, eight hundred million dollars.

Imagine asking a young Euro-American couple what they are going to do once they graduate from college and hearing from them that they were going to work on paying their school bills and their slavery restitution tax. The hours spent on paying this debt would leave a powerful impression to both the recipients and on those working for these funds. It is our goal, not to provide definitive solutions, but to stimulate the discussion on this important issue and foster debate that seeks to arrive at concrete solutions.

Economic Justice

The present emphasis on studying the poor and the Blacks implies that these are the 'problem' groups. The real problem resides in the 'haves' rather than in the 'have-nots.' What stands in the way of social advance is resistance to change on the part of the rich and the powerful; their reluctance to give up even a tiny fraction of their privileges.
—ALEXANDER THOMAS

One must question the values of a society that tolerates the kind of poverty that exists in the United States.
ANDREW YOUNG

Economic efforts are at the heart of justice initiatives. While some Euro-Americans fixate on passive multiculturalism, the economic gaps are widening at a troubling rate. While people talk about praying together for unity, economic realities go unmentioned. Immediately after the Civil War African-Americans owned only 0.5 percent of all of the total economic worth of the United States. That statistic is not too surprising given that most African-Americans had been slaves up to that point. What is the amount today after all of our progress? Conley observes:

By 1990, a full 135 years after the abolition of slavery, black Americans owned a meager 1% of all total wealth…(and) almost no progress had been made in terms of property worth. African-Americans may have won "title" to their own bodies and their labor, but they have gained ownership over little else… Over the course of the twentieth century there has been a dispersal of wealth-limited as it may have been-with the result that in 1994 the typical White family had a nest egg of assets totaling a median of $72,000.With a median net worth of approximately $9,800 in that year the typical black family had no nest egg to speak of. [Conley, 25]

African-Americans are less likely than whites to own homes in which they reside. In 1997, 28% of whites lived in central cities, compared with 55% who lived in the suburbs (the figures do not add up to 100% because they exclude rural residents). During that same year, the corresponding figures for blacks were almost a mirror image: 64 percent for urban residence and 31% for suburban residence. This spatial distribution is important because 72% of suburban residents owned their homes in 1997, compared to only 49% of their urban counterparts. The result of this combination is that in 1997 only 44% of blacks owned their homes in contrast to the 71% of whites according to the Harvard Joint Center for Housing Studies. [Conley, 38]

These statistics show that economic justice is needed in America. Until people can live without fear of economic disaster then their situation will be insecure. Poverty humiliates and leads to submissiveness. The problem of income inequality is accepted as normative when it is abusive and a whole group of people find themselves doing subsistence labor on behalf of the powerful because they feel that there is no alternative. Many people have to work two jobs to survive. Poverty fosters feelings of inferiority. The wealth of the United States comes at the expense of the poor. The rich impoverish the poor. Economic inequality in America goes on in a context of unparalleled economic growth. Ironically, the quality of many people's lives declines, their economic wealth increases.

Christians cannot merely lament the systemic nature of these problems. The Bible is replete with challenges that call believers to aid those who are lacking. Responsibility to those in need is a Christian virtue if not an American civil duty. Christians are called upon to make personal choices with their pocket-book and call on their institutions and constituencies to move proactively into social justice through economic redistribution. This might mean that Christians will identify, then boycott companies that are not supporting Affirmative Action in their hiring practices. Christians might boycott certain products or, alternatively, go out of their way to let employers know that their efforts to integrate their places of business are appreciated. Churches or colleges might distribute an African-American business directory for their area. These could be placed in the home or in the desk of office personnel. Actions have to be concrete and identifiable. For many the problem is not the 'color-line,' but the bottom line; not that their skin is black, but that their checkbooks are in the red. Unfortunately, many churches and colleges absorbed in three-fifths theology are also beholden to Mammon and economic greed. W.E. B. DuBois noted this connection when he stated:

> Let not the cloak of Christian mission enterprise be allowed in the future, as so often in the past, to hide the ruthless economic exploitation and political downfall of less developed nations, whose chief fault has been reliance on the plighted troth of the Christian church. [Magubane, 141]

What is our answer to DuBois? He continues: "Let the white world keep its missionaries at home to teach the Golden Rule to its corporate thieves. Damn the God of slavery, exploitation, and war...." [Magubane, 213] DuBois is responding to three-fifths theology. Our answer is to lift up an outward-looking faith that is focused on God's call for Biblical justice. Former missionary to Kenya, Vincent Donovan offers this challenge for building an "outward-turned Christianity":

> It is only by the imparting of an outward-turned Christianity that we have any hope in achieving Christianity. An inward turned Christianity is a dangerous counterfeit, an alluring masquerade. It is no Christianity at all. The salvation of ones soul or self-sanctification or self-perfection or self-fulfillment may well be the goal of Buddhism or Greek philosophy. But it is not the goal of Christianity. For someone to embrace the purpose of Christianity for self-fulfillment or self-salvation is, I think, to betray or to misunderstand Christianity at its deepest level. [Donovan, 104]

Inclusive Biblical Community or Exclusive American Injustice?

*A boat does not go forward if each person is
rowing his own direction.*
—Swahili Proverb

Americans claim to believe in justice. We repeat in the pledge of allegiance the phrase, "liberty and justice for all." Do liberty and justice always go together? Liberty is often opposed to justice. People who are free do not automatically experience justice. Reality tells us otherwise. Who is the "all" that pledge? Should the pledge be more accurately restated as "liberty and justice for some"?

Community, from a biblical and civil standpoint demands more from us. Injustice anywhere, Dr. King often said, is a threat to justice everywhere. As long as some suffer, all of us suffer. This is the idea presented to us in St. Paul's understanding of the Christian community as the body of Christ. The church, divided as it is in America (some claim there are more than 20,000 groups), can unite to a greater degree and thus become a potent force for progress in society. The church is not powerless. Racism is rooted in power and thus must be uprooted by the greater power of God and His determined people. Restitution and economic empowerment initiatives are only a few of the tools that can be used to express justice in concrete ways. Another is authoritative and administrative power-sharing. Very slowly, more Euro-Americans have African-American pastors or supervisors in other positions of authority over them. This pattern must grow exponentially.

Language is another area where justice needs to take root. For all Christians, the Bible is God's Word, whether it is spoken in King James English or in contemporary Ebonics. Euro-American linguists were quick to distinguish Ebonics as retrogressive to intellectual development just as many Euro-Americans are quick to downplay many other cultural differences. This is beginning to change. In the last twenty years this area has improved dramatically. Ebonics are now widely accepted as normative among early education reading specialists. John Rickford of Stanford University has written that it is a "systematic, regular and complex structure insofar as it involves a vocabulary or lexicon, a phonology or sound system and a grammar." [Shipler, 76] Language leads to antagonism among both cultures, and a paradigm shift from a demand for conformity to Eurocentric standards will be a positive step in the right direction.

Do these questions about issues like restitution and respect for Ebonics, for example, foster divisiveness? Certainly, they are uncomfortable to some. Do they actually create more problems than they solve? There are legions of important problems that remain unaddressed. Are we only African and Europeans? No: There is common ground. We can stand together as Americans and as humans and as Christians once mutual respect replaces Eurocentric demands for cultural conformity.

From Apprehension to Inclusion

We cannot dwell in a house together without
speaking to one another.
—Yoruba Proverb

Christianity holds the potential to break the fear, insecurity, and ignorance that some European-Americans have of African-Americans. There is no justice when there is fear and suspicion. Fear combined with power and ignorance means that people will continue to try to manipulate and exploit other people.

Justice theology could also be called "African-American Theology." What do we mean? If James Cone is right that "thinking of Christ as a non-Black in the twentieth century is as theologically impossible as thinking of him as non-Jewish in the first century" [Weiner, 170] and again, "If there is any contemporary meaning to the Anti-Christ than the white church seems to be a manifestation of it" [Griffin, 68], then only the coming of justice will free both oppressed and oppressor. Beyond viewing this as an exercise in asserting blame, Christians should take Cone's challenge to heart. The situation is often too polarized for progress. Moses in pharaoh's court wanted to help the Hebrew slaves and, in his willingness to help, killed a fellow Egyptian. The Hebrew onlooker responded to the gesture by wondering, "Will you now kill me also?" Moses had to divest himself of the robes of power and spend a few decades learning at the feet of the common people before he could have any credible voice among the people of Israel whom he claimed he wanted to help. His desire to help was as misguided as it was sincere. Euro-Americans who have Moses' sympathies should not respond rashly to either criticism or affirmations, but move slowly in partnership with African-Americans to avoid relational dynamics that lead to paternalism or abandonment.

The slave in the world's eyes is the ruler in God's eyes. Ephesians 2:10 reminds us that "we are God's workmanship." The greatest among you, the liberating Jesus explains, is the one who serves. There is one in America today who has served for 350 years. This Joseph-people will be the teachers and leaders for America's tomorrow. Euro-American children must now learn the wisdom of Native America and the wisdom of Africa. African-American theology is one of the most authentic voices in the American church. The African-American church has guarded the truth of God's love in this often hostile land and now, in this time of spiritual famine, is willing to share it again with the brothers who had sought his destruction. One European-American, Jon-Michael Spencer echoes James Cone's call to worship a "Black Christ":

> When people of European descent can accept and appreciate, love and worship a Jesus who in his pictorial representation is Black, then and only then will they have entered into the kind of therapy that alone can begin to alleviate their subconscious feelings of superiority and their inferiority claims against people of African ancestry. [Spencer, 99]

"No Choice" Christianity

The church is constantly tempted to be conformed to the world, to want influence that comes from power, prestige and privilege, and it forgets that its Lord and Master was born in a stable and that the messengers who announced his birth were rustic shepherds The church is always in the world but never of the world so that it can exercise its prophetic ministry. The church must be ever ready to wash the disciple's feet, a serving church, and not a triumphalistic church. A church that preaches the Gospel of reconciliation but works for justice because there can be no real reconciliation without justice....
—ARCHBISHOP DESMOND TUTU

Incarnational Christianity is "no-choice" Christianity. Many Americans have the notion that they can choose what will comprise their lives. They envision their lives as a smorgasbord of apparent choices. In fact, there is no choice in working for justice if one is to be a Christian. Again and again, African-Americans tell a familiar story of Euro-American colleagues who work closely with them only to veer off into a different direction when they have had enough of the "racial justice thing." Trust gives way to distrust. Distrust is a huge barrier in most relations between races in this country. But there is no choice in this area. There is no parachute or bailout option for a person who is following the liberating Jesus. In the past many Christians have shied away from politics and social action because it was corrupt or "of the world." Some have forged an unholy alliance with secular agendas. In these days, Christians must be proactively political without being partisan or caught up in the belief that social change is primarily political; and not moral and spiritual. We must get off the sidelines. The church can not be a social club or a private society. Christians must begin to reflect seriously on the issues. We must become progressive listeners.

Christians must develop a set of "credentials" that support platitudes about our desire for justice. People should be able to see what we believe by what we buy, where we live, how we spend our time, and with whom we relate. These credentials will help others determine whether we are trustworthy and truly seeking to follow the liberating Jesus. Stokley Carmichael, half mockingly asked Dr. King, shortly before his murder, why African-Americans had to be "more moral than white folks?" Why? Because of the claim of Christianity that "God was in Christ reconciling the world to Himself." Because it is not about ethnic injustice alone; it is also about incarnational revelation. Because the liberating message of Jesus is that the truth is inextricably bound to freedom.

The Bible reminds us that "God is not mocked. Whatever a person sows that will they also reap." Wholeness and holiness are complimentary. The writer of the revelator said that Christians overcame Satan by the "blood of the Lamb and the word of their testimony." Overcoming means an eternal salvation validated in temporal conditions. For African-Americans it means being "more moral" than many Euro-American Christians who are trying to overcome only by the "blood of the Lamb" and not the "word of their testimony!" Jesus speaks of "recovering sight to the blind."

Euro-American theology is in need of this healing touch if it wants to escape the confines of its blindness. Euro-American theology in its present forms may be eloquent; it may be aesthetically beautiful; it may be inspiring, but until it adds the respect of recognition and the obedience of justice that comes from following the liberating Christ it will remain nothing more than three-fifths theology.

Chapter Eight — Incarnational Christianity
Questions for consideration and discussion:

1. Why do many Christians frequently avoid focusing on issues of social justice? What does that say about Christianity as it has developed in the United States?

2. How is the biblical view of salvation comprehensive in a way that includes this life as well as the life in the world to come?

3. What would the prophet Amos or Haggai say if he were writing to the American church? What would you include in a contemporary version of one of the books by the minor prophets who focused on injustice in the Israel of his day. Write, as Dr. King did, a letter to today's American church.

Chapter Nine: Conclusion
American Christianity is Inexorably Linked to American Racism

We must be together. This is not a matter of doing something "for" Blacks or "for" Whites. It is a matter of making this country something viable in the future
—THOMAS PETTIGREW

We have seen in America what happens to a society when Christians begin to embrace three-fifths theology. People hold to a theology that absents itself from the realities of the society that it was called to transform. Sadly, the story of American Christianity is inexorably linked to the story of American racism. It was the Euro-American church that chose the path of segregation in its worship over integration and unity with all fellow Christians. It was the Euro-American church that, not only "made itself in the image of America," but also pushed those it abused from its midst. Out of chaos, the cosmos of a new church was born. The African-American church has often been a "prophetic adversary" of Euro-American Christianity. It has been the Elijah to King Ahab theology.

Three-fifths theology lies at the heart of the larger American social vision. From their Mayflower, the Puritan fathers launched a holy vision for a new land that held no place for Africans or Native Americans. These same religious leaders were also political leaders, and they were Christians who owned slaves. Their Christianity allowed them to own slaves. It allowed them to make a holy covenant with God without making any covenant with African-Americans or Native American people that they met when they arrived. The one-dimensionality of that kind of Christianity has been a distinguishing feature of self-serving three-fifths theology.

It is not Christianity that has done so much harm in America, but the theological aberration of three-fifths theology. It is not the Christianity of the Sermon on the Mount, but the Christianity that has as its holy scripture the Declaration of Independence and the Constitution. Constitution-Christianity taught that Africans are three-fifths of a person. Declaration of Independence-Christianity promised freedom for all at the same time that it excluded freedom for many. Thomas Jefferson, the high priest of this new American civil religion, taught: "You shall believe the lies and the lies will make you free to pursue individual happiness."

The solutions America needs will not come from a fractioned Christianity. It will rise instead from an Elijah people who have not "bowed their knee" to King Ahab's Baal's or to his false religion that joined political power with injustice. It is time to respond to the clarion message of Elijah: "If the Lord Be God then follow Him! But if the slave-owners be God then follow them and go to hell."

Christians in America must move from the place of genuine repentance that recognizes Euro-American culpability in our nation's injustices to that which biblical justice demands: to reparations and, only then, to reconciliation. The persistent double-edged American heresy of injustice and inequality must be reversed if Christianity is to have any credibility in this country. Paul wrote that the church is one body made up of many diverse components. Our diversity need not be a reason for division. The church of Jesus, which is one church in theory, must become one church in reality. Unity is not optional. Disunity reveals that the church is a human power structure and not a spirit-led dynamism. To be able to live comfortably with disunity; to be content with de-facto segregation in our churches is a clear expression of three-fifths theology at work.

"Woe to Those Who Are at Ease..." in America

What makes the road long is laziness to go.
— Bemba Proverb

If Proverbs 23:7 is right in stating that, "As a man thinks in his heart so is he," Americans have embraced three-fifths theology if they have not embraced God's call for justice in society. For the Christian, faithfulness to God is the primary concern. The dismantling of three-fifths theology will mean the end to the notion that de-facto segregation is not life threatening to Christian witness. Racist inequality and economic injustice are not only problems; they are America's national sins.

Pastors and lay people will begin to boycott any and all church meetings and functions that do not squarely address the need for America's Christian church to put an end to de-facto segregation and social injustice. The refutation of three-fifths theology will recognize that what is happening in lukewarm churches is rooted in disobedience and expressed in inauthentic worship. Three-fifths theologians may continue to call its members to opt for the drug of gradualism because it does not disturb their comfort zones. The Christian faith of the African-Elijah church must call all Christians to take a clear stand at our Mount Carmel.

The kind of comfort that three-fifths theology offers is the kind of comfort that a person dying in the cold experiences when the entire body goes numb. The body of Christ in America has been immobilized by three-fifths theology. The numbness that we are describing may help explain why American sociologists of religion note a preoccupation with the experience of the sensational, the miraculous, and the mysterious. At the bottom of their hearts, Christians in America know that to "something is rotten" in our churches. But a new cassette tape, new book or a new seminar will not bring the solution.

Until there is justice, three-fifths Christians will continue to be guilty of perpetrating "a form of godliness that denies the power" of God's reality. Three-fifths theology is ungodly in its expression, and it will continue to result in subjugation, degradation, division, and hypocrisy. American Christianity, must, perhaps for the first time as an entire community of believers from all cultures, become the religion of Jesus. Once "feel-good" meetings are over, one group returns to racial profiling while another returns to their insularity. This is not revolutionary faith. Jesus calls us to preach to the poor, to set at liberty all who are oppressed and to preach the acceptable year of the Lord's favor (Luke 4: 18). Christ lived his life fulfilling the Jewish injunction to "do justice and walk humbly and to love mercy" (Micah 6:8), and the call to obey God before offering the sacrifices of our own choosing (I Samuel 15:22).

A theology of liberation for American Christianity must, first of all, move from the theoretical to the applied; a theology of praxis. Our church is in a critical "state of emergency;" where there is no place for ease and isolation. The church must speak on behalf of the poor before those who are disenfranchised eventually resort to violence. Civil disobedience, the method of Dr. King, remains a vital tool in our efforts against racism in America. The primary way that this must be expressed is in economic terms. Imagine what would happen if American Christians boycotted the Christmas shopping frenzy and instead called the nation to address the need for reparations and greater economic justice. Prophetic Christianity will confront evil and will express itself in "non-racialist" structures. The church will be recognized by the world for what it does and not for what it says. God is calling His church to be a prophetic voice that understands the times in which it lives. The church must offer a message of hope in response to the prevailing despair rampant in our time.

Hope galvanizes us to action. Fighting three-fifths theology will be hard work as long as some Christians attempt to forge reconciliation without restitution; forgiveness without reparations; unity without contrition; community without power-sharing; and peace without justice. God's grace at work through us will not be contrived, superficial, sentimental, or theoretical; it will be love incarnationally expressed in action.

"What is Africa..." to Three-Fifths Theologians?

*To find the origins of the 'Negro Problem' we must
turn to the 'White Man's problem.*
—MARTIN LUTHER KING, JR.

*Black theology arises in a context of Black suffering at the hands of
rampant white racism. And consequently, Black theology is concerned with making sense theologically with the black experience
whose main ingredient is Black suffering in the light of God's revelation of Himself in the man Jesus Christ*
—DESMOND TUTU

Preaching the Luke 4:18 gospel cannot happen when one oppresses. A popular critique of mission was that the Europeans came with the Bible in their hands to African lands; and now the African has the Bible in their hands while the European has their land! European Christianity has not often been an agent of deliverance; rather it has been an instrument from which people needed to be delivered. The legacy of colonialism in Africa is well known: poverty and warfare have flourished in the wake of centuries of exploitation. We will cite only one reference. The following is an incident describing the "Christian Italian" terrorist response to calls for justice by "Christian Ethiopians" in 1936:

> The Italians ordered all the shops closed and suspended telegraph communications. Within an hour, Addis Ababa was isolated from the world...The slaughter began at midnight and continued through the next day. Ethiopians were killed indiscriminately, burnt alive in their huts, and shot as they tried to escape. Italian truckers chased people down and then ran them over, or tied their feel to the tailgates of their trucks and dragged them to their death. People were beaten until dead. Women were scourged, men emasculated and children crushed underfoot. Throats were cut. People were disemboweled and left to die or hung and stabbed to death. [Marcus, 48]

This on-going legacy of injustice in Africa must be amended before those who are the children of the colonizers are to be called "peace-makers."

True Christianity engenders holistic liberation. In Africa, three-fifths Christianity has bred in colonizing Christians the boastful assumption that they are more civilized than Africans. They have taught that the philosophies, cultures, arts, ideas, traditions and spiritualities of Africa could not possibly have been vessels that were able to contain God's revelation. The first non-Jewish convert was a eunuch from Africa . Three-fifths Christians are often similar to Phillip in Acts 8:26-40, who could not possibly imagine how God could bless the Ethiopian eunuch. Similarly, Peter was amazed by the response of the non-Jewish Jupiter-worshiping Gentile named Cornelius in Acts 10. Three-fifths Christians are also far from the attitude of Abraham in Genesis 14, when he met Melchizedek and bowed down to him, offering gifts of bread and wine. They do not act as if they believe Ecclesiastes 3:11 which proclaims: "God has placed eternity in the hearts of all people" or Romans 1 which affirms,"God is at work in all people." Many serve a god who is too small. Many try to crawl up onto God's Great Throne of Judgement and announce, on God's behalf, who is favored and who is condemned to eternal damnation.

Many three-fifth theologians have no problem accepting a processional understanding of revelation as it relates to Judaism. But they cannot countenance (or at least, largely ignore) the parallel equivalents to Moses and the ethical Ten Commandments could not be found in Confucianism in China or in traditional Nija of Africa. The very fact that many Chinese and many Africans can easily accept the liberating Christ, having once received this ethical and moral foundation shows that the "Ethiopian Eunuch/Cornelius factor" could be at work in their lives. This biblical perspective should foster respect for these ancient traditions. Instead, many are taught that any spirituality tradition, be it African or Asian, is retrogressive, and evil.

The alternative to three-fifths imperialistic Christianity's disdain for Africa is a view that acknowledges God's love for His beautiful creation in Africa. He has made Africans in His image and has led them through millennia to this time. Unfractioned Christianity sees people as complete people and not as fractions, concepts or theories.

A Vision for a Marooned People

By the rivers of Babylon we laid down and wept and cried, How can we sing the Lord's songs in a foreign land.
—PSALMS 134

When Malcolm X visited Ghana in 1964 he said that it had dramatically affected his life. Combined with his faith it rooted his identity in place. It was after this visit that he began to call himself an "Afro-American" instead of a "Negro,"and he gradually began to become aware of "Africa's wealth and of her power and of her destined role in the world." [Okpewho, 528]

Malcolm X began, at the end of his life, to understand his African heritage. His Sankofa insight rejected both the post-modern conspiracy to explode cultural identity and the dynamics of identifiable communities on one hand and the archaic residue of racial essentialism on the other. The latter, developed by Leopold Senghor, and William Blyden, is rejected as the fashioning of subjective constructions that fail to take African-American diversity into account. Spencer argues that they are inherently limited, because they were born as responses to the "master-slave dialectic." [Spencer, 66] The African diaspora is a phenomenon rooted in shared experiences and aesthetics; but it is in no way one-dimensional.

The marooned people of the African diaspora have been raised up by the Creator to keep a burning love for Africa in their hearts. The Bible tells us that the people in exile had their hearts filled with concern about their native land. Africans of the diaspora, as have Chinese, Irish, Armenians, and Jews of other diasporic peoples will serve as the voice in the world on behalf of the ancestral continent. The dual-allegiance concept of diaspora people gives them a sense of responsibility to both worlds. Cultural renaissance and economic development are usually the way this responsibility takes shape. Irish-Americans raised money, sang songs, and sent leaders to help launch the Irish Republic. President Mary Robinson of Ireland has said that it was the 70 million Irish worldwide who claimed some connection with Ireland that strengthened her country. The Irish diaspora, she glowed, is a "treasure of our society." [Okpewho, 8]

Today, the nation of Israel is supported financially and in many other respects by countless numbers of Jewish people who advocate on its behalf. It is those in exile who treasure precious legacies and, in God's timing, bring back the help and energy that the homeland requires. For centuries, the prayer of Jewish people has been, "next year in Jerusalem." This prayer proves to be a powerful engine for change. The connection with the homeland has never been lost. Jewish people have been able to guard their historical memory, religion, and culture.

God has empowered the marooned of the African diaspora to garner strength in character. Africa now needs the gift of those resources. There is an African proverb from the Ovambo people that states: "Place value on defending your own home." Diaspora Africans must speak for mother Africa. We must work on her behalf.

Africans in the diaspora have been living in an imperialistic world where others, usually Europeans, have set the limitations. European colonialism in Africa was a direct "extension of the economic logic of the slave trade." [Okpewho, 99] Colonialism utilized the same mechanisms that had been established in the Maafa. This dynamic is still at work among people of the diaspora today. A person's soul cannot not be captured or merchandised as often happens when people lose their community identity. The soul of the diaspora, born in slavery, has always struggled for freedom. Those enslaved sought to keep their hearts free from bondage. Today, our ancestors, the ocean people, still speak of this desire for freedom from the bottom of the cold Atlantic.

Confronting Three-Fifths Theology as it Seeks to Control

Americans of good will, the nice decent church people,
the well-meaning liberals, the good hearted souls who themselves
wouldn't lynch anyone, must begin to realize that they have
to be more than passively good-hearted, more than
church-goingly Christian, and much more than
word-of-mouth in their liberalism.
—LANGSTON HUGHES

Jesus, born to an unwed mother, was raised in poverty and marginalization among oppressed people in the Roman Empire. He left the security of a middle-class profession as a carpenter and took up the life of an impoverished itinerant preacher. He had no privilege to draw on except the support of those who also shared in his oppression. The Messiah also had all of the power of God at his command, and that power was greater than the power of social status and political and economic influence. A Christian is not a "victim" in any sense of the word, because he or she is not powerless. The victim is paralyzed and dependent. A Christian is empowered in the midst of difficult circumstances. Jesus lived as one who was "disinherited" (to use Howard Thurman's phrase) from worldly influence, but He was "rich in the things of God." Christianity teaches that spiritual power is often expressed through social powerlessness.

Incarnational Christianity empowers believers with God's power expressed in humility. Humility cannot be humiliated. It drives people to dependence on God and independence from false sources of power. Humility liberates. To quote Bob Dylan: "If you ain't got nothing'; you ain't got nothing to lose." Humility in life is as appropriate as it is intelligent but, in light of the tragedies of history, it is not an easy concept to embrace. In Christ, it is a liberating perspective on life that keeps people from idolatry and insularity. It is not an easy way to live life. It has been said that "if you think meekness is weakness; try being meek for a week!" The way of humility is a way that demands courage. This is not the groveling humility of the "house Negro" or the acquiescent accomodationalist. It is a biblical paradigm that springs from a new understanding of how humility relates to genuine spiritual power through dependence on God.

Dr. King could have led the quiet life of a scholar. Archbishop Tutu could have chosen safety in America after watching friends like Stephen Biko and others executed in South Africa. It is dangerous to be a Christian. It is costly in America. The liberating Christ calls us to take up the cross, not the sofa or the video game. He calls us to a life of suffering and promises us that in losing we will gain. We see in this country the clearest expression of this Sermon on the Mount Christianity in the Christianity of Dr. King, Fred Shuttelsworth and Medgar Evers. Their power was with God and not rooted in social understandings of priority and privilege.

Yet, in America, much of the church is not rooted in God's power. This raises an obvious question: Is American Christianity capable of dealing with racial injustice? Is Christianity an "other-worldly religion?" Three-fifths theology is a betrayal of Christianity's authentic version which ennobles the oppressed and heals the broken-hearted.

Confronting the Three-Fifths Theology of America's Sadducees

Evil must be attacked by the day-to day assault
of the battering rams of justice.
—MARTIN LUTHER KING, JR.

Song of Solomon 1:5—"I am black but comely"—in the King James Bible/"I am dark but lovely"—in the New English Bible. "I am dark but beautiful"—in the Living Bible/"I am very dark, but comely"—in the Revised Standard Version/"I am black but lovely"—in the New American Standard Bible/"Dark I am, yet lovely"—in the New International Version/"I am black and beautiful"

—in the New Revised Standard Version

The different renderings of the love poem from the Song of Solomon raises an interesting question as to how our faith is "translated" from its Hebrew and Afroasiatic "home" culture of the biblical world to the way that we understand the Bible in contemporary America. Felder calls this passage the "original I am black and I am proud statement in the Bible" [*The Original African Heritage Study Bible,* 991]. We must never lose sight of the fact that the liberating Christ of God calls us to live in a world-wide community of faith that is inclusive in scope. People from all cultures will one day stand around the throne of God in worship.

In Jesus' time there was a group of people, the Sadducees, who loved their religion. They also loved their security and comfort, and this love was greater than their devotion, causing them to reconfigure their faith so that it mirrored their selfishness. This was the three-fifths theology that Jesus would have encountered in his life. Whatever else one could say about these people it is certain that they were not very interested in confronting the injustices of their society. This was probably because to do that would have brought judgment against their own priorities. They were the direct beneficiaries of injustice and inequality in their society.

The "Sadducees" are a major group in American Christianity today. America does have its pharisees who clamor with dogmatic assertiveness. Three-fifths Christians, however, are more interested in their own security than in "rocking the boat." They call themselves moderates (neither hot nor cold) as opposed to the "fanatics" on either side of the spectrum. These "Christians," who follow a personal Savior and have a personal quest for personal peace and personal security. This has led them into a theological wilderness as free of social ethics as it is free from problems. They live in social isolation with indifference to injustice.

Jesus spent much of His time arguing with the Pharisees of his day. His love for them brought him into the arena of engagement with them. Jesus also loved the Sadducees, but they were not interested in challenging Him in any discussion. They were largely indifferent to His life. As a result it would seem, at least from the New Testament record, Jesus had little time for the Sadducees because they had little time for Him. Their profuse rhetoric was a smokescreen for inactivity. This did not fool Christ. They probably advocated interesting agendas, but it was all rhetoric without action. Big clouds but no rain! They were on the sidelines while the great revolution of their day went forward. They were like today's American sadducees who are "AWOL": "absent without love" from the challenges of our world. Incarnational Christian faith is about engagement. Spencer states that "racial fatigue is un-Christian." [Spencer, 62]

The Sadducees saw poverty in their world but claimed that they had no share in the responsibility of addressing it. The same kind of religion is alive today. Sadducees in America involve themselves in speaking against racism when it is good public relations to do so. They encourage people not to become agitated about the problem. Sentiment rules, and soothing voices prevail. Their recasting of the Golden Rule might have been: Whoever has the gold makes the rules. The Sadducees are more interested in maintaining the status quo and in their own personal comfort. It is a kind of religion that cannot allow itself to see the world's real discrepancies because these facts would interfere too much with the desires and aspirations of their own lives.

Incarnational Christianity, in contrast, proclaims a counter-cultural message. Dr. Martin Luther King wrote a powerful critique of the "white moderate" in his "Letter from a Birmingham Jail:"

> I have almost reached the regrettable conclusion that the Negroes greatest stumbling block in the stride toward freedom is not the White Citizens Councilor or the Ku Klux Klanner, but the white moderate who is more devoted to order than to justice; who prefers a negative peace, which is the absence of tension, to a positive peace, which is the presence of justice; who constantly says, "I agree with you in the goal that you seek but I cannot agree with your methods of direct action"; who lives by the myth of time and who constantly advises the Negro to wait until "a more convenient season. [in *I Have A Dream: Speeches of Martin Luther King, Jr.* 91]

The Incarnation as the Model for Unfractioned Christianity

If I your Lord and Master have washed your feet, so
ought you to wash one another's
—JESUS CHRIST

Have this mind in you which was also in Jesus Christ; who being in
very nature God did not consider equality with God something to
be grasped but made himself nothing and took on the very nature
of a slave and became obedient to death—even death on a cross
—St. Paul

Injustice and racism are disturbing truths in American society. Christians facing these truths will be set free, knowing what they need to do in order to respond to that reality in a way that brings honor to the liberating Christ. Three-fifths theology turns away from that reality and opts for indifference. Incarnational Christianity refuses to capitulate to hopelessness but, instead, looks for models and solutions even though the problems of this country seem "unsolvable." The unsolvability of human sin was met, according to Christian faith by the incarnation of God in the person of Jesus. Christ entered into the painful realities of His day and calls us in the same way to invest our lives with passion in the brokenness of our generation.

The incarnation shows Jesus hurled into the middle of a specific time and political/social conflagration and working for change. It is also "very inefficient." Americans have long touted the glories of efficiency. The American definition of efficiency, however, is narrowly based on the process of the work and not on the ultimate result. Cohen states:

> Efficient American farmers can produce many times more food for each hour of work than do third world peasants working by hand but they are in fact extremely wasteful of energy. For every calorie of food derived our efficient farming method requires the investment of many more times more energy than does any primitive system....Americans have fallen into the trap of measuring efficiency only in terms of dollar profits. [Cohen, 173]

It is easy for someone rooted in this kind of American paradigm to imagine a more "efficient" way for God to change the world than the incarnation of Christ. It is not very efficient to send one man in human flesh, to have Him live as a carpenter for thirty years and then to leave Him to die with a handful of fisherman in a backwater of the Roman Empire after only three years.

The incarnation of Jesus is an act of guerilla resistance that raises an assertive "no" to the status quo of self-interest and greed. The incarnation of Christ surmounts fear and rejects accommodation to evil and is an overt act of God expressing His love. It is action and not dogma that calls Christians to move beyond rhetoric and into lives given over to "following in Christ's steps." The pre-occupiers who wait for the Lord's return have forgotten God's call to address injustice. There can be no separation from the world and its challenges as long as we follow the incarnated Christ of God. We must take our world seriously and fill the common with the divine. The incarnation means that no Christian can compartmentalize the spiritual and the eternal from the material and the present. We can not live in luxurious spiritual ghettoes. The transcendent God of creation and power comes to walk among us in Christ. He will be known in dusty streets.

The incarnation is powerful and not theoretical. It is the initiative of the King of Heaven to forcefully establish the kingdom of God on the earth. All Christians are citizens of heaven and are "marooned" in a world of injustice and brokenness. The church is not earth-bound or earth-contingent in its origin or end-result. That is why the incarnation is the foundation for the hope that Christians can renounce three-fifths theology in its many guises and once again begin to follow the Nija of Jesus Christ, the Liberator. He is "our peace who has broken down every wall of division." This is our resolute conviction.

"Woe Is Me if I Preach Not the Gospel"

We, Tait and van Gorder, conclude with a story: While we were leaving Addis Ababa, Ethiopia we were invited to the home of a sixty-one year old patriarch of the faith. We were almost out of time and our flight was leaving later that day. We were exhausted and hungry. Then it began to rain. Nonetheless, we hailed a taxi and went to the home of Father Thomas.

The driving rain had made the muddy mountain path to the house barely passable. The occasional boulders that scraped the bottom of the car provided the only traction to be had among the ruts in the road.

Finally, through the heavy deluge we arrived at the small mud-brick house that was home to Father Thomas, his wife, his four children and three grandchildren. The shack consisted of three rooms: a communal bedroom, a small kitchen, and a dining room where we huddled from the storm. What struck us immediately when we came into the living room was the tattered banner on the wall that heralded: "Woe is me if I preach not the Gospel!"

We sat looking at each other across the gnarled old table. It had been a long and exhausting week in East Africa. We had struggled together over issues in the writing of this book as we had for months before. We had dealt with each others quirks in traveling and living together. Our interactions had often stretched us because we are two Americans who come from very different Americas and from very different experiences and assumptions. Ours is not an easy relationship. Nevertheless, in spite of our myriad of differences, we share a faith in Christ Jesus and the conviction that the liberating Gospel of Jesus can bring freedom and hope to life.

Father Thomas glowed with that same faith. After a few minutes he asked if he could "preach to us." We agreed. He got up from where he was sitting at the table and, standing in front of the sign began to tell us that it was, at all times and at all places, the duty of the Christian to preach the Gospel of Jesus. This, he said was the truth that would set people free and bring peace to troubled hearts and broken lives. It was Jesus alone who could solve the problems of Ethiopia and all of Africa as well as the problems of each of us in that room.

The message was his life. He looked us both in the eye and told us never to grow weary in our work for God. There would be a curse on us if we lived for ourselves and sought our own self-interests. Blessings and peace would come to us as we followed the liberating Christ in this world. Father Thomas reminded us it was a hard road but also a "freedom road." That is the road on which we invite you to join us. Listen to our brothers and sisters and to our fathers and mothers who have gone before us. Listen with us to our God and follow Him with us on this long and hopeful "freedom road."

Appendix One: Selected Bibliography

Additional Reading for Chapter One: Afrocentricity

Akbar, Nai'im. *Know Thyself*. Tallahassee: Mind Productions, 1998

Anyike, James C. *Historical Christianity African Centered*. Chicago: Popular Truth, 1994

Asante, Molefi Kete. *Afrocentricity*. Trenton, N.J.: Africa World Press, 1988.

Asante, Molefi Kete. *The Painful Demise of Eurocentrism*. Trenton, N.J.: Africa World Press, 2001.

Ashby, Muata. *Egyptian Yoga: The Philosophy of the Enlightenment*. Miami: Cruzian Books, 1995.

Barber, Benjamin. *Jihad vs. MacWorld: How Globalism and Tribalism are Reshaping the World*. New York: Ballantine Books, 1996.

Bates, Robert H.; V. Y. Mudimbe; and Jean Barr. *Africa and the Disciplines: The Contributions of Research in Africa to the Social Sciences and the Humanities*. Chicago: University of Chicago Press, 1993.

Ben Jochannan, Y. *Africa: The Mother of Civilization*. New York: Alkebula Press, 1971.

Berkely, Bill. *The Graves are Not Yet Full: Race, Tribe and Power in the Heart of Africa*. New York: Basic Books, 2001.

Bernal, Martin. *Black Athena: The Afroasiatic Roots of Classical Civilization*. New Brunswick, N.J.: Rutgers University Press, 1987.

Bujo, Benezet., *African Theology in its Social Context*. Translated by John O' Donohue. Maryknoll, N.Y.: Orbis Books, 1992.

Cleage, Albert B. *Black Christian Nationalism: New Directions for the Black Church*. New York: William Morrow and Co., 1972.

———— *The Black Messiah*. New York: Sheed and Ward, 1969.

Costen, Melva Wilson. *African-American Christian Worship*. Nashville: Abingdon Press, 1993.

Davidson, Basil. *African Civilization Revisited*. Trenton, N.J.: Africa World Press, 1991.

————. *Black Mother: The Years of the African Slave Trade*. Boston: Little Brown and Co., 1961.

Desai, Ram, ed. *Christianity in Africa as Seen By Africans*. Denver: Alan Swallow, 1962.

Diop, Cheikh Anta. *The African Origins of Western Civilization*. Translated by Yaa-Sengi EEMA Ngemi. Westport, CT: Lawrence Hill, 1987.

————. *Civilization or Barbarism: An Authentic Anthropology*. Translated by Yaa-Sengi EEMA Ngemi. Westport, CT: Lawrence Hill, 1991.

Donders, Joseph G. *Non-Bourgeois Theology: An African Experience of Jesus*. Maryknoll, N.Y.: Orbis Books, 1985.

Ela, Jean Marc. *My Faith as an African*. Translated by John Pairman Brown and Susan Perry. Maryknoll, N.Y.: Orbis Books, 1988.

Hammond, Dorothy and Alta Jablow. *The Africa That Never Was: Four Centuries of British Writing About Africa*. Prospect Heights, IL: Waveland Press, 1992

Johnson, John. *The Black Biblical Heritage*. Nashville: Winston Derek Publishers, 1993.

James, George. G. M. *Stolen Legacies*. San Francisco: Julian Richardson Publications, 1976.

Karenga, Maulana. *Introduction to Black Studies*. Los Angeles: University of Sankore Press, 1992.

———. *Selections from the Husia: Sacred Wisdom from Ancient Egypt*. Los Angeles: Kaiwada Press, 1981.

Lefkowitz, Mary. *Not Out of Africa: How Afrocentrism Became an Excuse to Teach Myth as History*. New York: New Republic Books, 1996.

McKissic, William Dwight and Anthony Evans. *Beyond Roots: If Anybody Asks You Who I Am?* Wenonah, N.J.: Renaissance Productions, 1994.

Mengisteab, Kidane. *Globalization and Autocentricity in Africa's Development in the Twenty-First Century*. Trenton, N.J.: Africa World Press, 1996.

Mudimbe, V.I. *The Idea of Africa*. Bloomington: Indiana University Press, 1994.

Murray, Charles and Richard Herrnstein. *The Bell Curve: Intelligence and Class Structure in American Life*. New York: Harper and Row, 1989.

Parratt, John. *A Reader in African Christian Theology*. London: SPCK, 1987.

Rutstein, Nathan. *Healing Racism in America: A Prescription for the Disease*. Springfield, MA: Whitcomb Publishing, 1993.

Sanneh, Lamin. *Piety and Power: Muslims and Christians in West Africa.* Maryknoll, N.Y.: Orbis Books, 1996.

——. *West African Christianity: The Religious Impact.* Maryknoll, N.Y.: Orbis Books, 1983.

Sindima, Harvey J. *Drums of Redemption: An Introduction to African Christianity.* Westport, CT: Greenwood Press, 1994.

Shorter, Aylward. *African Christian Spirituality.* Maryknoll, N.Y.: Orbis Books, 1980.

Snowden, Jr. Frank M. *Before Color Prejudice: The Ancient View of Blacks.* Cambridge, MA: Harvard University Press, 1983.

Tarabrin, E.A. *Neocolonialism and Africa in the 1970s.* Moscow: Progress Publishers, 1978.

Taryror, Nya Kwiawon. *Impact of the African Tradition on African Christianity.* Chicago: Strugglers Community Press, 1984.

Waters, John W. "Who Was Hagar?" *in Stony The Road We Trod.* Cain Hope Felder, editor. Minneapolis: Fortress Press, 1991.

Wilmore, Gayraud. *African American Religious Studies: An Interdisciplinary Anthology.* Durham, N.C.: Duke University Press, 1989
Wilson, Amos. *The Falsification of African Consciousness.* New York: Afrikan World Information Systems, 1993.

Additional Reading for Chapter Two:
The Stow-away Rats of European Racism

Allen, Theodore. *The Invention of the White Race.* London: Verso Publications, 1994.

Ani, Marimba. *Yurugu: An African Centered Critique of European Cultural Thought and Behavior.* Trenton, N.J.: Africa World Press, 1994.

Barnes, Annie. *Everyday Racism.* Naperville, IL: Sourcebook Publishing, 2000.

Cohen, Mark Nathan. *Culture of Intolerance: Chauvinism, Class and Race in the United States.* New Haven: Yale University Press, 1998.

Doyle, Bertram Wilbur. *The Etiquette of Race Relations in the South: A Study in Social Control.* New York: Schocken Books, n.d.

Emerson, Michael O. and Christian Smith. *Divided By Faith: Evangelical Religion and the Problem of Race in America.* New York: Oxford University Press, 2000.

Griffin, Paul. *The Seeds of Racism in the Soul of America.* Cleveland: Pilgrim Press, 1999.

Holloway, Karla F. C. *Codes of Conduct: Race, Ethics and the Color of Our Character.* Rutgers, N.J.: Rutgers University Press, 1995.

Knoble, Dale T. *Paddy and the Republic.* Middletown, CT: Allison Press, 1986.

Pinkey, Alphonso. *Lest We Forget: White Hate Crimes-Howard Beach and Other Racial Atrocities.* Chicago: Third World Press, 1994.

Schutte, Gerhard. *What Racists Believe: Race Relations in South Africa and the United States.* London: Sage Productions, 1995.

Segal, Charles. *Dionysiacs, Poetics and Euripedes Bacchae.* Princeton: Princeton University Press, 1982.
Terry, Robert. *For Whites Only.* Grand Rapids, MI: Eerdmans Publishing, 1975.

Turner, Jonathan H.; Royce Singleton; David Musick. *Oppression: A Socio-History of Black White Relations in America.* Chicago: Nelson Hall, 1992.

Walker, Clarence E. *De-romanticizing Black History: Critical Essays and Reappraisals.* Knoxville, TN: The University of Tennessee Press, 1991.

Wood, Forrest G. *The Arrogance of Faith: Christianity and Race from the Colonial Era to the Twentieth Century.* New York: Alfred A. Knopf, 1990.

**Additional Reading for Chapter Three:
Rethinking American History**

Asante, Molefi Kete, and Abu S. Abarry, eds. *African Intellectual Heritage: A Book of Sources.* Philadelphia: Temple University Press, 1996.

Bennett, Lerone. *Before the Mayflower: A History of Black America.* New York: Penguin Books, 1988.

Berkeley, Bill. *The Graves are Not Yet Full: Race, Tribe and Power in the Heart of Africa.* New York: Basic Books, 2001.

Dyson, Michael Eric. *Making Malcolm: The Myth and Meaning of Malcolm X.* New York: Oxford University Press, 1995.

Ehrlich, Walter. *They Have No Rights: Dred Scott's Struggle for Freedom.* Westport, CT: Greenwood Press, 1979.

Epps, Archie, ed. *The Speeches of Malcolm X at Harvard.* New York: William Morrow and Company, 1969.

Fehrenbacher, Don E. *Slavery, Law and Politics: The Dred Scott Case in Historical Perspective.* New York: Oxford University Press, 1981.

Finkleman, Paul. *Slavery and the Founders: Race and Liberty in the Age of Jefferson.* Armonk, N.Y.: M.E. Sharpe, 1996.

Garrow, David J., ed. *Martin Luther King, Jr.: Civil Rights Leader, Theologian and Orator:* New York: Carlson Publishing, 1989.

Gourevitch, Philip. *We Wish to Inform You that Tomorrow We Will Be Killed with Our Families: Stories from Rwanda.* New York: Farrar Straus and Giroux, 1998.

Hilliard, Asa G. *SBA: The Reawakening of the African Mind.* Gainseville, Florida: Makeare Publishers, 1977.

Hopkins, Vincent C. *Dred Scott's Case.* New York: Athenaum Press, 1967.

Kaminsky, John P. *A Necessary Evil? Slavery and the Debate over the Constitution.* Madison, WI: Madison House, 1995.

Kelley, Robin D. and Earl Lewis. *A History of African-Americans: To Make Our World Anew.* New York: Oxford University Press, 2000

Klammer, Martin. *Whitman, Slavery and the Emergence of Leaves of Grass.* University Park: The Pennsylvania State University Press, 1995.

Lewis, Rupert. *Marcus Garvey: Anti-colonial Champion.* Trenton, N.J.: Africa World Press, 1988.

Littlefield, Daniel F. Jr. *Africans and Seminoles: From Removal to Emancipation.* Westport, CT: Greenwood Press, 1977.

Loewen, James. *Lies My Teacher Told Me: Everything Your American History Textbook Got Wrong.* New York: Simon and Schuster, 1995.

Mbali, Zolile. *The Churches and Racism: A Black South African Perspective.* London: SCM Press, 1987.

Newman, Richard, and Marcia Sawyer. *Everybody Say Freedom: Everything You Need to Know about African American History.* New York: Penguin Books, 1996.

Oubre, Claude F. *"Forty Acre's and A Mule" The Freedmen's Bureau and Black Land Ownership.* Baton Rouge: Louisiana State University Press, 1978.

Sanneh, Lamin Osman. *Abolitionists Abroad.* Cambridge, MA: Harvard University Press, 1999.

Sbacci, Alberto. *Ethiopia under Mussolini.* London: Zed Books, 1985.

Spencer, Jon Michael. *Sing a New Song: Liberating Black Hymnody.* Minneapolis: Fortress Press, 1995.

**Additional Reading for Chapter Four:
America's New Subtle Racism**

Cohen, Mark Nathan. *Culture of Intolerance: Chauvinism, Class and Racism in the United States.* New Haven: Yale University Press, 1998.

Franklin, John Hope. *Racial Equality in America.* Chicago: University of Chicago Press, 1976.

Franklin, Robert Michael. *Liberating Visions: Human Fulfillment and Social Justice in African American Thought.* Minneapolis: Fortress Press, 1990.

Fredrickson, George M. *The Comparative Imagination: On The History of Racism, Nationalism, and Social Movements.* Los Angeles: University of California Press, 1997.

Hecht, Michael. *African American Communications: Ethnic Identity and Cultural Interpretation.* London: Sage Publications, 1993.

Kelley, Robin D. G. *Yo Mama's Dysfunctional! Fighting the Culture Wars in Urban America.* Boston: Beacon Press, 1997.

Lambert, Wallace E., and Otto Kleinberg. *Children's Views of Foreign People.* New York: Appleton Century Publishers, 1967.

Lincoln, C. Eric. *Coming Through the Fire: Surviving Race and Place in America.* Durham, N.C.: Duke University Press, 1996.

MacInnes, Gordon. *Wrong for All the Right Reasons: How White Liberals Have Been Undone by Race.* New York: New York University Press, 1995.

Marable, Manning and Leith Mullings, eds. *Let Nobody Turn Us Around: Voices of Resistance, Reform and Renewal: An African-American Anthology.* New York: Rowman and Littlefield Publishers, 2000.

Munford, Clarence J. *Race and Civilization: Rebirth of Black Centrality.* Trenton, N.J.: Africa World Press, 2001.

——. *Race and Reparations: A Black Perspective for the 21st Century.* Trenton, N.J.: Africa World Press, 1996.
Outlaw, Lucius. *On Race and Philosophy.* New York: Routledge Press, 1996.

Shull, Stephen. *A Kinder, Gentler Racism: The Reagan and Bush Legacy on Race.* New York: M. E. Sharpe, 1993.

Steinberg, Stephen. *Turning Back: The Retreat from Racial Justice in American Thought and Policy.* Boston: Beacon Press, 1995.

Thomas, Alexander and Samuel Sillen. *Racism and Psychiatry.* New York: Carol Publishing, 1993.

Wilson, William J. *The Bridge over the Racial Divide: Rising Inequality and Coalition Politics.* Los Angeles: University of California Press, 1999.

Wright, W. D. *Racism Matters.* Westport, CT: Greenwood Press, 1998.

Zook, Kristal Brent. *Color by Fox: The Fox Network and the Revolution in Black Television.* New York: Oxford University Press, 1999.

Additional Reading for Chapter Five: Sankofa and Ujima

Adeyemo, Tokunboh. *Salvation in African Tradition.* Nairobi, Kenya: Evangelical Publishing House, 1979.

Asante, Molefi. *The Afrocentric Idea.* Philadelphia: Temple University Press, 1989.

———. *Kemet, Afrocentricity and Knowledge,* Trenton, NJ: Africa World Press, 1990.

Butler, Johnnella E. *Black Studies: Pedagogy and Revolution, A Study of Afro-American Studies and the Liberal Arts Tradition Through the Discipline of Afro-American Literature.* New York: University Press of America, 1981.

Browder, Anthony T. *Survival Strategies for African Americans: 13 Steps to Freedom.* Trenton, N.J.: Africa World Press, 1996.

Carruthers, Jacob and Maulana Karenga. *Kemet and the African World view.* Los Angeles: University of Sankore Press, 1984.

Costen, Melva Wilson. *African-American Christian Worship.* Nashville: Abingdon Press, 1993.
Diop, Cheikh Anta. *Cultural Unity of Black Africa.* Chicago: Third World Press, 1976.

Fanon, Frantz. *The Wretched of the Earth.* New York: Grove Press, 1965. Lawrence Hill Publishing, 1974.

Gundaker, Grey, ed., *Keep Your Head to the Sky: Interpreting African American Home Ground.* Richmond: University of Virginia Press, 1998.

Hood Robert E. *Must God Remain Greek? Afro Cultures and God-Talk.* Minneapolis: Fortress Press, 1990.

Idowu, E. Bolaji. *African Traditional Religion: A Definition.* London: SCM Press, 1973.

Karenga, Maulana. *Kawaida Theory.* Los Angeles: Karenga Press, 1980.

Keto, C. T. *African-Centered Perspective on History.* Blackwood, N.J.: K&A Publishers, 1989.

Kofi, Buenor Hadjor. *Another America: The Politics of Race and Blame.* Boston: South End Press, 1993.

Maquet, Jaques and Joan Rayfield. *Africanity: The Cultural Unity of Africa.* New York: Oxford Press, 1972.

Mbiti, John S. *The Bible and Theology in African Christianity.* Nairobi: Oxford University Press, 1986.

Mendelsohn, Jack. *The Martyrs: Sixteen Who Gave Their Lives for Racial Justice.* New York: Harper and Row, 1966.

Mengisteab, Kidane. *Globalization and Autocentricity in Africa's Development in the Twenty-first Century.* Trenton, N.J.: Africa World Press, 1996.

Nyamiti, Charles. *Christ as Our Ancestor: Christology from an African Perspective.* Gweru, Zimbabwe: Mambo Press, 1984.

Paris, Peter J. *The Spirituality of African Peoples: The Search for a Common Moral Discourse.* Minneapolis: Fortress Press, 1995.

Perkins, Useni Eugene. *The Afrocentric Self-Inventory and Discovery Workbook for African-American Youth*. Chicago: Third World Press, 1989.

Rodney, Walter. *How Europe Underdeveloped Africa*. Washington, D.C.: Howard University Press, 1980.

Sanneh, Lamin Osman. *West African Christianity: The Religious Impact*. Maryknoll, NY: Orbis Books, 1983.

Schucter, Arnold. *Reparations: The Black Manifesto and its Challenges to White America*. New York: Lippincott Publishers, 1970.

Wiley, Ralph. *Why Black People Tend to Shout*. New York: Penguin Paperbacks, 1997.

Woodson, Carter G. *The Mis-Education of the Negro*. Washington, D.C.: Associated Publishers, 1933.

Young, Josiah Ulysses. *A Pan-African Theology: Providence and the Legacies of the Ancestors*. Trenton, N.J.: Africa World Press, 1992.

Zahan, Dominique. *The Religion, Spirituality and Thought of Traditional Africa*. Translated by Kate Ezra and Lawrence Martin. Chicago: University of Chicago Press, 1979

Additional Reading for Chapter Six:
The Rip Van Winkle Syndrome

Berry, Wendell. *The Hidden Wound*. Boston: Houghton and Mifflin, 1989.

Burgess, John M. *Black Gospel: White Church*. New York: Seabury Press, 1982.

Caditz, Judith. *White Liberals in Transition*. New York: Spectrum Publications, 1976.

Carter, Robert L., Dorothy Kenyon, Peter Marcuse and Loren Miller. *Equality*. New York: Pantheon Books, 1965.

Cuomo, Chris J. and Kim Q. Hall. *Whiteness: Feminist Philosophical Reflections*. London: Rowan and Littlefield Publishers, 1999.

Delgaldo, Richard and Jean Stefanicic. *Critical White Studies: Looking Behind the Mirror*. Philadelphia: Temple University Press, 1997.

Ellul, Jacques. *The Technological Society*. New York: Random House, 1967.
Fanon, Frantz. *Black Skin, White Masks*. New York: Grove Press, 1967.

Forman, Seth. *Blacks in the Jewish Mind: A Crisis of Liberalism*. New York: New York University Press, 1998.

Fredrickson, George M. *The Black Image in the White Mind: The Debate on Afro-American Character and Destiny, 1817–1914*. New York: Harper and Row, 1971.

Holloway, Joseph. *Africanisms in American Culture*. Bloomington: Indiana University Press, 1990.

Lipsitz, George. *The Possessive Investment in Whiteness: How White People Profit from Identity Politics*. Philadelphia: Temple University Press, 1998.

McPherson, James M. *The Abolitionist Legacy from Reconstruction to the NAACP*. Princeton, N.J.: Princeton University Press, 1975.

Perkins, Spencer and Chris Rice. *More Than Equals: Racial Healing for the Sake of the Gospel*. Downers Grove, IL: InterVarsity Press, 1993.

Ridgeway, James. *Blood in the Face: Ku Klux Klan, Aryan Nations, Nazi Skinheads and the Rise of A New White Culture.* New York: Thunder's Mouth Press, 1990

Swift, David E. *Black Prophets of Justice: Activist Clergy Before the Civil War.* Baton Rouge: Louisiana State University Press, 1989

Tucker, Sterling. *Black Reflections on White Power.* Grand Rapids, MI: Eerdmans Publishing, 1969.

Van Ausdale, Debra and Joe R. Feagin. *The First R-How Children Learn Race and Racism.* New York: Rowan and Littlefield, 2001

Weiner, Eugene, ed. *The Handbook of Interethnic Coexistence.* New York: Continuum Publishing Company, 1998.

Additional Reading for Chapter Seven:
Desegregating Reality with Respect

Anderson, Claude. *Powernomics: The National Plan to Empower Black America.* Bethesda, MD: Powernomics Corporation, 2001.

Anthony Baez Foundation. *Stolen Lives Killed by Law Enforcement.* New York: The Stolen Lives Project, 1999.

Baker, Houston, A. *Black Studies: Rap and the Academy.* Chicago: University of Chicago Press, 1993.

Bass, S. Jonathan. *Blessed are the Peacemakers: Martin Luther King, Jr., Eight White Religious Leaders and the Letter from Birmingham Jail.* Baton Rouge: Louisiana State University Press, 2001

Blassingame, John W. *New Perspectives on Black Studies.* Urbana, IL: University of Illinois Press, 1998.

Boxill, Bernard. *Blacks and Social Justice.* London: Rowman and Allanheld Publishers, 1984.

Brooks, Dana and Ronald Althouse, editors. *Racism in College Athletics: The African American Athlete's Experience.* Morgantown, W.V.: Fitness Technologies, 2000.

Burgess, John M. *Black Gospel/White Church.* New York: Seabury Press, 1982.

Carnoy, Martin. *Education as Cultural Imperialism.* Pittsburgh: Educational Policy Planning and Theory Series, University of Pittsburgh, 1981.

Chapman, Mark. *Christianity on Trial: African American Religious Thought Before and After Black Power.* Maryknoll, N.Y.: Orbis Books, 1996.

Dalton, Harlon. *Racial Healing.* New York: Doubleday Publishing, 1995.

Donovan, Vincent. *Christianity Rediscovered.* Maryknoll, N.Y.: Orbis Books, 1978

Goldberg, David Theo. *Racial Subjects: Writing on Race in America.* New York: Routledge, 1997.

Hill, Robert B. *The Strength of African American Families: Twenty-Five Years Later.* Langham, MD: University Press in America, 1999.

Jenkins, Adelbert H. *Psychology and African Americans: A Humanistic Approach.* Needham Heights, MA: Allyn and Bacon, 1982.

Lincoln, C. Eric, ed. *Is Anybody Listening to Black America.* New York: Seabury Press, 1969.

Matthews, Donald H. *Honoring the Ancestors: An African Cultural Interpretation of Black Religion and Literature.* New York: Oxford University Press, 1998.

Moltmann, Jurgen. *Experiences in Theology: Ways and Forms of Christian Theology* (translated by Margaret Kohl). Minneapolis: Fortress Press, 2000.

Oppenheimer, Martin, and George Lakey. *A Manual for Direct Action: Strategy and Tactics for the Civil Rights and all Other Non-Violent Protest Movements.* Chicago: Friends Peace Committee, 1965.

Thomas, Alexander and Samuel Sillen. *Racism and Psychiatry.* New York: Citadel Press, 1972.

Walker, Theodore. Jr. *Empower the People: Social Ethics for the African American Church.* Maryknoll, N.Y.: Orbis Books, 1991.

Wimberly, Anne Streaty, and Edward P. *Liberation and Human Wholeness: The Conversion Experience of Black People in Slavery and Freedom.* Nashville: Abingdon Press, 1986.

Additional Reading for Chapter Eight: Incarnational Resurrected Christianity-"When Justice Flows Down Like Rivers"

Boesak, Willa. *God's Wrathful Children: Political Oppression and Christian Ethics.* Grand Rapids, MI: Eerdmans Publishing, 1995.

Carson, Cottrel R. *Do You Understand What You Are Reading?: A Reading of the Ethiopian's Story (Acts 8:26-40) From A Site of Cultural Maroonage.* New York: Union Theological Seminary Doctoral Dissertation, May 1999.

Cone, James. *Martin and Malcolm and America.* New York: Harper Torchbooks, 1983.

Douglass, Kelly. *The Black Christ*. Maryknoll, N.Y.: Orbis Books, 1993.

Dyson, Michael Eric. *Between God and Gangsta Rap: Bearing Witness to Black Culture*. New York: Oxford University Press, 1996.
Evans, James H. *We Have Been Believers: An African American Systematic Theology*. Philadelphia: Fortress Press, 1992.

Felder, Cain Hope. *Stony the Road We Trod*. Philadelphia: Fortress Books, 1994.

————. *Troubling Biblical Waters: Race, Class and Family*. Maryknoll, N.Y.: Orbis Books, 1997.

Franklin, Robert. *Another Day's Journey*. Philadelphia: Fortress Press, 1997.

Hildebrand, Reginald F. *The Times were Strange and Stirring: Methodist Preachers and the Crisis of Emancipation*. Durham, NC: Duke University Press, 1995.

Paris, Peter. *The Social Teaching of the Black Churches*. Philadelphia: Fortress Press, 1995.

Raboteau, Albert J. *A Fire in the Bones: Reflections of African American Religious History*. Boston: Beacon Publishers, 1995.

Roberts, J. Deotis. *The Prophethood of Black Believers*. Louisville, KY: Westminster John Knox Press, 1991.

Stewart, Carlyle Fielding. *Soul Survivors: An African American Spirituality*. Louisville, KY: Westminster John Knox Press, 1997.

Taylor, Edward C., ed. *The Words of Gardner Taylor, volume I: NBC Radio Sermons, 1959-1970*. Valley Forge, PA: Judson Press, 1998.

Thurman, Howard. *Jesus and the Disinherited*. Boston: Beacon Publishers, 1996 (1946).

Wilmore, Gauyard. *Black Religion and Black Radicalism*. Maryknoll, N.Y.: Orbis Books, 1985.

Wolfe-Devine. *Diversity and Community in the Academy*. Langham, MD: Rowman and Littlefield, 1997.

Young, Josiah Ulysses. *Black and African Theologies*. Maryknoll, N.Y.: Orbis Books, 1986.

Young, Joshua Ulysses. *A Pan-African Theology: Providence and the Legacies of the Ancestors*. Trenton, N. J.: Africa World Press, 1992.

Additional Reading for the Conclusion

Adegbola, E.A. Ade, ed. *Traditional Religions in West Africa*. Nairobi: Uzima Press, 1983.

Akbar, Nai'im. *Breaking the Chains of Psychological Slavery*. Tallahassee, FL: Mind Productions, 1996.

———. *Visions for Black Men*, Tallahassee, FL: Mind Productions, 1998.

Appiah-Kubi, Kofi and Sergio Torres, editors. *African Theology Enroute*. Maryknoll, N.Y.: Orbis Books, 1979.

Asante, Molefi Kete. *Malcolm X As A Cultural Hero and other Afrocentric Essays*. Trenton, N.J.: Africa World Press, 1993.

Ben-Jochannan, Yosef. *African Origins of the Major Western Religions*. Baltimore: Black Classic Press, 1991.

Cannon, Katie Geneva. *Katie's Cannon: Womanism and the Soul of the Black Community*. New York: Continuum Publishing, 1995.

Cone, James H. *Speaking the Truth: Ecumenism, Liberation and Black Theology*. Grand Rapids, MI: Eerdmans Publishing, 1986.

Dawson, Michael. *Behind the Mule: Race and Class in African American Politics.* Princeton, N.J.: Princeton University Press, 1994.
DuBois, W. E. B. *The Souls of Black Folk: Essays and Sketches.* New York: Blue Herron Press (1903), 1953.

Eberhardt, Jennifer L., and Susan T. Fiske. *Confronting Racism: The Problem and the Response.* London: SAGE Publications, 1998.

Forbes, Jack. *Black Africans and Native Americans: Color, Race and Caste in the Evolution of Red-Black Peoples.* New York: Basil Blackwell, 1988.

Franklin, John Hope. *The Color Line: Legacy for the Twenty-First Century.* Columbia, MO: University of Missouri Press, 1993.

Hooks, Bell. *Killing Rage: Ending Racism.* New York: Henry Holt Publishers, 1995.

Kenon, Randall. *Walking on Water: Black American Lives at the Turn of the Twenty-First Century.* New York: Alfred A. Knopf, 1999.

Magubane, Bernard. *The Ties That Bind: African-American Consciousness of Africa.* Trenton, N.J.: Africa World Press, 1987.

Massey, Douglas, and Nancy A. *American Apartheid: Segregation and the Making of the Underclass.* Cambridge, MA: Harvard University Press, 1993.

Nelson, Angela. *This is How We Flow: Rhythm in Black Culture.* Los Angeles: University of Southern California Press, 1999.

Okpewho, Isidore, Carole Boyce Davies and Ali A. Mazrui. *The African Diaspora: African Origins and New World Identities.* Bloomington: Indiana University Press, 1999.

Segal, Ronald. *The Black Diaspora.* New York: Farrer, Straus and Giroux, 1995.

Tlhagle, Buti. *Hammering Swords into Ploughshares: Essays in Honor of Archbishop Mpilo Desmond Tutu.* Trenton, NJ: Africa World Press and Grand Rapids, MI: Eerdmans Publishing, 1986

Tutu, Desmond Mpilo. *Hope and Suffering.* Grand Rapids, MI: Eerdmans Publishing, 1984.

Van Certima, Ivan. *They Came Before Columbus.* New York: Random House, 1976.

Wade-Gayles, Gloria. *Rooted Against the Wind.* Boston: Beacon Publishers, 1996.

Williams, Richard. *They Stole It but You Must Return It.* New York: HEMA Publishers, 1990.

Ziegler, Dhyana. *Molefi Kete Asante and Afrocentricity: In Praise and in Criticism.* Nashville: Winston Publishing, 1995.

Appendix Two
A Survey for Starting Conversations with Euro-Americans

Answer Yes/ No or True/False
1. I would call myself a racist or, a "recovering racist." ____
2. I am intentionally working against racism. ____
3. I am a direct beneficiary of slavery and see its effects today. ____
4. I intentionally support African-American businesses. ____
5. It troubles me that slave-owners are on American dollar bills. ____
6. I can name two civil rights leaders beyond King and Malcolm X ____
7. I can name two of the principles of Kwanzaa. ____
8. I am directly accountable to people of color. ____
9. Racism is America's most pressing social problem. ____
10. I have at least 5 African-Americans in my address book. ____
11. I have stayed overnight in an African-American home. ____
12. I am a descendent of people from Africa. ____
13. Racism is declining in America. ____
14. Alexander Hamilton was an African-American. ____
15. Multiculturalism is the goal of race relations in America. ____
16. The first slave owners in America were New England Puritans. ____
17. Abraham Lincoln was a strident abolitionist. ____
18. My parents chose to raise me in a segregated environment. ____
19. I would welcome inter-racial dating in my family. ____
20. I usually say "white and black" to describe some people ____
21. I usually say Egypt is in "North Africa" instead of in "Africa." ____
22. Egypt, and not Greece, is the cradle of European Civilization. ____
23. I have confronted the fact that my ancestors caused the murder of millions during the Maafa. ____
24. Restitution should be given for descendants of the Maafa. ____
25. I have been a victim of "profiling" while shopping/driving. ____
26. I can "visit" the race issue in America whenever I choose to do so. ____
27. My church is at least 20 percent African-American. ____

28. Segregated Christianity is an inauthentic expression of Christianity ____
29. I participate in segregated American Christianity. ____
30. Jesus was a person of color. ____

Respond to the following quote from novelist James Baldwin:

The fear that I heard in my father's voice when he realized that I believed that I could do anything that a white boy could do and had every intention of proving it, was not at all like the fear that I heard when one of us was ill. It was another fear, a fear that a child, in challenging the white world's assumptions, was putting himself in the path of destruction.

Appendix Three
Glossary of African and Arabic Terms

These terms are for your consideration in light of what Molefi Asante calls the *Nomo* (Swahili), the "creative, generative power of words" to reconfigure paradigms. Reconstructing ways of thinking is a basic task in the dynamic of developing an Afrocentric world-view.

Abayah – (Mandinka) – gown/robe
Asante Sana – (Swahili) – Thank You
Askiya – (Songay) – ruler/king
Barakah – (Arabic) – merit, grace
Danka – (Mandinka) – curse, evil spell
Dar al-Harb – (Arabic) – sphere of strife/enmity
Griot – ("French" West African) – story teller/poet/prophet
Habari Gani? (Swahili) – "What is happening?"
Hurumbee – (Swahili) – togetherness; loyal support
Imam – (Arabic) – Prayer Leader; Imani – (Swahili) – faith/devotion
Jambo (Swahili) – A greeting "hello" or "goodbye"
Jangugol – (Fulani) – reading/study
Jihad – (Arabic) – to engage in struggle (for righteousness).
Kemet/Kemetic – (Ancient Egyptian) – pertaining to "Kem" or Egypt
Kuumba – (Swahili) – creativity
Kujicahagulia – (Swahili) – self-determination
Maafa – (Swahili) – great suffering or deep anguish
Maat – (Ancient Egyptian) – righteousness
Malaika – (Swahili) – a beautiful one
Mambe/Mambo – (Kongolese)–song
Mu'allim – (Arabic)/*Mwalimu* – (Swahili) – teacher
Nia – (Swahili) – purpose/goal
Nija – (Swahili) – path/the way
Nyancho – (Mandinka) – a royal warrior clan
Oluku Mi – (Yoruba) – My Friend

Sankofa – (Akan) – to remember/draw strength from the past
Sarki – (Hausa) – ruler/leader
Tajdid – (Arabic) – gradual/peaceful reform
Teranga – (Wolof) – hospitality/ care for visitors
Ubuntu – (Zulu) – community
Ujaama – (Swahili) – collective economics;
Ujima – (Swahili) – collective responsibility
Umoja – (Swahili) – unity
Windugol – (Fulani) – writing
Yatim – (Arabic) – orphan
Yirwa – (Mandinka) – blessing/virtue
Yurugu – (Swahili) – "white man"/one who is disfigured

Appendix Four
Readings in African Spirituality

1. An African Creed
From Christianity Rediscovered by Vincent Donovan.

We believe in the one High God, who out of love created the beautiful world and everything good in it. He created humanity and wanted all people to be happy in the world. God loves the world and every people and nation on the earth.

We have known this High God in the darkness and now we know him in the light. God promised in his word, the Bible, that he would save the world and all the nations and peoples of the earth.

We believe that God made good on his promise by sending his son Jesus Christ, a man in the flesh, a Jew by tribe, born poor in a little village, who left his home and was always on safari doing good, curing people by the power of God, teaching about God and humanity and showing that the meaning of religion is love.

Jesus was rejected by his people, tortured and nailed, hands and feet to a cross and died. He lay buried in the grave but the hyenas did not touch him and on the third day he rose from the grave. He ascended into the skies. He is the Lord.

We believe that all of our sins are forgiven through him. All who have faith in him must be sorry for their sins, be baptized in the Holy Spirit of God, live the rules of love and share the bread together in love to announce the good news of others until Jesus comes again.

We are waiting for him. He is alive. He lives. This we believe. Amen.

2. A Prayer for Africa
From a young man in Ghana quoted in African Christian Spirituality

O Lord, O Ruler of this world, O Creator, O Father, this prayer is for Africa. For our brothers in the South, for our brothers in the North and for those far away from us.

Lord, you know that the white brothers have made their black brothers second class people. This hurts so much. O Lord, we suffer from this. You have given us a dark skin so that we may better bear your strong sun. Why have our brothers done this to us? They are no better than we and we are not better than they. What comfort is it to us that you always love most those who suffer the most?

We call ourselves Christians on both sides. But we go to different churches, as if there were also different heavens. The white men still have some power over us. Help them to use their power wisely and accept us as brothers. Take the mistrust out of their hearts and minds and make them share with us. This is our continent, or, more truly, yours.

You have marked us for this continent. O Lord, we also pray for ourselves that you will keep our hearts free from hatred and let us be grateful for what we have. Let us be united among ourselves and let all of our children know that you have died for them. You died for all and are risen for all. Hallelujah!

We praise you, our Father, who are greater than Europe and Africa and who loves where we hate and who long ago could have destroyed us but you did not because you love us so much! Praise be to you, O Lord!

3. An African Creation Story, I – Zora Neale Hurston, *Mules and Men*, 1935.

High riding and strong armed God!
Walking across His globe creation, hah!
Wid de blue elements for a helmet and a wall of fire 'round his feet...
And Oh-Wid de eye of Faith I can see Him standing out on de eaves of

ether breathing clouds from out His nostrils, blowing storms from 'tween his lips, I can see!
Him seize de mighty axe of his proving power and smite the stubborn space,
And laid it wide open in a mighty gash—Making a place to hold the world, I can see him!
Molding de world out of thought and power and whirling it out on its eternal track,
Ah hah, my strong armed God!
God shook his head and a thousand million diamonds flew out from his glittering crown and studded the evening sky and made de stars....

So God A'mighty, Ha! Got his stuff together—
He dipped some water out of the mighty deep and He got Him a handful of dirt from de foundation sills of de earth.
He seized a thimble full of breath from the drums of the wind, ha!
God, my master!
Now I'm ready to make man! Aa-aah!

4. An African-American Creation Story, II. – James Weldon Johnson, in *God's Trombones*, 1927.

And God stepped out on space and He looked around and said: I'm lonely-I'll make me a world. And far as the eye of God could see darkness covered everything, blacker than a hundred midnights down in a cypress swamp.

God smiled and the light broke, and the darkness rolled up one side, and the light stood shining on the other, and God said: "That's good!"

Then God reached out and took the light in His hands and God rolled the light around in his hands until He made the sun; and He set that sun a blazing in the heavens. And the light that was left from making the sun God gathered it up in a shining ball and flung it against the darkness, spangling the night with the moon and stars.

Then down between the darkness and the light he hurled the world; and God said: "That's good!"

And God walked, and where He trod his footsteps hallowed the valleys out and bulged the mountains up.... And He spat out the seven seas-He batted His eyes, and the lightning flashed-He clapped his hands and the thunder rolled-And the waters above the earth came down, the cooling waters came down.... And God smiled again and the rainbow appeared, and curled itself around His shoulder.

Then God raised His arm and waved His hand over the sea and over the land and He said: "Bring Forth! Bring Forth! And quicker than God could drop his hand, fishes and fowls and beasts and birds swam the rivers and the seas, roamed the forests and the woods, and split the air with their wings.

And God said: "That's good!" Then God said, "I'll make me a man...."

The Great God Almighty who lit the sun and fixed it in the sky, who flung the stars to the most far corner of the night, who rounded the earth in the middle of His hand; This Great God, like a mammy bending over her baby, kneeled down in the dust toiling over a lump of clay till he shaped it in His own image

Both excerpts are quoted in Theophus H. Smith, Conjuring Culture: Biblical Formations for Black America. New York: Oxford University Press, 1994.

Appendix Five
About the Authors

The **REVEREND DR. LEWIS T. TAIT, JR.** is the founder and pastor of the New Life United Church of Christ in Stone Mountain, Georgia. Before this he was the founder and pastor of the Harambee United Church of Christ in Harrisburg, Pennsylvania, from 1993 until 1999. He also served as an associate pastor with his father for seven years at the Faith Bible Church of Washington, D.C.

Tait received his doctorate of divinity degree in Afrocentric Pastoring and Preaching from the United Theological Seminary of Dayton, Ohio. He also received a certificate in the study of Muslim-Christian relations at the Mansefield College, Oxford University in Oxford, England. Reverend Tait received his bachelor of arts degree in business administration from Hardin-Simmons University in Texas and his masters of divinity degree from the Howard University School of Divinity in Washington, D.C. Lewis T. Tait, Jr. was born in Washington, D. C. He has two children and lives in Atlanta.

Professor **A. CHRISTIAN VAN GORDER** has been a professor of Asian Religions and World Christianity at Messiah College in Grantham, Pennsylvania since 1997. Before that he was a Professor at the Yunnan University in Kunming, Yunnan, China and served for nine years with Bethany Fellowship and Open Doors With Brother Andrew in Singapore, Northern Ireland, and in the Netherlands.

Van Gorder received his doctorate of philosophy degree in Muslim-Christian Comparative Studies at the Queen's University of Belfast, Ireland , with external examiner Andrew Walls. He also completed courses of study at Trinity College, Dublin and at the National University of Singapore's Chinese Language and Research Center. Professor van Gorder completed a bachelor of arts degree in literature at Oral Roberts University in Oklahoma and his masters of arts degree in world religions at the Asbury Theological Seminary in Kentucky. Chris was born in Pittsburgh, Pennsylvania. He has four children and lives in a Pennsylvania town that was once an important stop on the Underground Railroad.

Index